Trends in Corrections

Interviews with
Corrections Leaders Around the World

International Police Executive Symposium Co-Publications

Dilip K. Das, *Founding President-IPES*

Interviews with Global Leaders in Policing, Prisons, and Courts Series

PUBLISHED

Trends in Corrections: Interviews with Corrections Leaders Around the World
By Jennie K. Singer, Dilip K. Das, and Eileen Ahlin, ISBN: 978-1-4398-3578-4

Trends in Policing: Interviews with Police Leaders Across the Globe, Volume Three
By Otwin Marenin and Dilip K. Das, ISBN: 978-1-4398-1924-1

Trends in Policing: Interviews with Police Leaders Across the Globe
By Dilip K. Das and Otwin Marenin, ISBN: 978-1-4200-7520-5

FORTHCOMING

Trends in Policing: Interviews with Police Leaders Across the Globe, Volume Four
By Bruce F. Baker and Dilip K. Das, ISBN: 978-1-4398-8073-9

Justices of the World: Their Views, Opinions, and Perspectives
By Cliff Roberson and Dilip K. Das, ISBN: 978-1-4200-9978-2

Trends in Corrections

Interviews with
Corrections Leaders Around the World

Edited by
Jennie K. Singer
Dilip K. Das
Eileen M. Ahlin

International Police Executive
Symposium Co-Publication

CRC Press
Taylor & Francis Group
Boca Raton London New York

CRC Press is an imprint of the
Taylor & Francis Group, an **informa** business

CRC Press
Taylor & Francis Group
6000 Broken Sound Parkway NW, Suite 300
Boca Raton, FL 33487-2742

First issued in paperback 2019

© 2013 by Taylor & Francis Group, LLC
CRC Press is an imprint of Taylor & Francis Group, an Informa business

No claim to original U.S. Government works

ISBN-13: 978-1-4398-3578-4 (hbk)
ISBN-13: 978-0-367-86515-3 (pbk)

Library of Congress Cataloging-in-Publication Data

Trends in corrections : interviews with corrections leaders around the world / edited by Jennie K. Singer, Dilip K. Das, and Eileen Ahlin.
    p. cm.
Includes bibliographical references and index.
ISBN 978-1-4398-3578-4
    1. Corrections. 2. Corrections--Cross-cultural studies. 3. Criminal justice, Administration of--Cross-cultural studies. I. Singer, Jennie K. II. Das, Dilip K., 1941- III. Ahlin, Eileen.

HV8665.T74 2013
364.6--dc23   2012015445

Visit the Taylor & Francis Web site at
http://www.taylorandfrancis.com

and the CRC Press Web site at
http://www.crcpress.com

To Mitch, Nicole, Brianna, and Leo

JKS

To Lowy (Marlow Torrance Das), beloved
granddaughter of Ana and Dilip

DKD

To Matthew and Sarah Payne

EMA

Table of Contents

Series Preface

The International Police Executive Symposium, in collaboration with CRC Press/Taylor & Francis Group, has launched a series entitled Interviews with Global Leaders in Policing, Prisons, and Courts. The objective is to produce high-quality books aimed at bringing the voices of the leading criminal justice practitioners to the forefront of scholarship and research. These books, based on interviews with leaders in criminal justice, are intended to present the perspectives of high-ranking officials throughout the world by examining their careers, insights, visions, experiences, challenges, perceived future of the field, and related issues of interest.

True, the literature is replete with scholarship and research that provides academic interpretations of the field, its practices, and its future. However, these publications often appear in difficult-to-access journals and are written from the perspective of the academic, with little interpretation or feasible action items for those professionals working in the field. A comprehensive literature discussing the on-the-ground, day-to-day understanding of how police, courts, and prison systems work, do not work, and need to be improved, is lacking. This series provides "inside" information about the systems as told to respected scholars and researchers by seasoned professionals. In this series, the dialogue between scholar/researcher and practitioner is opened as a guided yet candid professional discussion, providing the opportunity for academics to learn from practitioners, whereas practitioners also learn and are provided an outlet for the expression of their experiences, challenges, skills, and knowledge.

Throughout the world, the criminal justice field is at juxtaposition, and the time is ripe for change and improvements. Many countries throughout the world have long-standing policies that have been successful for their culture and political climate or are in need of serious revamping due to budgetary concerns or corruption. Other countries are at a precipice and are beginning to establish new systems. In all of these situations, the international criminal justice field stands to benefit from an accessible, engaging, and enlightening series of frank discussions of the personal views and experiences of leaders in the field.

The current volume, *Trends in Corrections: Interviews with Corrections Leaders Around the World*, sets the stage to enhance readers' understanding of correctional programming and management styles used throughout the world from an insider's perspective. The correctional leaders interviewed in this volume represent a variety of cultures, political environments, and economic systems. Representatives from the Americas (Canada, Mexico, and the United States), Asia (Singapore), Australia, the Caribbean (Trinidad and Tobago), and Europe (England, Hungary, and Bosnia–Herzegovina) are interviewed. The Introduction acquaints the reader with the issue of international corrections and the need for a forum to discuss corrections from the perspective of noted corrections officials. Chapters 1 through 12 each provide the transcribed interview of a corrections leader as conducted by the scholar/researcher. A brief portrait of the corrections system in that jurisdiction is also provided. The final chapter is a reflection on the interviews and is a summary of the common themes evident throughout the book.

Thus, *Trends in Corrections: Interviews with Corrections Leaders Around the World* continues the work of the International Police Executive Symposium (IPES) and CRC Press Interviews with Global Leaders in Policing, Prisons, and Courts series by advancing knowledge about the corrections system, examining comparative corrections from the perspective of correctional leaders in a variety of countries, and opening a dialogue between scholars/researchers and practitioners. It is anticipated that this addition to the series will facilitate discussions within and between countries' correctional systems to add value to their current operations and future directions. It is hoped that this series will also bridge the gap of knowledge that exists between scholars and researchers in academia and practitioners in the field. We invite correctional scholars, researchers, and practitioners across the world to join in this venture.

Dilip K. Das, PhD
Founding President, International Police Executive Symposium
Founding Editor-in-Chief, Police Practice & Research:
An International Journal (PPR)
Series Editor for
Advances in Police Theory and Practice, CRC Press
Interviews with Global Leaders in Policing, Prisons, and Courts, CRC Press
PPR Special Issues in book format, Routledge

Foreword

Corrections is the arm of the criminal justice system that has a history of being an enigma to the general public. Yet, it plays an enormous role in public safety and has become an increasingly large expenditure of government funds. This fact has led to increased scrutiny. Politicians and the general public demand to know why the burgeoning use of tax funds for corrections is required and how these funds are used.

Corrections practitioners are reaching out to one another across geographic, national, and cultural boundaries in search of viable ways of ensuring that the practices they engage in are effective and efficient and affect offenders to the greatest degree, thus justifying expenditures and moving toward the least amount of supervision and incarceration necessary or commensurate with the safety of communities and the interdiction of victimization.

Collaboration with the academic community to assist with research, utilizing practitioners in teaching students and generally opening up the corrections community to colleges and universities, is on the increase. Furthermore, a new understanding of corrections within the law enforcement community, victims' groups, advocacy agencies, religious entities, civic organizations, the business community, and the judiciary has enabled the corrections systems to call on and cooperate with these outside groups. These partnerships support several mutual goals, including the success of probationers before they become an incarceration statistic and the success of parolees upon release.

The scarcity of resources continues to force the evaluation of all aspects of the corrections profession. As a result, underperforming programs and efforts are eliminated or modified, with the efficacy of strategies being at the forefront of decision making. This has set a tone throughout the profession of a thirst for knowledge of "what works," so the adoption of the most effective endeavors in managing offenders and preincarceration and postincarceration can lead to success.

In addition, as broader knowledge is gained about offenders and the predisposing and precipitating factors that have brought them to the criminal justice system, the necessity of collaboration continues to cut across other public service entities such as mental health, social service, and health agencies. This has given rise to a deeper understanding and cooperation across agencies that has promise to increase offender success.

The Trends in Corrections series (and this first volume on corrections in the series, Interviews with Global Leaders in Policing, Prisons, and Courts) builds on the various international changes that occur within the corrections community and opens a dialogue across countries that can be a catalyst for creative approaches that cross boundaries and enhance success with offenders as well. For humanitarian, fiscal, and victimization reasons, we as practitioners need to be open to learning from others' successes and failures, irrespective of the country of origin. The public demands this, and it is the ultimate responsibility of each of us to employ proven techniques as a moral imperative. *Trends in Corrections: Interviews with Corrections Leaders Around the World* moves us in these directions accordingly and also provides readers with unique insight into the leaders who are deeply involved in the practical aspects of corrections, as well as their visions, experiences, successes, challenges, and failures.

George Lombardi

Acknowledgments

This volume would not exist without the concerted efforts of the numerous authors and corrections leaders who contributed interviews. We wholeheartedly thank authors Elena Azaola, Clare Beckett, Lauren Benton, József Boda, Sharon Casey, Andrew Day, Laurence Armand French, Goran Kovacevic, Ann-Claire Larsen, Mary Maguire, Zsolt Molnár, Elias Mpofu, Danielle Murdoch, Rick Parent, Rodd Rothwell, Joanna Spink, and Dianne Williams for their superb chapters.

Of course, none of these chapters would have been possible had it not been for the generosity of the contributors: Robert Ambroselli, Michael Boileau, Luke Grant, Sue Hall, Robert Jennings, Lt. General Antal Kökényesi, Timothy Leo, John Pastorek, John Rougier, Hazael Ruiz, Dusko Sain, and CM. We genuinely appreciate you for taking time out of your very busy schedules to share your stories with us.

We also thank George Lombardi, director of the Missouri Department of Corrections, for providing an insightful foreword for this volume.

Special thanks to Dusan R. Sipovac for providing the International Police Executive Symposium (IPES) account information.

The editors, authors and interviewees wish to express sincere thanks to Carolyn Spence, senior editor at CRC Press/Taylor & Francis Group, for her steadfast and enduring editorial support during this project.

Editors

Jennie K. Singer, PhD, graduated *magna cum laude* in English from San Diego State University, San Diego, CA, in 1989 and received a PhD degree in general clinical psychology from California School of Professional Psychology, San Diego (now part of Alliant International University) in 1995. She has worked in several clinical settings, with children, adolescents, and adults in both outpatient and inpatient settings. In addition, she has held several positions as a psychologist with the Federal Bureau of Prisons and the California Department of Corrections and Rehabilitation. Dr. Singer is a faculty member in the Division of Criminal Justice, California State University, Sacramento. She teaches courses in corrections, criminal theory, and research methods. Dr. Singer worked as a key researcher with the California Sex Offender Management Board from 2007 to 2009 and published several government reports on sex offender management. In addition, Dr. Singer has published articles and chapters on corrections, intelligence assessment, and sex offender policy. She is currently a researcher and an advisor to a new cognitive behavioral life skills diversion program, Ascend, which is implemented in California as part of AB 109, a plan to divert some state prisoners to local jails.

Dilip K. Das, PhD, has years of experience in police practice, research, writing, and education. After obtaining his master's degree in English literature, Dr. Das joined the Indian Police Service, an elite national service with a distinguished tradition. After 14 years in the service as a police executive, e.g., as a chief of police, he moved to the United States, where he achieved another master's degree in criminal justice and a doctorate degree in the same discipline. Dr. Das is a professor of criminal justice, a former police chief, and a human rights consultant to the United Nations. He is the founding president of the International Police Executive Symposium (IPES), where he manages the affairs of the organization in cooperation with an appointed group of police practitioners, academia members, and individuals from around the world. Dr. Das is also the founding editor-in-chief of *Police Practice and Research: An International Journal*. He is the author, editor, or coeditor of more than 30 books and numerous articles. Dr. Das has received several faculty excellence awards and was a distinguished faculty lecturer.

Eileen M. Ahlin, PhD, is a senior study director with Westat, with more than 15 years of research experience. She has directed multisite and statewide evaluations, including randomized intervention trials. Dr. Ahlin's research has focused on evaluations of community corrections including kiosk supervision of probationers, adult treatment drug courts, family treatment courts, the effectiveness of countermeasures to driving while intoxicated and criminological theory. Her recent publications have appeared in the *American Journal of Public Health*, the *Journal of Criminal Justice*, the *Journal of Experimental Criminology*, *Traffic Injury Prevention*, and *Accident Analysis and Prevention*. She has conducted interviews with incarcerated homicide and drug offenders for the Pittsburgh Youth Study and served as a mentor to inmates preparing for release. Dr. Ahlin teaches courses in criminological theory and corrections. She received her PhD degree in criminology and criminal justice from the University of Maryland, College Park, in 2010.

Contributors

Elena Azaola, PhD, is a senior investigator with the Center for Advanced Studies and Research in Social Anthropology, Mexico City, where she received her PhD degree in social anthropology. She also graduated as a psychoanalyst. She was an advisor with the National Commission of Human Rights (1991–1993) and is a current council member of the Commission of Human Rights of Mexico City. She has published more than 125 works in Mexico, as well as in other countries. Most of Dr. Azaola's research has been in juvenile and women's justice institutions, human rights, and violence. Her research on commercial sexual exploitation of children (1999–2003) was sponsored by the United Nations Children Fund (UNICEF). She co-coordinated a National Report on Violence (2004) sponsored by the World Health Organization (WHO), and the European Commission project for street children in Mexico (1997–1999). Since 2001, she has conducted several research projects on Mexico's police forces. She is the board chair of the Institute for Security and Democracy, which won the 2007 McArthur Award for Creative and Effective Institutions.

Clare Beckett is senior lecturer with the University of Bradford, Bradford, England, U.K. She received her doctorate degree from Leeds Metropolitan University, Leeds, England, in 2003. Her previous nonacademic roles included work with Inquest, where she explored deaths in custody and provided support for the families of prisoners, work with Gingerbread, a campaigning group for single parents, and work supporting the Citizen's Advice Bureau's tribunal assistance unit. She now provides program leadership for the University of Bradford's contribution to probation training and is a member of the Criminal Justice and Social Science Division. Her current research focuses on the relational factors between offenders and offender managers that contribute to desistance.

Lauren Benton, B. Hlth. Sci, M. Rehab. Clng is a graduate in rehabilitation counseling from the Faculty of Health Sciences, University of Sydney, Sydney, NSW, Australia. Her research interests include the study of the correctional system and vocational settings, which enable individuals with injury, disability, or health conditions to reenter the work force. She has a particular interest in establishing an understanding of human behavior and the ways in which difficulties faced throughout an individual's life can be overcome. Since leaving the university, she has been employed with the Australian Government's Commonwealth Rehabilitation Service, where she is a rehabilitation consultant.

József Boda is the director general of the Special Service for National Security (SSNS), the "young" organization in the national security structure in Hungary (established in 1996). SSNS provides technical support and some intelligence services to law enforcement agencies. Dr. Boda has 35 years in the law enforcement service, having started his professional career in the Hungarian National Army. He joined the Hungarian National Police in 1991 as the deputy commander of the Hungarian Special Police Force (Counterterrorist Unit). Since 1997, he has been acting in the police training field mainly on international dimensions as the Hungarian director of the International Law Enforcement Academy (ILEA), Budapest, Hungary, and later on, as the director general of the International Training and Civilian Crisis Management Centre, Budapest. He has been a trainer for decades to military and police personnel in Hungary and on the mission areas (e.g., Azerbaijan or Afghanistan). He was the chair of the European Police College (CEPOL) during the Hungarian European Union (EU) Presidency.

Sharon Casey is a senior lecturer with the School of Psychology, Deakin University, Melbourne, Victoria, Australia. Prior to taking up this position, Dr. Casey was the program director of the master of psychology (forensic) program at the University of South Australia in Adelaide, Australia. Her recent research consultancy projects for the Singapore Prison Services have included rehabilitation program review and evaluation, development of a criminogenic needs assessment tool, and the development of a rehabilitation program delivery framework.

Andrew Day is a clinical and professor of psychology at Deakin University, Melbourne, Victoria, Australia. He is interested in all aspects of offender rehabilitation, particularly in relation to the treatment of involuntary clients (notably violent offenders), readiness for treatment, juvenile justice, and offenders from indigenous cultural backgrounds.

Laurence (Larry) Armand French, PhD, served as a senior Fulbright scholar with the Faculty of Criminology, Criminal Justice and Security Studies, University of Sarajevo, Saravejo, Bosnia and Herzegovina, during the academic year 2009–2010. He holds BA, MA, and PhD degrees in sociology/ criminology from the University of New Hampshire, Durham, and a PhD degree in cultural psychology from the University of Nebraska, Lincoln. He is a professor emeritus of psychology with the Western New Mexico University,

Silver City, NM, and is a senior research associate with the Justiceworks Institute, University of New Hampshire.

Goran Kovacevic was born in Sarajevo in the former Yugoslavia in 1982 and earned his MS degree from the Faculty of Law, University of Sarajevo, Saravejo. He is currently completing his doctorate degree in the Faculty of Criminology, Criminal Justice, and Security Studies, University of Sarajevo, where he also serves on the faculty as a teaching assistant.

Ann-Claire Larsen, BA, LLB, LLM (Human Rights), PhD, is a sociologist with a law background. She is a senior lecturer with the School of Law and Justice, Edith Cowan University, Perth, WA, Australia. Dr. Larsen's research interests include policing, corrections, family violence, human rights, and technologies in health care. She teaches international human rights and professional ethics.

Mary Maguire, PhD, is an associate professor of criminal justice with California State University, Sacramento. She has an MA degree in psychology and MSW and PhD degrees in social work and social research. She has 12 years of research experience measuring clinical models and behaviors of high-risk populations and 15 years of professional experience in behavioral health. She worked in research for the Oregon Department of Corrections and has written about correctional staff attitudes and inmate assault. In addition, she contributed to the statewide research project for the standardization of the California Department of Corrections and Rehabilitation. Dr. Maguire has published in the areas of policing, corrections, and sex offender policy.

Zsolt Molnár is a police education expert at the Ministry of Internal Affairs (MoI) and has 20 years of service in the Hungarian National Police Force. Dr. Molnár started his career in the Investigation Department, specializing in crimes against properties. In 1996, he joined a United Nations Mission in Bosnia–Herzegovina (UN International Police Task Force). After 15 months in the Srebrenica area, he returned to the police trial investigation unit, focusing on economic crimes. In 2001, after finishing his degree from the Faculty of Law, Dr. Molnár was assigned to be the head of Crime Prevention Department, and 3 years later, he was assigned as the head of the Crime Prevention Academy of the MoI. He participated in the Council of Europe–sponsored program with the International Organization for Migration (IOM) in the CARDS Regional Police Project (CARPO) as a curriculum developer on the subject of human trafficking and smuggling, and trained police and community leaders in Georgia in a United Nations Mission in Georgia. Dr. Molnár is a guest lecturer at the International Law

Enforcement Academy, Budapest, Hungary, and has given presentations in Azerbaijan and Turkmenistan at the invitation of the Organization for Security and Cooperation in Europe (OSCE). His national trainings focused on crime prevention, human rights, fighting against hate crimes, and community development. Dr. Molnár has published studies in the subject of data protection, security strategy, rules of engagement, community policing, and human dimension of defense. Since 2009, Dr. Molnár has been a member (from 2010, a department chair) of the Working Group on Learning of the European Police Academy (CEPOL WGL).

Elias Mpofu, PhD, DEd, CRC, is a professor and the head of the Discipline of Rehabilitation Counseling, University of Sydney, Sydney, NSW, Australia, providing teaching, research, and service leadership to graduate programs in rehabilitation counseling. Formerly a professor of rehabilitation services with Pennsylvania State University, University Park, he has an international reputation in the scholarship of teaching with service-learning and research on community-oriented health interventions.

Danielle Murdoch received her MPhil degree in criminological research from the University of Cambridge, Cambridge, U.K., and is a doctoral candidate in the School of Criminology, Simon Fraser University, Burnaby, BC, Canada. Her teaching and research interests include institutional and community corrections and international criminal justice issues, in particular, criminal justice reform in post-conflict and transitioning environments.

Richard Parent, PhD, is an assistant professor of police studies with the School of Criminology, Simon Fraser University, Burnaby, BC, Canada. Dr. Parent has recently completed 30 years of service as a police officer in the Vancouver area. He is also a former police recruit instructor and recently spent more than 8 years as a crisis negotiator, assigned to a regional emergency response team. His area of research includes police ethics and accountability, crisis negotiations, police recruiting and training, and the police use of deadly force. Dr. Parent is a frequent provider of training to various police agencies in Canada. Dr. Parent also provides expert opinion evidence to attorneys in the United States and Canada pertaining to the police use of deadly force and the phenomenon of "suicide by cop."

Rodd Rothwell, MA, MA(Hons), PhD, has been senior lecturer in rehabilitation counseling and behavioural science at the University of Sydney for many years. His background work experience has been in psychology in the corrective service system and in drug and alcohol services. His research and teaching have centered on drug and alcohol rehabilitation, rehabilitation history and philosophy, clinical reasoning, and public offender rehabilitation.

He has authored many articles and book chapters on these topics in international publications. Recent chapters have been published in the Butterworth Heinemann series on clinician reasoning in the health professions.

Joanna Spink has been an academic with the Department of Social Sciences and Humanities University of Bradford, West Yorkshire, England, U.K., since 2000. Her background is in sociology and social psychology, and she worked for several years in health-related qualitative research, particularly in two diverse areas: elderly patients' self-analysis of their health care and the links between stroke and subsequent depression and/or anxiety. In 2004, She started working exclusively in criminal justice, establishing placement opportunities for undergraduate students with criminal justice agencies as the centerpiece of the applied criminal justice studies (BA Hons) degree. She also has a particular interest in the relationship between crime and media and has taught a course on this subject for 8 years.

Dianne Williams, PhD, is the coordinator of the Criminology Unit, University of the West Indies, St. Augustine. She also coordinates the Unit for Social Problems Analysis and Policy Development, a research unit under the umbrella of the Department of Behavioural Sciences. She is a certified criminal justice specialist, certified by the American College of Certified Forensic Counselors in 2004 in the Division of Counseling. She is currently a consultant criminologist for the Ministry of National Security of Belize and is one of the Caribbean criminology experts of record for the Organization of American States. She currently and has recently completed projects as an author of the *Analysis of Firearms Legislation for the Caribbean* and by providing expert opinion on the risks faced by homosexuals in Trinidad and Tobago for the Refugee and Migrant Justice Service of the United Kingdom.

Interviewees

Robert Ambroselli received the BS degree in organizational management from the University of La Verne, La Verne, CA. He has more than 23 years experience with the Department of Corrections and Rehabilitation, having held numerous field and administrative positions in both the Parole and Institutions divisions. He is currently the director of the Division of Adult Parole Operations, where he provides ongoing administration functions for the California State Parole, which includes 3550 employees and a budget of approximately $863 million. He is charged with managing the division's High-Risk Sex Offender supervision and establishing one of the largest global positioning systems for the supervision of sex offenders in the nation. He oversees many rehabilitative programs that assist parolees' successful reintegration into society and has established the California Parole Apprehension Teams, which have been responsible for the apprehension of thousands of parolees at-large and the most significant reduction in the absconder population in the history of the division. He is also a member of the California Sex Offender Management Board, which addresses issues, concerns, and problems related to the community management of adult sex offenders.

Michael Boileau is the warden of Matsqui Institution, a federal prison that is part of Correctional Service Canada, located in an eastern suburb of Vancouver, BC, Canada. He began his career with the federally based Correctional Service Canada in 1987 and rose through the ranks to the position of warden. He is experienced as both a correctional officer and as a parole officer. While working full time, he entered a university program that was offered at the Justice Institute of British Columbia and successfully completed his bachelor of general studies degree. Warden Boileau also served in the Preventative Security Department of Correctional Service Canada and has completed several assignments at the National Headquarters, Ottawa, ON, Canada.

Luke Grant, MSc, was appointed as the assistant commissioner of offender services and programs in June 2006. Previously, he was the assistant commissioner of offender management beginning in December 2000. He has held a number of positions in corrective services in the areas of inmate classification, programs, and education and comes from a background in tertiary education. As the assistant commissioner of offender services and programs, he is responsible for offender services and programs in custody and in the community, including Corrective Services Industries and inmate classification and case management.

Sue Hall is the chief executive of West Yorkshire Probation Trust. She studied modern languages (German and Russian) at Girton College, Cambridge, U.K. She qualified as a probation officer from the University of Cardiff, Cardiff, Wales, U.K., in 1979 and was awarded an MBA from the Open University in 2002. She started as a probation officer in Grimsby in 1979 and spent 20 years with Humberside Probation Area. She moved to West Yorkshire as a deputy chief probation officer in 2000. She has been a chief officer since 2004, first with South Wales and, since 2005, with West Yorkshire. In April 2010, Sue was appointed as a chief executive for the new West Yorkshire Probation Trust, the fourth largest Probation Trust in England and Wales. She is a member of the Yorkshire and Humberside Criminal Justice Board, where she is the lead for Reducing Reoffending. Sue is currently the chair of the Probation Chiefs Association, which promotes the professional voice of senior probation managers in England and Wales. She is the PCA lead for International Probation.

Robert Jennings left the U.K. aviation industry and studied in Nottingham. He worked as a probation officer in the United Kingdom and joined the Corrections Department in Western Australia in 1981. He was the first lateral-entry prison administrator appointed in Western Australia. Then, he worked in a number of prisons, including Bandyup Women's Prison and the Victorian era Fremantle Prison. In 1998, he took over the Canning Vale complex and headed up the amalgamation of the two prisons into what is now Hakea Prison. This was the world's first experience to keep two maximum security facilities running while they are joined. He returned to Casuarina in 2004 and retired in October 2010.

Lt. General Antal Kökényesi conducted the compulsory military service and then started his police career in 1979. Dr. Kökényesi graduated from the Horticultural University in 1976, from the Police College in 1984, and from the Faculty of Law, Eötvös Loránd University (ELTE), Budapest, Hungary, in 1991. During his career, he was a station commander in some police stations of the Metropolitan Police in Budapest beginning in 1991. He was assigned to be the chief of the Metropolitan Police in 1998. From 1999, he was promoted to the first general rank: brigadier general. He became a major general in 2001. In 2003, he was the head of the Crime Prevention Department, Ministry of Interior, and from 2004, he was the chief of Borsod County Police

Headquarters. In 2007, he became the general director of the Investigation Bureau of the National Police Force as the deputy chief of police. In 2008, he was promoted by the President of the Republic of Hungary. Lt. General Kökényesi was assigned to be the commander of the Hungarian National Prison Service at that time.

Timothy Leo is the chief psychologist with the Singapore Prison Service. Leo is responsible for the development of psychological services and psychological-based programs throughout the Singaporean prison system, and he has been a key driver behind the rehabilitation policies that now characterize the service. Leo is a Singapore national who completed his postgraduate education in Auckland, New Zealand, before working as a clinical psychologist in forensic mental health and with the family court.

John Pastorek has worked with BC Corrections for more than 34 years in both female and male correctional facilities. He has held management positions since 1987, including his role as the project manager during the design, construction, and commission of BCCW, a female provincial/federal facility with a strong programming focus. Throughout the years in his roles as both deputy warden and warden, he has also been involved in a number of facility design projects.

John Rougier has been the commissioner of prisons in Trinidad and Tobago since July 1, 2005. He expects to proceed with preretirement leave before the end of 2011. Rougier is a 38-year veteran of the Trinidad and Tobago Prisons Service. He worked his way up through the ranks, having joined the service as a prison officer trainee. Rougier holds a BSc degree in sociology and an MSc degree in human resource management.

Hazael Ruiz is an attorney and has experience of more than 15 years in the Federal District Penitentiary System. He served as the deputy director of criminological studies and the director of Oriente and Santa Martha Acatitla Male Preventive Prisons and was Mexico City's former secretary of the Prison System. Nowadays, he writes the analytical column "Cuidémonos" for the newspaper *El Sol de México*.

Dusko Sain earned his graduate degree from the Department for Social Self-Protection, Prevention and Resocialization of Persons with a Behavioral Disorder, Faculty (College) for Defectology, University of Belgrade, Belgrade, Serbia. He began his current position as the head of the Department for Supervision of Penal/Correctional Institutions in the Ministry of Justice for the Republic of Srpska in December 2007. His prior experiences include working as an educator at the reformatory in Banja Luka (1987–1992). From 1992 to 2005, he was the head of the Department for Admission and Discharge at the Correctional Facility in Banja Luka, in addition to being the assistant director for security and treatment. In 2006, he was with the Ministry of Justice as an inspector for treatment. From May to December 2007, he was the director of the Criminal Correctional Home in Foca. He also serves as the president of the Association of Penologists of the Republic of Srpska.

Introduction

The field of corrections is an exciting, changeable profession, and countries are dealing with similar areas of challenge, triumph, and disappointment around the world. Corrections is a global phenomenon, as each country and their jurisdictions are responsible for the treatment of its offending populations. This treatment includes housing inmates for periods of incarceration, developing offenders' skills and educational background, and rehabilitative programming aimed at improving individuals' abilities to live a law-abiding life after supervision by the correctional system has ended. Issues such as overcrowding, prisoners' rights, adherence to evidence-based programs, the availability of rehabilitation programs, and correctional officer's buy-in to new offender management plans affect prison systems around the world. This book details, through individual interviews, how each country handles its population of offenders both within the prison system and out in the community.

All correctional practitioners are charged with ensuring the public's safety while also ensuring inmates' safety and preparing them for release back into the community. However, it is the correctional leaders throughout the world who are at the forefront of incorporating theory, evidence-based practices, and real-world experience into the day-to-day management of their correctional institution, regardless of whether it is a prison or a prison system, the agency responsible for overseeing parolees or probationers, or rehabilitative programming dealing with issues related to reintegration and reentry to society. Correctional leaders are the heart of the corrections system, and it is important for scholars, researchers, and other practitioners to understand their viewpoints in order to move the field forward.

Despite the importance of examining the day-to-day operations of the corrections field through the lens of its leaders, the extant literature does not address this topic. Furthermore, the field lacks an international understanding of correctional leaders' ascendency to top positions in their respective agencies, how they approach their job managing staff and inmates while also balancing political pressures from the government and public, and their visions for the future. There are numerous books, book chapters, and journal articles that address these issues from the perspective of scholars and researchers—persons who have a vested interest in the topic but reside outside the corrections system. The perspective of the correctional insider is not only missing but may also provide the most informative and useful contributions to the literature for use by scholars, researchers, and, perhaps more importantly, other practitioners. Comparative corrections is best addressed by getting inside information from a variety of seasoned practitioners throughout the world. It is through their firsthand observations, reflections, and forecasts that others may benefit and learn about their trials and tribulations, as well as their successes and plans for the future. This current volume is the first step toward providing the knowledge necessary for moving the comparative corrections field forward in the twenty-first century.

The chapters in this book provide a rare, unabashed look at the field of corrections from the viewpoint of 12 high-ranking correctional leaders in nine countries throughout the world. Each chapter contains an interview with a corrections official who leads a correctional institution or key department/agency related to the field of corrections. These interviews were conducted by well-respected scholars/researchers who are familiar with the correctional system in the country where the correctional leader worked. The interview structure was flexible but aimed at gathering information about career paths, the correctional leaders' personal views about the corrections system in their country/jurisdiction, and how international correctional practice informs their work. This series provides practitioners with an outlet for voicing their perspectives on how the corrections system works (and areas of needed improvement) while accommodating their busy work schedules, priorities, and other demands by having scholars compile their reflections into this volume.

The interviews cover areas such as the correctional leaders' background, education, and career in corrections. The reader gains an understanding of how the corrections leader came to be involved in the field, what kept them motivated to climb the ranks, and how they used their education, training, and experience to improve the correctional institution for which they work. The correctional leaders interviewed in this volume also discuss important changes and problems, as well as successes, they have experienced over the years of their service. They discuss the ubiquitous challenge of balancing the seemingly competing goals of corrective control and rehabilitation and how they have handled the ebb and flow of both public support and research evidence for each strategy.

In Chapter 1, Hazael Ruiz, ex-director of the Penitentiary System in Mexico City, talks about how they are struggling with the overcrowding of inmates and how the lack of upward mobility for correctional officers makes having a prison career less than desirable. Ruiz details Mexico City's ability to treat only a few of the massive number of drug-addicted inmates, poor community supervision, which leads to much recidivism or "relapsing" after prison, and almost no use of intermediate sanctions; prison is the punishment given in most cases. Ruiz cites the need to create other sanctions for those who do not need prison and could benefit from lesser punishment.

In Chapter 2, assistant commissioner Luke Grant of Offender Services and Programs in New South Wales, Australia, states that the media gives a negative portrayal of prisons, which results in poor community attitudes toward corrections, and ignorance of what corrections seek to achieve. This negative media coverage also stigmatizes prisoners and fuels community fear and a reluctance to provide practical assistance and support to those exiting prison. He discusses how the community would be less reactive if they understood more details, such as how much prisons cost, where the funds are being used, and the outcomes or alternatives for people who commit crimes.

In Chapter 3, Dusko Sain, director of corrections for the Republic of Srspka, talks about beginning his position the day after war crimes suspect Radovan Stanković escaped from prison and the challenges this posed to his administration. He discusses the problems with the previous legal system in his country and how the current government is supportive of moving forward through the use of effective change. Post-Balkan war era improvements include staff training and a better operating budget. Sain also expresses his desire for input from the staff and inmates, including complaints that are fully investigated to remove any notion of a repressive environment.

In Chapter 4, Dr. Antal Kökényesi, a lieutenant general and the commander of the Hungarian National Prison Service, stated that overcrowding in the prisons has led to an increase in alternative sanctions and an increase in building modern prisons. In 2008, the Hungarian Prison Service launched a new strategic development program where the aim was to examine the strengths and weaknesses of the organization. This new strategic program has modernized the future objectives and mission of the Prison Service. Dr. Kökényesi also discusses his proactive strategies to engage the media and change the public's image of the corrections system.

In Chapter 5, John Rougier, the commissioner of prisons of Trinidad and Tobago, sees a need to modernize the prison system. He talks about the philosophical change in Trinidad and Tobago from a punitive philosophy of corrections to one that encourages restorative justice. Rougier has met with resistance but is steadfast in his belief that a change is necessary. He sees prison programming and reentry services as important functions in a holistic approach to handling offenders and ensuring they have the best chance at a recidivism free future. He also discusses the combined use of theory and practice and sees the need to replace programs that are not working to reduce recidivism and improve the offender.

In Chapter 6, John Pastorek, the warden at North Fraser Pretrial Centre (NFPC), operates a remand facility opened in British Columbia in 2001. NFPC incarcerates offenders who have been remanded in custody pending trial or sentencing, as well as individuals on immigration detention, and conducts the assessment and classification of offenders who receive a term of imprisonment of 30 days or more from a Lower Mainland court. Because most offenders in the NFPC serve only 1–3 months, few services can be provided, and little help is provided for the offenders to reintegrate into the community, as they are not incarcerated for very long. He talks about issues related to overcrowding, difficulty for those waiting for trial finding privacy to prepare for their trial, and the lack of adequate programming for an increasingly higher risk population of remanded individuals.

In Chapter 7, Michael Boileau, the warden of Matsqui Institution, Correctional Service Canada, Vancouver, BC, talks about the differences between the provincial and federal systems in Canada. He discusses the delicate tightrope that needs to be walked when dealing with several groups of people (the public, the corrections staff, and the inmates) in support of a common goal. By engaging people and seeking mutually beneficial solutions to issues, Boileau encourages outcomes that allow all parties to achieve their goals. He supports meaningful programs that remove the warehousing effect of prisons and aid offender development as inmates prepare for release.

In Chapter 8, Robert Jennings from the Western Australia Corrective Services discusses the overcrowding in his jurisdiction and his dislike of warehousing prisoners. According to Jennings, many inmates should not be incarcerated, and some may be better served through other programs (e.g., mental health). He acknowledges the need to run prisons like a business, without taking into account popular opinion, although he does support a team mentality in his facility. All staff are held accountable for the management of offenders and the successful operation of the prison. Jennings also believes that the goals of corrections extend beyond the point of incarceration and into the community as offenders reenter society.

In Chapter 9, Timothy Leo, the chief psychologist with the Singapore Prison Service, talks about the ongoing changes in his country. There is increased interest in the development of evidence-based practices and the need for a risk–needs–responsivity approach to offender assessment and rehabilitation. Leo also describes the Singapore Prison system as one that uses intermediate sanctions that keep lower risk offenders in the community. He has engaged the community and garnered support for the rehabilitation of offenders and reintegration and acceptance of them once they are released back into the community.

In Chapter 10, Sue Hall, the chief officer of West Yorkshire Probation, provides a community corrections perspective to this volume. She talks about how probation is now part of the entire criminal justice system in Britain. Her main aims in probation are to protect the public while reducing offending behavior by the probationer. Hall is outcome focused, paying necessary attention to the process and time associated with attaining desired outcomes while zeroing in on the end goal. She achieves this by investing resources in her staff through training and requiring that they meet academic and practical qualifications. By instilling a sense of vocation, Hall believes that her probation staff can make a difference.

In Chapter 11, Robert Ambroselli, the director of parole of the California Department of Corrections and Rehabilitation, is in charge of the largest corrections system in the United States, now under a series of lawsuits, which currently deals with issues of overcrowding. Ambroselli believes that parole needs to be reinvented and discusses how returning ex-offenders to prison for technical violations may be missing the real purpose of parole. He also recognizes the need to reduce the rate of incarceration and use feasible alternatives to jail and prison. Ambroselli speaks to the traditional legacy of the corrections field that has a culture of its own that is resistant to change. However, he believes that changes are necessary to progress.

In Chapter 12, "CM" in the United Kingdom has worked for years to help ex-offenders get employment or skills to facilitate employment. He provides perspective on reentry initiatives and programs available during imprisonment that facilitate offender reintegration into society upon release. CM is a proponent of employability skills and believes that employment among ex-offenders will help reduce recidivism. He also recognizes that imprisonment can be detrimental to the entire family and supports programs that keep the family unit together during periods of confinement (e.g., mother/baby units and overnight visits with family members).

Although each country faces its own unique set of challenges and rewards, the same themes are woven throughout most of the interviews. Most countries must deal with overcrowded prison facilities; resistance to change despite the knowledge of evidence-based practices and programs; difficulty procuring funding sources, especially when they have to compete with healthcare and educational priorities; and difficulty with "revolving door" inmates who come and go from prison so quickly such that there is no time to help them inside the prison or to ease their way back into the community and learn job skills or other ways of desisting from further offending. In each chapter, the corrections leader speaks about his or her unique system within the broader framework of shared global challenges.

Transnational relations and interactions with corrections institutions in countries outside one's own are becoming increasingly important because of the globalization of society and proliferation of useful knowledge throughout the world. The correctional leaders interviewed in this volume reflect on international interactions they have experienced and discuss how they have incorporated these encounters into their work with the correctional institutions in their home countries. The purpose of this volume and the subsequent volumes is to gain a personal understanding of how correctional systems operate in the field, in the real world, not what the official rhetoric dictates or pontificates. The interviewers ask correctional leaders about their personal (not the establishment's) correctional philosophy, as well as how they incorporate theory and best or evidence-based practices into their work. It is through this candid discussion that corrections scholars, researchers, and practitioners can develop an appreciation for transnational operations in the field from an insider's perspective and begin to reinvigorate the nature of their work.

Jennie K. Singer
Dilip K. Das
Eileen M. Ahlin

Interview with Hazael Ruiz, Ex-Director of the Penitentiary System in Mexico City

1

ELENA AZAOLA

Contents

Introduction

Mexico is a democratic, federal, and representative republic, integrated into 31 free states and a Federal District, the capital, also known as Mexico City. Each state, as well as the Federal District, has its own laws and penal codes and its own prisons. There are 431 penal institutions in the Mexican Republic, which, according to the type of authority responsible for each of them, are distributed into seven federal prisons, 322 state prisons, 92 municipal prisons, and 10 prisons in the Federal District. Mexico has 107 million inhabitants, and the total population in the prison system was 230,000 inmates at the end of 2009.

During the last decade, the prison population in Mexico has increased at an exceptional rate. Today, Mexico has a rate of 200 inmates per 100,000 inhabitants, whereas 10 years ago, it was 140 inmates per 100,000 inhabitants. Mexican prisons today have an overpopulation rate of 33% on the average, and there are states in which the prison overpopulation is at 100% of their capacity. This is the case for the Federal District, which has 20% of the population of local jurisprudence. Regarding gender, 96% of the prisoners are men, and 4% are women. This proportion has been steady at least during the past 30 years, since 1980 and is similar in other developing countries with the same level of development.

Regarding the legal situation of the inmates in the country, 59% are convicted, and 41% have been incriminated but not convicted; these percentages have been kept more or less the same for the last decade. Twenty-three percent are in the prison system because of a federal crime, and 77% are in prison for crimes pertaining to local jurisprudence. This percentage has not changed significantly for the last decade either.

Among the factors that have influenced the increase in population in the prison system of the country, the following can be included: 1) an increase in the crime rate; 2) reforms to the penal codes, making sentences stronger; and 3) administrative measures that make the length of stay longer.

Interview with Hazael Ruiz, Ex-Director of the Penitentiary System in Mexico City

The interview was carried out in three work sessions, done in three afternoons during January 2010. It lasted 6 h in total. The ex-director of the Mexico City Prisons was kind enough to accept our offer of going to our office at a center for social anthropological studies in the south area of the city. Both of us thought that that would be more convenient, because it would allow us to concentrate on the interview, with no interruptions from the normal work in offices that are in charge of defining policies for the Penal Centers of the City, where the ex-director still works.

He responded to my questions with interest, and the interview developed in a climate of confidence and cordiality, in which, according to what we were able to perceive, he expressed openly and sincerely his points of view. Below, he answers the topics we addressed.

Q: What can you tell us about your career?

A: I have been working in the penitentiary system in Mexico for 14 years, from 1995 to 2009. My career developed in the prisons of Mexico City. I started as a criminologist doing studies of personality with the inmates. Then, I was Executive Director in the Office of Criminology, and later, I became Director General in the same office for the Eastern Prison (*Reclusorio Oriente*) of Mexico City. Because I did a criminological study of a famous woman delinquent, "La Paca," a woman who claimed she knew of several crimes because she was clairvoyant, I was promoted to be the leader in that office. A little later, there was a riot in the Northern Prison (*Reclusorio Norte*), and I was commissioned as director in the Department of Observation and Classification (*Departamento de Observación y Clasificación*) in that prison. Later, I was promoted to assistant director of Criminological Studies in the Direction for Enforcing Penal Sanctions (*Estudios Criminológicos de la Dirección de Ejecución de Sanciones Penales*), which is the office that controls the 10 prisons in the Mexico City area. Later on, there was another strike, and I was commissioned to technical assistant director in the penitentiary, and, sometime later, director of the Eastern Prison. Then, I was promoted to technical director of several prisons in the city (*Reclusorios*), and when a convict escaped from the penitentiary, I was sent there as director. I consider that period of my life as being my best moment, the one I have enjoyed the most, in spite of being promoted later to be director of all the prisons in Mexico City.

Regarding my education, I studied law in Mexico City and then criminology at the University of Buenos Aires (*Universidad de Buenos Aires*) and at the University of Law and Penal Enforcement of Salamanca (*Universidad de Derecho de Ejecución Penal en Salamanca*). When I came back to Mexico and started working at the penitentiary system, I started doing tests of personality with delinquents, and I got passionate about it; I felt I was doing what I wanted to do. The positions I held afterward were more administrative or political, and that made me leave behind what was really of interest to me: criminal behavior. Actually, all the promotions that I had were unexpected; I thought I was going to remain studying criminal behavior and did not have in mind to hold administrative and political positions. Nevertheless, I was happy in those positions too.

My interest in this field started when I was 10 years old, as I was working in my father's company, and a coworker was arrested; at that time, I thought I would like to be a lawyer. When I was studying law, I had a criminologist teacher, and that contributed to enhancing my interest. Then, I was lucky to have an invitation to study in Argentina from a very distinguished family in the area of law, and there, I had the opportunity to meet great teachers in the field.

In spite of all the problems that one has to face being in charge of prisons, I felt quite satisfied with my career; I have been doing what I like and putting into practice the knowledge I have acquired. Truly, I did not have other opportunities than those I took, and I never refused any offer to occupy the different positions that were presented to me. At this point, I have ended my time as director general, and I work as a counselor for those who have that office in the Ministry of Government in Mexico City.

Q: What do you see as the most important changes that have occurred in the field of corrections over the course of your career (philosophies, organizational arrangements, specializations, policies and programs, equipment or technology, methods of rehabilitation, methods of community supervision, intermediate sanctions, personnel, and diversity), and so on?

A: Among the most important changes in the penitentiary system in Mexico, I would point out a greater openness that has made possible collaborations with academics and with civil, religious, and human rights organizations. There was a time when none of these organizations were allowed to get into the prisons. At least they could raise questions about what was happening there. Today, we have to be very attentive to the observations they make of us, particularly those from the human rights organizations. There is also a greater concern for the rehabilitation of the inmates, although the results cannot be good when we have more than 40,000 inmates in the prisons in Mexico City. We have to take into consideration that two of the prison centers here have more than 12,000 inmates. The overpopulation has the result that all programs for care and rehabilitation are totally insufficient. We also have to point out that the content of these programs have not been modified for many years; the only difference is that before, the government used to carry out these programs, and now, it allows the participation of specialized organizations, like those who take care of addictive behavior problems.

There have been changes also with regard to the normative aspect, but nothing substantial has changed, for instance, with regard to the abuse of preventive confinement. An important change happened when the local government was allowed to give benefits of prerelease; it used to be that only authorities from the federal government could do that. Nevertheless, the local system started to work having no experience nor qualified personnel, so it had to start following the old model imposed by traditional penitentiary officials. That brought up the lack of necessary generational relievers, as all the directors of penal facilities have come up from the old schools. There has not been any possibility of establishing training for civil service, where personnel receive ongoing training from high-quality professionals. In this environment, designations are made more for political or friendship reasons rather than based on the merits and knowledge of people. The same directors occupy the same positions over and over again.

Several external changes can be mentioned as the constant hardening of sentences, something that has induced overpopulation in the penal facilities as well as an increase in violence and lack of employment for the inmates due to the fact that society is not willing to collaborate with their recovery.

The poor work conditions of the personnel also stands out and contributes to the low self-esteem and lack of interest in their work, as their job is not professionalized, and they do not get any motivation. The great majority of workers do not have vocation for the work done in the penitentiaries. The penitentiary work has become bureaucratic, and nowadays, the only people who seek work in the penitentiary system are idealists or those who seek to make wealth through corruption. Nobody is interested in doing his/her career in the penitentiary system, as they know that is not the way to be promoted to occupy posts in the direction. Neither are there students interested in going to work in the prisons. The only way out now is to build a new prison facility where things can be done differently from the beginning, as it is very difficult to change old institutions. There is no solution for them.

There have been several isolated efforts to change, but they have not come to fruition, as they get diluted in such big populations. That is the case of treatments for addictions from specialized institutions that can only take care of a limited number of individuals (e.g., 60 inmates) when the estimation is that 20,000 inmates have addictive problems. Four years ago, two new prisons were built, but today, they are already overpopulated. The lack of funds is constant. Money is invested in the most basic things only: payroll, gas, food for inmates, and urgent reparations. There can be good intentions, but the lack of funds makes it impossible to put them into practice.

The main problem is overcrowding, which has induced deterioration in the life conditions of the inmates. Rates of homicide and suicide in prison have risen significantly. The problem is not the goodwill of officials in the prisons but the security policies that increase the punishments indiscriminately, which have led to over-population in the prisons. Not everything can be fixed by sending people to jail; prisons cannot change the conditions and deficiencies from the social environment of delinquents. As a former director of a prison, getting results is now much more difficult than it used to be. In 12 years, the population has tripled. The inmates themselves realized that the officials are overwhelmed. There is abuse of the prison punishment. Prisons should be only for those representing a real social risk. It has been said that inmates receive training for committing more crimes when they are in prison. Those who manage to come out of prison have overcome many tests and are ready for anything; they want to go out to show others that they are capable of surviving prison.

Q: What is your philosophy of the personnel in the prisons? What do you think should be the role of prison, jail, and community supervision officials in society?

A: The role of the personnel in the prison should be that of a first-class public servant, acknowledged for his/her capacity and honesty. He/She should be aware of the great social responsibility deposited in him/her to rehabilitate criminals. I think they can be of service if they give a good example; delinquents have not been able to assimilate adequate behavioral parameters, and if they manage to be aware of a good example in an official, seeing him/her as a normal civil person, they would like to be like him/her. Then, one must serve as an example to inmates, and also, one must be aware that custodians do not commit abuses. In other words, first comes the way one treats inmates and then comes the treatment. There should be penitentiary officials with a good training, with a degree; but specialists from other organizations should also be allowed inside the prison, for instance, people who know how to deal with addictions. We should stop pretending that we can do everything. Modern prisons cannot do without the support of external organizations or institutions that can give work and training to inmates, and even without those who offer cultural and sport activities. This contact with the outside world also encourages the prison to work in a transparent way, less closed into itself. Nevertheless, these programs must be revised continually so that they do not lose their objectives. Their appropriateness needs to be revised, as well as the degree of quality and the benefit they contribute for helping inmates in reintegrating into society. Evaluation of these programs is very important, although it has not been done in a systematic way until now. Another instance that does not exist in Mexico is the community supervision of the prisons, although this function is carried out continuously by the public human rights institutions that have been getting stronger and specialize in this task. Their visitors are very experienced.

The existing organization in the prison is a formal state organization; nevertheless, prisons also operate with informal codes, and inmates meticulously take care of making sure they are respected. That is the case, for instance, of the rules those inmates who share a dormitory impose on themselves or the behavioral codes established regarding their family members. It is easier for an inmate to violate a formal rule than to violate one imposed by them themselves. Inside the prisons, there is complicity, which can be positive or negative; there is comradeship, but there are also abuses.

There should be a higher selectivity to send to prisons only those who really deserve to be bereft of their freedom. Nevertheless, legislators have not done this work, as they litigate guided by political considerations, not by technical ones. Also, it can be said that what has prevailed is a "punitive populism"; that is, the idea that if more people are taken to prisons, criminal rates will decrease. Other kinds of strategies are needed, such as cleaning the police corps, being stricter in abiding by the norm, and updating and revising the norms. The corps of custodians also needs to be depurated, to be made more professional, to carry out more strict processes, and to perform good selections. In these tasks, experts from other institutions, such as human rights institutions, attorneys' offices, and other nongovernmental institutions, should take part. In this way, responsibility will be shared and not be only in the hands of the penitentiary system.

Prisons are responsible for almost all of the services they have: food, custodians, medical services, and those of psychologists and social workers. Exceptions are work and training (for inmates) in which we always need support from other institutions. What is offered in the area of work and education is always insufficient. The education we can offer is not of the highest quality and generally does not take into account the special characteristics of the population in prison. The inmates go to the classes, because if they do, they obtain other advantages such as permission to have a television set or to be granted an intimate visitor. They do not go to the courses because they are interested in them but for the additional benefits. The offer of higher education is scarce. There are only 280 inmates enrolled, which represents less than 1% of the population. Medical attention is also inefficient and insufficient. Personnel are not often there and have very little motivation. Family visits are allowed four times a week, but the number of family members that go is such that the service is exceeded. Two of the prisons that have more than 12,000 inmates each are totally saturated on the visit days. The facilities are totally insufficient to take care of the population. Water and electricity are also insufficient. It is a system that was borne from good intentions but, nowadays, is very difficult to manage. Even in this situation, the length of the sentences tends to rise, and more people are taken to prison; in a few words, because of punitive populism.

Certain services have been started to be commissioned as private institutions, for instance, food, but that has not solved the problem. The managers do not supervise adequately, nor is there adequate quantity or quality of food, and if food is not secure, there is a risk that inmates might riot.

Regarding postpenitentiary supervision for inmates, it is done more for the sake of police control than for contributing to social rehabilitation. It should be granted that ex-inmates who would request it could be enrolled in one of the social programs that the government of Mexico City sponsors. Otherwise, with not enough support nets, they are more prone to relapse. There is no adequate supervision for ex-inmates, and this is one of the factors that has contributed to the increasing relapses, as well as the violence that is involved in crimes in the last few years. Many inmates go out feeling resentful, because some officials treated them as if they were invisible; they realize the food is bad, the medical staff does not fulfill its function, their families do not receive any help, and as all this happens, it seems to them that everybody pretends nothing is wrong.

Although intermediate sanctions have been contemplated in the law, in practice, the system to apply them has not been developed, so prison is the punishment for everybody. That is the reason why prisons are overpopulated with people who could have been sanctioned through programs in freedom.

Q: In your experience, what policies or programs have worked well, and which have not? Can you speculate for what reasons?

A: The policy of increasing sentences indiscriminately has been a mistake, and a policy of intermediate sanctions should be developed. There used to be a program for sending all the young people who committed a crime for the first time to another prison. Unfortunately, this has been cancelled, and the new young ones are mixed again with all types of criminals. There have also been problems with giving anticipated freedom, because there have been a lot of cases of corruption, people who pay the officers to grant them freedom without having the right to it. Another problem is the use of substances and the officers participating in getting drugs into the prison. Addiction is much stronger inside than outside; being outside, the person can be addicted and functional, but inside, the person stops being functional.

Seven thousand people work in the prisons in Mexico City, and this number is insufficient to take care of the 40,000 inmates. We are outside the norm in all the parameters. Although the capacity of the facilities is for 20,000, we have doubled that number. Corruption in these circumstances is very difficult to fight; it seems that it can only be eradicated if these institutions are closed and new ones are opened. Other things cannot be eliminated either, like the tradition of putting tents in the yards so inmates can have intimate relations with their partners, given the fact that the facilities for that purpose are insufficient.

Internal and external changes have to go in parallel, and both are very difficult to achieve. Externally, it is very difficult to modify codes and criminal policies and to obtain more funds. Nevertheless, without these funds, it is impossible to try to achieve any internal change. There have not really been any successful programs, only isolated and small efforts in relation to the size of the population.

Q: In your view, what should be the relationship between theory and practice? What can practitioners learn from studying and applying
theories, and what can those who create theories of punishment
gain from practitioners?

A: This is an essential combination, and without it, it is impossible to function: Academics need to listen to the experiences of the people who
work in the field. At the same time, people who work in the field
should look into the theory to make better methods to use in their
work. In the last few years, the government has been more willing
to be evaluated by academics; nevertheless, a constructive relationship has not been achieved. New theoreticians are needed, there
are some very old ones who have monopolized the field and are
organized into a very close group, not welcoming new specialists.
They designed the laws and the models for treatment that are still
in use. They formed a group, took the topic for themselves, and
pretended that they are the only ones who can "certify" other specialists and they are the only ones who can say who is a specialist in
the field and who is not. They occupy the directive posts in several
states. There is no new input for their frames of reference or for
generational change.

There is a need for research in many subjects. For example, several studies have been done with the inmates, but very little has
been done regarding the staff in the prisons. It would be good to
know their profile and why they have so little interest in their work.
There is also a need for new manuals; the ones that are in use are
from 30 years ago and are obsolete. Some studies have been done,
but then, they are not disseminated enough; they only get to the
hands of a small elite. Researchers need to disseminate their work
widely. Nevertheless, it is true that those who work for the penitentiary system have no motivation; they are not interested in reading
the theoreticians. It would be good if some joint studies were carried out, where personnel in the institutions and academics participate. Many subjects need to be studied.

There are very few scientific journals in this field, and they are
not widely disseminated. I would rather read specialized journals
instead of books that soon become obsolete. The personnel in the
prison system do not have money to buy books either but probably
could buy journals if these attracted their interest. If there would
be a journal that could give voice to them, somewhere where they
could express their problems, their concerns, then, probably, they
would be interested in getting it.

Q: In your experience, has your state's correctional system made use of various evidence-based programs? Do you feel that it is best to use

evidence-based practices (or "what works") or that this focus is not important?

A: The programs and policies that are carried out in the prisons have been the same for many years; we have not left behind the traditional penitentiarism—we have not evolved. There have not been legislative reforms allowing new policies to develop. In this sense, we don't have a penitentiary system based on evidence, as it would be desirable. This is one of the more abandoned sectors, and very little funds are given to it each year. More investments have been done in other aspects of security, like in police corps and technology, but in the prisons, there have not been any changes, and even less profound, meaningful changes. Officials responsible for penitentiary institutions are not used to looking at new information or new studies; only a few who have the interest to do it, but they are the exception. It is not something institutionalized, only isolated efforts. On my part, I find relevant information especially in the Institute for Legal Research from the National University (*Instituto de Investigaciones Jurídicas de la Universidad Nacional*).

There is a need for a National Institute for Penitentiary Training so that there will be a unique criterion about training for personnel. Nowadays, each state in the republic does what it can, but there is not even one uniform model to follow when doing criminal studies of inmates. If there were a journal, a discussion for all these topics could begin, but this has not happened yet.

Q: Regarding transnational relations, how have you been affected by the following in your organization's work by developments outside the country (human rights demands, universal codes of ethics, practical interactions with corrections officials from other countries, personal experiences outside the country, programs developed by other countries, new sentencing laws, political strife, or war in your or neighboring countries)?

A: It can be said that officials in the prisons of my country almost do not have any opportunities to relate and know what officials in other countries do. There are very little opportunities for exchange. This exchange seemed to me very useful at the time of my formation; later, as an official, it was not encouraged. We have to take into consideration that what is done in other countries is not always possible to apply here. For instance, in the United States, some technologies (such as scanners, which are used for controlling entrances) have not worked here, because the equipment is not taken care of, they do not last long, and their maintenance is costly. The same happened with the equipment installed for inmates not to make use of cell phones. Custodians sabotage the system and allowed inmates to make calls with cell phones, as inmates use them to extort citizens; it is a good business for custodians.

Q: Are you basically satisfied or dissatisfied with developments in the field of corrections?

A: Despite all this, the penitentiary system in Mexico has some acceptable features. The design of the prisons in the 1970s was good, although nowadays, it has been surpassed. The system is not that bad; the main problem is overpopulation—inside policies do not work mainly because of this. If it were in my hands, I would make legislative changes for establishing a more selective use of the prison and not as the only sanction in all cases. I would also do a better classification of the centers, and depending on the profile of each center, I would design a scientific treatment for the inmates. I would do programs for minimal imprisonment with follow-ups and tutorials from the State. I would change the system of custodians, the profile for recruitment, and the training. I would avoid the contamination of inmates who have a low criminology index, because this increases when living with others who represent a higher social risk. Also, prerelease has failed, because it has not been used in the right way; there are people who deserve an opportunity, and this is not granted; there are also others who do not deserve it but pay for it.

I have to acknowledge, nevertheless, that the dominant policy points us in the right direction, opposite to the one that demands more severe sentences and no tolerance. This last issue affects the results of the penitentiary institutions. Given the current conditions, officials are not in a situation where they can rehabilitate inmates who go back to society with a higher degree of social resentment.

Once inmates go back to society, there should be guidelines for contention and a follow-up, less for police control, and more based on support through social programs. This has not happened in the country, except for a few isolated experiences that have not managed to last. The current norms even make it difficult for ex-inmates to socially reincorporate when it imposes the compelling rule of having to go to sign in periodically. This makes ex-inmates have to take absence from their jobs, in case they have found one. A system of intermediate sanctions and house arrests should also be developed, as well as halfway houses, support programs for ex-inmates, and other specific programs for women who come out of prison. These supports are necessary, especially if we take into consideration that not all ex-inmates tend to escalate to more serious crimes but continue stealing out of poverty and alienation, which can be stronger when coming out of jail. Many inmates are not worried about when they will come out of prison but about what they will do when they come out. It should be good to ask the industry to take advantage of the ex-inmates for employment, assume the commitment of giving them a job once they are granted their freedom.

If conditions in the prisons were better, they would be less harmful, for inmates and for their families. Currently, the environment contaminates, and it does not make sense to submit to it those who have committed minor crimes, including traffic accidents.

The changes that will have greater impact in transforming prisons are those of legislative order which are feasible, except for the criminological policies currently dominating, which emphasize punitive populism. Besides reducing overpopulation, infrastructure should be adapted, and personnel should be increased. In the same vein, this subject should again be a priority in the political agenda, just as the people in charge of prisons of the past managed to do when the prisons were designed in the 1970s. Nowadays, politicians do not touch this subject, and we should convince them of the importance of doing it.

Conclusion

In general terms, the logic followed by the ex-director of the penitentiary centers of Mexico City is congruent with what academics have pointed out in their studies and clearly reflect some of the most severe problems in the penitentiary system of the whole country. The picture he delineates is that of a stagnant system, incapable of transforming itself and of offering alternatives in front of the avalanche of a growing population that surpasses, by far, the capacity of their funds and facilities. As the ex-director points out, the solutions have to come from a redesign of the criminological policies, which have not managed to put into practice a system of punishments alternative to prison, do not have among their priorities the investment in programs of social assimilation of ex-inmates, and do not have a system of incentives for personnel who are committed to their work.

In a situation such as in Mexico, in which the increasing rates of criminality are a key subject, it is imperative that the State and the society revise the role that the abandonment of our prisons has played in this issue. As the ex-director pointed out, the time has come for prisons to occupy a relevant place in the agenda of important issues in security policies.

Interview with Assistant Commissioner Luke Grant of Offender Services and Programs in New South Wales

2

LAUREN BENTON
ELIAS MPOFU
RODD ROTHWELL

Contents

Correctional services in Australia operate within a complex legislative environment that is governed by independent state government statutes. The majority of criminal law is codified in state government legislation, and although there is a federal criminal law code, it is responsible for the incarceration of a relatively small number of individuals. There is no federal correctional jurisdiction in Australia. In the state of New South Wales (NSW), the corrections authority, Corrective Services New South Wales (Corrective Services NSW), is part of the Department of Justice and the Attorney General and is headed by a commissioner.

For the purpose of this research, a series of interviews were conducted with Luke Grant, Assistant Commissioner of Offender Services and Programs— Corrective Services NSW (Asst. Commissioner Grant), at the organization's headquarters in Sydney, NSW. Asst. Commissioner Grant is responsible for, among other things, offender services and programs in custody and in the community, including correctional services industries, inmate classification, and case management. He was interviewed on multiple occasions (around

6 h in total) and, throughout, was extremely forthcoming about the correctional system, as he was very keen to increase community understanding of the correctional system in NSW. He evidences well-grounded knowledge in this field and is passionate about the developments that can be made to the correctional system.

Over the course of three meetings, a range of questions and topics were put to Asst. Commissioner Grant. Where possible, these were kept relatively consistent with those being used elsewhere in the overall compilation of interviewee results. His responses have been summarized as follows. The points presented are not intended to be a verbatim representation but have been kept as close as possible to his comments.

Career

I have read your biographical details and current responsibilities profile listed on your organization's web site, but can I ask you to restate what your current role is and what your responsibilities are?

The following remarks characterized Asst. Commissioner Grant's response to this question. He observed that there are several drivers and disconnected elements associated with the current role of Assistant Commissioner of Offender Services and Programs. These roles include

- Responsibility for all activities within the organization, including correctional centers' probation and parole, which pertain to the rehabilitation of offenders. The activities consist of the provision of services and programs to promote the health and well-being of prisoners while also reducing their risk of reoffending.
- Policies affecting offenders both in custody and in the community through the offender policy unit.
- The correctional services industries, including commercial business units and service areas employing inmates that provide opportunities to develop and practice vocational skills that will assist with employment post-release. This area also deals with food services for inmates.
- Social equities and how they affect offenders, including responsibilities for Aboriginal, women, and disabled offender management, and the implementation of specific policies and services that directly connect people to services outside the organization.
- Inmate classification, which determines in which security regime an inmate is managed, the correctional center they are placed, and if they are suitable for external leave programs, including work release, education leave, and weekend leave.

- Offender case management, which ensures an individualized approach to offender management, linking offenders to services and interventions that promote their well-being, and addresses the underlying causes of their offending. This also entails the creation of reports that are provided to courts and/or the state parole authority.
- Restorative justice programs.
- Victims' services such as the community partnerships initiative, which looks at strategies that the whole government may be interested in, along with interagency relationships. Other victims' services included responsibility for chaplaincy, spiritual guidance, and advisers/counselors operating within prisons.

How long have you worked for this department? Can you also describe what else you have done and how your career trajectory has brought you to where you are today?

Asst. Commissioner Grant first worked in corrective services in the early 1980s. As a university student, he worked on a casual basis for about 4 years as a community service organizer at the Newtown and City District Probation and Parole offices. The job function was to interview offenders to whom the courts had issued a community service order, to match the individuals to a community work project, and to monitor compliance with the conditions of the order.

In 1990, Asst. Commissioner Grant pursued an opportunity to work at the Long Bay Correctional Complex as a numeracy teacher within the facility's Remand Center. The experience was very positive, and he recognized that the combination of obvious opportunities for improvement in the system and an organization that was receptive to change had the potential for providing a challenging and stimulating work opportunity. When a position as a senior educational officer at Long Bay Jail became available, he was appointed to this position and departed from his previous occupation as an academic at the University of Sydney.

A later promotion from a role in the jail to a position in the organizational executive came about through broader recognition of his experimentation with new approaches to the initial custody handling procedures. He initiated systems at the front end that assisted in reducing the rate of unnatural deaths in custody. This approach was endorsed by the State Coroner, Kevin Waller, who had conducted a statewide review of deaths in custody. As a consequence, the present commissioner, Ron Woodham, directed that Asst. Commissioner Grant implement this approach throughout all correctional centers within NSW. Grant was subsequently given responsibility for the reception and screening process, suicide prevention strategies, and the case management framework process statewide. From there, he became the director of Inmate Classification and Mass Management, which led to broader responsibilities for programs, classifications, and industries in all NSW jails. This last role, in turn, led him to the current position of Assistant Commissioner of Offender Services and Programs, with expanded responsibilities for the equivalent activities in both correctional centers, court cells, and community offender services in NSW.

Is there anything in your career path that is very different from what you expected it would be, and if so, can you explain that for me?

He initially came into the organization with negative preconceptions about the way offenders were treated and the opportunities and scope for rehabilitation. However, he later came to appreciate that much of the prison system was misrepresented and misunderstood by the community. From an initial viewpoint, in which he thought he would advocate for change, he later sought to participate in change and, in that way, have more impact. His ambitions remain the same today: to make prisons more effective with improved outcomes that balance the safety of the community with humane management of offenders.

He has maintained a particular interest in analyzing and challenging prevailing orthodoxies and prison myths, particularly those informed by ideology as opposed to evidence, including the strongly held perception in the community that Aboriginal people in custody are basically "killed" by the "system" or, at the very least, that this population has a higher rate of deaths in custody than do non-Aboriginal inmates. In reality, there is a lower rate of Aboriginal deaths in custody compared with non-Aboriginal deaths, with the overrepresentation of Aboriginal people being incarcerated.

Another misconception is that there was nothing a prison could do to improve a person's prospects upon release. Although there is still concern regarding the negative impact a prison sentence can have, he is now more confident of the benefits of some interventions that are being applied to prisoners in jail. However, if it is a question of putting more resources into early intervention, such as improving preschools or high school retention rates, he would still argue that this would be the best stage to intervene. However, given that jails do exist and people are in jails, significant positive outcomes can be derived from connecting offenders to programs and services within the jails. These include the connection to good health services, proper assessments for mental health problems, and acquiring educational skills or a more prosocial orientation.

What motivated you to enter the field of corrections?

His initial interest was aroused by exposure to the experiences of a friend who worked within the probation and parole system. To an extent, the motivation was quite "voyeuristic" (his own words) in that he was curious about the hidden world of jails and intrigued by the personal stories of people living on the fringes of society and the nature of the microcosm in which they live.

Did you develop any specific specializations along the way, and how have they been important to your involvement in this area?

Asst. Commissioner Grant came into the career with no specific skills in corrections, and therefore, along the way, he had to acquire the skills that are relevant to performing his role. He had been a lecturer at university; however, he was not part of the students' pastoral care system while a university employee. He had studied psychology as an undergraduate student at a university, which assisted him in understanding the psychological theories and practices applicable to the corrections environment. As a scientist, he had also acquired a sound knowledge of empirical methods and a capacity for critically reviewing hypotheses and their supporting evidence.

Since moving into the field of corrections, he has had to develop a new array of skills. He has comprehensively researched the literature on penology, gaining a broad and detailed knowledge of correctional practice. This has enabled him to contribute to the knowledge base though publishing in academic journals. It was through his critical thinking surrounding the available literature that he has been able to filter through ideas relevant to correctional practice. Finally, he has acquired vital skills in the politics of corrections systems and corrections reform from working with political leaders and parliamentary ministers. Asst. Commissioner Grant is happy with his current position and is not inclined to move past it to the next job.

What are the real problems of performing your role?

One major issue for the corrections system is not having the opportunity to get positive information into the public domain through the media. Currently, the organization is fairly powerless when it comes to the media. There is an overemphasis on gratuitous stories relating to issues such as sex, drugs, or high-profile criminals. The fact that the media give a negative portrayal of prisons results in poor community attitudes toward corrections and ignorance of what corrections seek to achieve. It also stigmatizes prisoners and fuels community fear and a reluctance to provide practical assistance and support to those in prison. He feels that the community would be less reactive if they understood more details such as how much prisons cost, where the funds are being used, and the outcomes or alternatives for people who commit crimes.

A second area of frustration is the slow pace of change in corrections, which mitigates against timely and creative solutions. He may start with a visionary idea, develop a model or framework that is well informed, and then be unable to operationalize it in the short term. One of the obstacles to implementation is finding staff with the skills to match his expectations. As an example, recruiting qualified experienced managers who have a good fit with the organization and who can deliver on key correctional outcomes is often a daunting task, as people with such skills have other opportunities in less challenging work environments.

Changes Experienced

What do you see as the most important changes that have occurred in the field of corrections over the course of your career?

One key change is that his work peers and those in positions of influence have started to develop more of an appreciation of evidence-based outcomes, which guides investment of effort in programs that reduce reoffending and importantly determines what approaches should be abandoned. In the past, the reduction of reoffending was believed to be produced by enhancing self-esteem. However, in Asst. Commissioner Grant's view, this is a flawed concept, with evidence suggesting that this has little or no impact on rehabilitation and recidivism rates. Therefore, in recent times (since around the late 1990s), the approach has changed from an intrapsychic, individualized approach to a skills training–oriented rehabilitation service based on literature and evidence for success in the prison system. There is now more interest in models and theories of change and how these aspects inform corrections practices.

Another important change expressed by Asst. Commissioner Grant is requiring custodial staff to have a case load and the embedding of the concept of "duty of care" into the way correctional staff approach their responsibilities. When he first took a job within the correctional system, custodial staff did not have a case load, and when an inmate was distressed, it was the responsibility of the professional staff (i.e., nurse or psychologist) to assist the inmate. Today, there is a greater breakdown in the divisions within those roles. Prison officers now accept that they have a responsibility to contribute to positive outcomes in the longer term and not just to manage offender's reaction to a punitive custodial environment and to incapacitate. This has led to a balanced approach in which it is recognized that there is a responsibility to develop programs that will produce better outcomes for the community by reducing reoffenders and by treating prisoners more reasonably. A case management system that required prison officers to take on a case load, to record informal observations of behavior, and to formally interview and write at least one case note per offender per month detailing their positive interaction with inmates was introduced in 1994. By creating such relationships, officers were enabled to anticipate potential problems and to consider potential prisoner-centered approaches.

Officers require ongoing training and support to properly apply a case management approach. Nonetheless, there are positive steps in the right direction. An emphasis on training workers in specialized skills and functions helps reduce the gap between an organization's vision and its delivery by the staff.

The Canadian correctional system has been particularly influential on correctional practices in NSW (and in Australia). The Canadians have invested a large amount of money in research and have encouraged partnerships with universities around correctional methodology and outcomes. This has produced very robust findings about approaches to correctional interventions and practices that do and do not work. Central to this is the "risk–needs model," which recognizes the importance of determining each individual's risk of reoffending and their specific criminogenic needs before allocating the individual to a program. This approach recognizes that, to have an appreciable effect on a high-risk individual's behavior, they will require a higher dose of treatment. Therefore, some programs are now administered over a longer period of time, are more in-depth and, therefore, have a greater impact on the individual's long-term behavior.

Changing the quantum and ratio of staff in different functions has also proved to be important. Over the time that Asst. Commissioner Grant has worked in this field, there has been a significant increase in the provision of rehabilitation activities. Today, there are around 170 psychologists who work in the organization, whereas when he started, there would have been around 40. There needs to be sufficient staff with the right qualifications to have an impact and create change. The organization has been successful at increasing the number of staff in areas such as psychology, program facilitation, and education along with gaining increased funds for these activities.

Recent changes within the organization include the move toward the integration of community and custodial practice. Previously, probation and parole and prisons consisted of two discrete sections. This was associated with separate information systems and mistrust between the arms of the agency. There is now a more integrated approach to managing offenders, with case workers managing individuals throughout their sentence—creating a greater sense of continuity. This concept is called the "throughcare concept" and intended for implementation in the entire NSW correctional system.

There is also now an appreciation of the importance of community involvement and of targeting interventions at individuals on community-based orders at an earlier stage in an individual's criminal career. Coupled with this is the recognition that offenders require a lot more support in their transition back to the community at the expiration of a prison sentence. This has resulted in moving significant resources from custody to community. There is also a greater recognition now that incarceration is not always the best intervention, and oftentimes, community-based orders have a greater impact with better outcomes and a decrease in the distress brought about by incarceration on both individuals and their families and also better outcomes from treatment programs.

What changes in external conditions have had a significant impact on current correctional practices and policy?

According to Asst. Commissioner Grant, the current philosophies underpinning the corrective services operations in NSW have their origins in a major commission of inquiry into corrective services conducted by Justice Nagel in the 1970s. This was in response to complaints about staff malpractice, violent treatment of prisoners in a number of jails, and very bad living conditions leading to violent incidences of unrest, disobedience, and riots from within the jail system. Activism from proinmate civic organizations sprouted community interest in correctional system practices, particularly regarding the treatment and living conditions of prisoners. To reform the entire system, the Nagel Royal Commission Report (1978) laid the foundations for the way prisons operate in NSW today. The important principles adopted included the emphasis on rehabilitation services and adoption of the philosophy that deprivation of liberty should be the extent of the punishment. New approaches to correctional care included the provision of improved health treatment and chaplaincies. These changes were widely adopted throughout Australia. Asst. Commissioner Grant observed that correctional policies are often influenced by a chain of events arising from a single incident in which, fueled by media coverage, the community is outraged, precipitating "moral panic" and forcing reactive legislative change.

There were also changes in antidiscrimination legislation in which community issues inform and impact the way that inmates are now dealt with. Social and political activism has also fueled a range of parliamentary inquiries into the size of the prison populations and the way children of inmates and women visitors are managed. These inquiries have contributed to changes in legislation and challenges to traditionally held views and beliefs.

Corrupt practices have also been addressed over the years. A major event of the 1980s leading to change was the exposure of corruption among a number of people in the legal system, including magistrates and lawyers, famously resulting in the imprisonment of the Minister for Corrective Services, Rex Jackson. The corruption surrounding the system of remissions saw that, after a parole period, some inmates had their sentence reduced. This process was abused by a number of people within the system, and as a consequence, it gave rise to a different sentencing regime called the "truth in sentencing regime," which commenced in 1989. This meant that inmates had to serve the entirety of their sentence, with no opportunity for an early release. This was the direct consequence of the community's dismay around the corruption.

Within the last 10 years, influenced by the "new managerialism" permeating government activities, there has been a significant shift to increase emphasis on public accountability and efficient management in which outputs are measured, and there is greater oversight by external bodies; at the same time, the government has demanded measures of outcomes. The current thinking is that harsh punitive correctional systems do not produce effective outcomes. Changing behavior requires evidence-based and accredited education- and psychological-based programs.

Overall, has the quality of the corrective system in the state of New South Wales improved or declined over the past 10 years?

The major improvements within the NSW correctional system include goals to reduce reoffending and enhance community safety. This has led to a whole range of results that are planned and include reducing the risk of reoffending and providing safe, secure, humane management of offenders; community support; successful reintegration; and better resource management. This has led to improvements in measurable outcomes such as escape rates, assaults on prisoners, and rates of deaths in custody due to unnatural causes. From 2000, there have been significant improvements on almost every measure. Escape rates have been dramatically reduced. In the 1990s, there were nearly 200 people escaping from NSW jails every year, and the population was significantly lower (i.e., 40%) than it is now. There are now only about 10 escapes per year—a dramatic decline. This is not only due to the changing physical environments of jails but also to the quality of decision making around how people are managed. There is a behavioral profiling or classification system that is quite rigorous and uses an actuarial risk assessment instrument to formulate an individual case plan.

All of the prison officers in correctional centers in NSW below a certain rank have to have a case load. Prior to 1993, prison officers performed a very static function that was more about security and discipline; they were run in a highly regimented way in which the interactions between the officer and inmate were required to be minimal and authoritative. Around 1993, the case management system was introduced and required all prison officers to have a case load in which there were case plans about managing the inmates safely and being aware of the needs of the inmates as well as reducing their likelihood of reoffending. The new case load system enables prison officers to anticipate problems and to improve rehabilitative outcomes for inmates.

The cost of running the correctional system has increased due to the cost of living and the increased need for services. However, at the same time, within the community side of the organization, the cost has tripled in the last 3 years due to changes in the rostering community corrections staff, with unannounced home visits, increased drug testing, and more compliance and monitoring of people on community-based orders. Therefore, the cost of providing an improved service is quite significant.

The dialogue around the success or failure of corrections, particularly where interstate or international comparisons are being made, is often compromised by the lack of consistency in the agreed definition of "recidivism." The most common measure is whether the person returns to prison within a 2-year period. This is a very blunt measure, because it provides no indication of changes in the severity of offending, volume of crime, or time until the first offense. It is also influenced by policing, changes in legislation, and court processes. Return to prison does not capture offenders who reoffend but receive community-based orders and therefore underestimates the scale of reoffending. A better measure is to focus on the "return to corrective services" (adopted in NSW in 2000), which captures repeat offenders who are reconvicted and receive any type of corrective services administered order.

The general quality of life has improved within prisons. The general quality of the built environment has improved in response to new philosophies of design. Improvement of inmate food, better work programs for inmates, good workplace safety record, and the quality of the staff have had a positive impact. These improvements have led to a change in the quality of programmes for inmates in that correctional policy is now guided by an evidence-based practice framework based on rigorous pretesting and quality oversight.

Another area of improvement is improved relationships with other agencies. There is now an expectation on the exchange of information as people pass from one agency to the next. For example, if a person comes from police custody to correctional services, there will be information supplied from police observations of the individual and whether there is a risk of self-harm. Other relevant information is handed over in every case. Information about social security payments, housing and tenancy arrangements, debt, and physical and mental health are now exchanged with regard to privacy provisions with the relevant agencies.

Finally, in the last 20 years, the quality of health services provided in the correctional system has dramatically improved. The inmate health surveys compiled every 3 to 4 years have provided the evidence regarding the health needs of inmates, allowing better targeting of health services. NSW has been particularly innovative in harm minimization, which has ensured better health outcomes for intravenous drug users.

In general, is it more or less difficult to be a correctional officer now than in the past?

Asst. Commissioner Grant indicated it is much more difficult to be a corrections officer these days because of the requirements of accountability. For example, there is now more access to information and greater transparency requirements. Individuals can more easily make complaints about agencies, and the Ombudsman's Office can take up cases of grievance. The Minister can appoint visitors external to the department to check on the performance of correctional services. Other external bodies such as the Human Rights Commission and Antidiscrimination Commission have oversight and the capability to have matters brought before the Supreme Court. They can also challenge administrative decisions, and there is increased scope for civil litigation. All these aspects are intended to improve the system and resolve problems. However, the extensive external scrutiny adds to the performance demands on staff who must be wary of accountability and the complexities of their overall work requirements. The complexity of a correctional officers' role has also increased with the advent of case management and the introduction of new technology.

Personal Correctional Philosophy

What do you think should be the role of correctional centers and community supervision officials in society?

The correctional system plays an important role in contributing to public safety. Although the symbolism of corrections, in particular, prisons, is inextricably linked to the maintenance of public order and the notion that there is a consequence for persistent antisocial behavior, there is little evidence for the effectiveness of prisons as a specific or general deterrent. Correctional agencies have become increasingly important places of intervention in the lives of individuals who suffer a range of social and health deficits and perform the role of a true human service agency with respect to the most marginalized populations in the community.

Within the community, there is an increasing emphasis on providing people with close supervision so that, if someone has a series of conditions attached to their order, then the duty of the corrections staff is to provide good support and supervision to enable the individuals to meet their conditions.

Both correctional center and community supervision officers have a responsibility to provide the best advice to the community, including questions relating to the value and purpose of programs. In particular, community-based officers have a role in providing advice to the courts in a manner that will maximize the number of people on community-based orders rather than increase incarceration rates. There is recognition within the organization that imprisonment can harm and should be avoided if possible. However, it should not be done at the cost of exposing the community to people who have not been or cannot be rehabilitated.

What policies does Australia have regarding relations with the community, political groups, and other criminal justice organizations, and do these policies work well?

There is no specific policy in place; however, there are practices in place in relation to liaising with community groups. There are a number of mechanisms for this, as it is too vast to set up a single forum to ensure that all community interests are represented across all layers of the organization. A forum was established to deal with Aboriginal communities and recognizes the importance of involving them in decisions about how programs and services should be established. There are also external bodies that manage the needs of those within the community so that there is an independent voice in the process.

In addition, at each correctional center, there is a requirement to have a community consultant or council forum in which a representative will participate regularly at the correctional center level to discuss the impact of how things could be done. Correctional services are trying to encourage opportunities to communicate with other sectors by hosting public seminars so that the general public can express their ideas. It is difficult to address disparate views within the community, but there are systems to ensure that groups or stakeholders are listened to.

How would you prefer sentencing laws to be modified to have prisons and jails include the individuals most deserving of incarceration?

In NSW, on any day, there are twice as many people serving sentences in the community than in custody. There is scope, however, for more emphasis to be placed on noncustodial sanctions. The majority of other states in Australia place less reliance on incarceration. Any change to the emphasis on incarceration needs to maintain community safety as the paramount consideration. The effectiveness of community supervision and treatment, however, would suggest that it is in the community's interest to place a larger number of offenders on community-based orders. The use of actuarial risk assessment instruments to discriminate between an individual who has a very high likelihood of reoffending and those least likely to offend is an important element of moving in this direction.

To create the changes needed, more resources will need to be provided for community treatment and support. This is not just about changing the law but about creating adequate and appropriately resourced alternatives that will allow the court to avoid incarceration and minimize the cost and damage that this creates for individuals, their family, and the community.

Problems and Successes Experienced

What would you consider to be the greatest problem facing the correctional system at this time?

According to Asst. Commissioner Grant, increases in sentence length, increases in the utilization of prison sentences, and changes in the presumption in favor of bail have contributed to a massive increase in the full-time inmate population. It is often difficult to get the community engaged in correctional issues, because there is a tendency to demonize and pathologize criminals, and the fear that is experienced by the community is often out of proportion to the totality of risk from those people who are in custody. This community fear then translates into an expectation that people will be given longer sentences to keep them away from the community, without considering the consequences and benefits. Therefore, it appears that incarceration is more likely to satisfy the desire for retribution.

Community ignorance about what happens within corrections and their ill-informed views on the adequacy of sentencing place pressure on politicians to react conservatively to sentencing reform. People also assume that the justice system is a solution for a lot of health and social problems. A justice sanction is not always the best solution to a social problem. An aberrant behavior can often be a consequence of other issues such as mental health, drug and alcohol problems, cognitive impairment, or employment problems, and therefore, jailing in these circumstances only exacerbates the problem. The inadequacy of community-based health services, particularly mental health, can result in larger numbers of people placed in custody. If early intervention and services are provided in the community, then crime may be avoided.

Theory and Practice

In your view, what should be the relationship between theory and practice?

In relation to the rehabilitation side of corrections, which is his primary interest, it is essential to have a sound theoretical basis. The failings of rehabilitation in corrections around the world in the last 50 years often result from a lack of a sound theoretical basis and for informing practice. The use of instinctive and intuitive approaches not deeply imbedded in appropriate and sound psychological or other theory results in having "feel-good" programs that emphasize self-esteem and not the skills and relapse prevention strategies necessary to maintain behavioral change. A sound theoretical basis for making any decision in the correctional world is absolutely imperative.

What the NSW correctional department has attempted to do is to have an accreditation process that incorporates a requirement for a sound theoretical base underpinned by research evidence of effectiveness. However, there is often a big gap in the correctional world between theory and practice in terms of implementation with resourcing, training, and integrity, compromised by the focus on outputs and getting something going in short time frames.

Does the department of corrections you work for conduct research on its own? If so, on what types of issues or questions?

Within the organization, there is an extensive commitment to research internally and a number of research partnerships with universities and external agencies. Corrective Services NSW has a "Corporate Research Evaluation and Statistics Branch." Within this branch, about 14 people are devoted to that function. In terms of research, there are various streams: some are evaluative, whereas others focus on monitoring and ensuring that statistical information is available for responding to questions in parliament or from the media. Part of the research function is to ensure that the organization has built up appropriately finessed information that can be used for political purposes, public statements, decisions, or planning for the future. The second aspect is the evaluation of programs and intervention to determine whether they are having the intended effect. In addition, NSW corrections has various staff members who are completing doctorates or postgraduate work to encourage them to participate in research in the area in which they are working. In addition, individuals, such as Asst. Commissioner Grant, participate as a coinvestigator in partnership with universities on studies in areas such as mortality, sexual behavior of prisoners, and a clinical trial on the use of antidepressants to treat impulsive behavior.

There is also an ethics committee that looks at issues arising from the proposed research. The ethics committee's approval is essential before research can be conducted.

Where do you find theory-based information?

There are several ways that the information can be accessed. First, Corrective Services NSW subscribes to online journals and has an excellent research library. In addition, Asst. Commissioner Grant has created positions within the organization that are "thinking positions" or advisers such as principal advisers in psychology, family and community, women, alcohol, and drugs. These advisers are tasked with keeping on top of the literature so that, when information of relevance comes up, it is circulated across the organization.

He also attends both national and international conferences and sponsoring seminars that allow him to be up-to-date with the most modern views, theories, and thinking. The staff also have a culture of sharing and disseminating research articles and reporting back on conference presentations they may have attended. The Department also sponsors conferences and seminars to provide opportunities for local and international experts to share their knowledge.

Evidence-Based Corrections

In your experience, has New South Wales' correctional system made use of various evidence-based programs?

All programs are under a process of ongoing evaluation; each has pre-program and postprogram measures or targets of treatment and outcomes to measure changes that have occurred over time, as well as refinements occurring throughout the process to improve on that program.

According to Asst. Commissioner Grant, it is essential for the correctional system to use evidence-based programs, and the programs from within the correctional area allow evidence to inform what they think should be done based on both international evidence and the generation of the organization's own evidence on the implementation and the refining of the approach while, at the same time, dismissing approaches that are shown not to produce good effects.

General Assessments

Are you basically satisfied or dissatisfied with developments in corrections?

The field of corrections is a dynamic system. It is never a static environment, so it is satisfying to see the results and moving forward in new directions. There is recognition that there can always be improvements. The frustrations come from the fact that you never have enough resources to do everything that is possible and there is often not a good alignment between the evidence and the reality of what the community expects. However, it is an area that is constantly moving and changing in its approaches in a positive way.

What are the developments you see as most likely to happen in the next few years?

There will likely be a decreased reliance on incarceration as the main investment strategy in justice. This means that community-based interventions would be applied. There is also the recognition that early intervention is essential for successful rehabilitative corrections and that this responsibility is communitywide. At the earliest possible intervention stage, there needs to be a strategy that does not consist of punishing the individual but addresses the issues within his/her familial circumstance and community, which will lead to a broader holistic approach.

Second, the range of possibilities that arise from technology have not been exploited, such as using more interactive technologies for offenders in custody. This would create a greater level of autonomy and responsibility for one to find solutions to their own issues.

Conclusion

Overall, Asst. Commissioner Grant was of great assistance throughout the interview. He was extremely forthcoming and prepared to discuss all aspects of the corrective system in depth. The major themes that continually emerged throughout the process was the diversity and constant changing nature of his career, the ongoing issues and improvements within the corrective system, and the extreme importance of early intervention in producing lower risks of incarceration and reoffending. Finally, there is a high level of importance in combining both theory and practice with a strong evidence base for producing the most effective outcomes. He subscribes to a holistic approach that incorporates both the prison system and community mediation. He is a strong believer in keeping up with modern approaches and technology to assist in producing a stronger and better functioning corrective system in the long term.

Glossary of Terms or Events Mentioned

- The Department of Justice and Attorney General assists the NSW Government, Judiciary, Parliament, and the community to promote social harmony through programs that protect human rights and community standards and reduce crime.
- Long Bay Correctional Centre is located in the suburb of Malabar, Sydney, NSW, Australia. Long Bay comprises six institutions: four maximum security and two minimum security.

- Kevin Waller—A former NSW coroner.
- Ron Woodham—Commissioner, NSW Corrective Services.
- Ole Ingstrup—Commissioner, Correctional Service of Canada.
- Risk–need–responsivity model—Developed in the 1980s and first formalized in 1990, the risk–need–responsivity model has been used with increasing success to assess and rehabilitate criminals in Canada and around the world.
- "Throughcare concept"—Holistic approach to managing offenders, in which the whole system has been joined together, and a better recognition that people who are in jail are being managed by somebody on the committee side of the organization at the beginning and end of their sentence.
- "Nagle Royal Commission"—Commission of enquiry into NSW Corrective Services conducted by Commissioner Justice Nagle between 1976 and 1978.
- Antidiscrimination legislation—NSW Antidiscrimination Act 1977.
- Rex Jackson—Minister for Corrective Services in NSW from October 1981 to October 1983, Jackson was sent to prison for 10 years after conviction on charges of conspiracy in relation to the early release of prisoners.
- "Truth in sentencing rayim" (NSW 1989)—Stated that an inmate had to serve the entirety of their sentence with no opportunity for an early release.
- NSW Ombudsman—An independent and impartial watchdog whose job it is to ensure that the agencies that are watched over fulfill their functions properly and improve their delivery of services to the public, make agencies aware of their responsibilities to the public, act reasonably, and comply with the law and best practice in administration.
- The Australian Human Rights Commission—Established in 1986 by an act of the federal parliament and is an independent statutory organization that oversees the application of federal legislation in the areas of human rights, antidiscrimination, social justice, and privacy.
- Civil litigation—A legal dispute between two or more parties that seek money damages or specific performance rather than criminal sanctions.
- "Corporate Research Evaluation and Statistics Branch"—NSW Corrective Services' internal research branch.

Interview with Dusko Sain, Director of Corrections for the Republic of Srspka

3

LAURENCE ARMAND FRENCH
GORAN KOVACEVIC

Contents

Introduction

Bosnia–Herzegovina is a fractured state that was divided in 1995 into two major entities and a small enclave known as the Brcko District, in compliance with the Dayton Peace Accord, which ended open hostilities that began in 1991. The Federation of Bosnia–Herzegovina (FBiH) is the largest entity, comprising about 51% of the landmass, and represents a loose confederation of Muslim Bosniaks and Catholic Bosnian Croats, with the former being the majority dominating 7 of the 10 cantons located within the entity. The Republic of Srpska (Republika Srpska, RS) makes up the remaining 49%, with the exception of the minimal landmass making up the sectarian-mixed Brcko District situated along the Croatian/Serbian border within the RS. One of the contentious areas of penal sanctions was the death penalty, which existed in the former Yugoslavia until the Balkan Wars of 1991–1999 broke up the Communist nation. In 2001, Serbia's prime minister Zoran Djindjic wanted to indict the former head of state Slobodan Milosevic and his wife for murder. However, the establishment of the International Tribunal for the Former Yugoslavia discouraged the continuation of capital punishment, given that it contained no provision for the death penalty. Indeed, in October 1997, the Council of Europe Summit called for the universal abolition of the death penalty, which was to extend to all new member states of the Council of Europe, to which the former Yugoslavian states belong, eventually hoping to join as full members of the European Union (EU). Slovenia (in 1989) and

31

Croatia (in 1990) abolished the death penalty for all crimes, followed by the republics of the Socialist Federation of Yugoslavia and Bosnia–Herzegovina in 2001, and then by Serbia in 2002, whereas Montenegro reiterated its stance when it separated from Serbia in 2006.

The Yugoslavian penal system was established in July 1945 during the Second World War, in which prison sentences were divided into two categories: 1) regular incarceration or 2) incarceration with hard labor. The first completed regulations on the administration of criminal sanctions were passed in 1948 (revised in 1951 and again in 1961). In 1968, jurisdiction over the enforcement of criminal sanctions was transferred from the Minister of Internal Affairs to the Ministry of Justice. At this time, the jurisdiction over penal sanctions was decentralized from the federal level and transferred to the six republics comprising the Socialist Federation of Yugoslavia, hence the reason that Slovenia and Croatia were able to abolish the death sentence while it remained in the republics of Yugoslavia. In 1974, the Law on the administration of Criminal Sanctions was devised, providing a classification for penal facilities to include correctional institutions, district prisons, educational-correctional institutions, and prison hospitals. These facilities were further designated as being either "open," "semiclosed," or "closed." Sentences of up to 6 months are served in district prisons whereas those exceeding 6 months are served in correctional institutions. This was the Yugoslavian penal system until the start of the Balkan War in 1991. When the Republic of Srpska emerged as a legal, semiautonomous "entity" in 1995, it retained much of the old system within its borders, with six penal institutions: three district prisons (Doboj, Bijeljina, and Trebinja), one closed correctional institution at Foca, and two semiclosed correctional institutions in Banja Luka and Eastern Sarajevo. In 2010, the district prisons were abolished, and thus, all inmates are now housed in the correctional institutions (RS prisons).

Distrust and corruption were common elements after the end of the conflict, with the Dayton Accord in 1995 resulting in extralegal activity, including assisting high-profile criminals escape from custody. The Stankovic case illustrates this phenomenon. Radovan Stankovic was the first war crimes suspect convicted by the Hague Tribunal to the Court of Bosnia and Herzegovina. He was found guilty for his role in the capture, torture, rape, and murder of non-Serb civilians from April 1992 until February 1993 when he was a member of the Miljevina Battalion with the Foca Tactical Brigade. He was convicted and sentenced to a 20-year prison term to be served at the correctional institution at Foca Prison in RS. He escaped from the prison in Foca on May 25, 2007 and remains at large. If he is found in Serbia, Montenegro, or Croatia, he is expected to be returned to Bosnia–Herzegovina in accordance with the Agreement on the Execution of Criminal and Legal Sanctions. Sain became head of RS corrections the day after Stankovic's escape.

Interview

Q: Could you tell us about your work history?

A: My name is Dusko Sain. I am the head of the Department for Supervision over the work of penal correctional institutions at the Ministry of Justice for the Republic of Srspka (RS). Before that, I worked from 1987 until 1992 as an educator in the Educational–Reformatory Home in Banja Luka, and from 1992 to 2005, I was the head of the Department for Admission and Discharge of the correctional home in Banja Luka and assistant director for security and treatment. In 2006, I worked at the Ministry of Justice as an inspector for the treatment of offenders. From May 2007 to December 2007, I performed the duties of the director of the Criminal Correctional Home at Foca. My current position as the head of Department for Supervision began in December 2007, where I am in charge of all penal correctional institutions in RS. I am also currently the president of the Association of Penologists for the Republic of Srpska.

Q: What is your educational background?

A: I graduated from the Faculty (College) for Defectology in Belgrade, Serbia, in the Department for Social Self-Protection, Prevention and Resocialization of Persons with a Behavioral Disorder. My degree is in special education. I also attended a series of courses and training within the penal correctional institutions in treatment and security. I have also organized and participated in a large number of courses and training in these fields. I have been a permanent member of the Joint Steering Group of the Council of Europe for the reformation of the prison system in Bosnia–Herzegovina since its inception. In this capacity, I have had the opportunity to study prison systems in other countries, including Poland, France, Italy, Sweden, and Finland.

Q: Since you have been working within the former Yugoslavia, when the penitentiary system of Bosnia and Herzegovina was first established, what do you see as the latest changes in the penitentiary system since 1995, in BiH in general and in the RS in particular?

A: Before the war, the Bosnia–Herzegovina penitentiary system was the same in all the federal republics of the former Yugoslavia. At that time, this system was considered progressive (other than the politics involved). Some of the leading European democracies, such as Sweden, modeled their laws on those of Yugoslavia. However, when the Balkan War broke out (1991–1999), these progressive standards dissolved, and as early as 1992, new rules began to emerge at the

State level, entity level, and in the Brcko District as part of new laws regarding detention and prisons.

Currently, the prison system of the RS is composed of six prisons, whereas the FBiH, to my knowledge, also has six prisons. The Brcko District, although an autonomous legal entity, does not have its own prisons and therefore allows the inmates to choose from cooperative correctional agencies within RS for their sentencing obligations. A state (National) prison is currently under construction and will be a function of the state courts and will contract with the entities so that convicts can serve their sentences within the entity prisons as well, if they choose. Therefore, we are obliged to treat these prisoners according to the Law on Execution (administration) of Criminal Sanctions BiH.

The major changes that occurred between 1992 and 1995 in RS and in the entity's prisons are based on the laws for the administration of criminal sanctions and are standardized for the most part. The existing legislation and readaptation of existing facilities' conditions are created in accordance with the European Prison Rules as far as the RS is concerned. Every day, we work on implementing these rules and inserting them into our laws. We have improved our security and tracking systems and have better equipped facilities that far exceed the conditions that existed in the former system (Yugoslavia). We now provide ongoing training for our personnel in accordance with the European Council and other international organizations. These are some of the basic changes that have occurred from 1995 and onward in relation to the prewar period, with the aim of introducing the modern system of enforcement of criminal sanctions.

Q: How do you see these new changes in relation to the former state penitentiary system? Are they better or worse?

A: Better, mainly, because there are now six different types of penal institutions that are categorized according to certain criteria, including being closed or open systems, so I can say that the conditions for the implementation of criminal sanctions are far better than during the pre-war era in that our staff is better trained and we have a reasonable operation budget. We strive to meet basic standards in the administration of the laws governing penal operations.

Q: Do you see strong support for these new changes, and do you see any difference in cooperation between the entities and the Brcko District?

A: The Law for the Execution (administration) of Criminal Sanctions in the RS came into effect in 2001. Prior to that, we operated under the laws derived in 1994. However, I will focus on the period since 2001. In this law, for the first time, we introduced the recommendations of the Council of Europe. Since then, there have been other changes as well. In 2008, a new law regarding the administration of criminal sanctions with even more mandatory standards was passed. These standards mandated that the majority of our (RS) officers, serving within the penal/correctional system, attend various training seminars to be better acquainted with both our penal system as well as those of other countries. Besides, our prisoners are not the same today as they were 10 years ago. In the past, there were many complaints regarding adequate treatment within the old legal system. In order to bring about effective changes to address these abuses, a working group was established, and I must say that we have had excellent support from the Minister and the Government and assessed the situation resulting in changes—modern, model changes—so that today, there are essentially no differences between our (RS) system of penal sanctions and those of most European countries.

In 2009, the Law on Execution (administration) of Criminal Sanctions, the Law on Special Regime (office) for the Enforcement of Criminal Sanctions, the Law on Juvenile Perpetrators of Criminal Acts, and the Law on Forfeiture of Property (for criminal acts) were passed. All these laws have a direct influence on public safety in the RS. As for support, we were united in our efforts to implement these changes in our criminal and juvenile laws. Indeed, our new Law on the Execution (administration) of Criminal Sanctions in the RS was assessed by the Council of Europe and the Organization for Security and Cooperation in Europe (OSCE) as being one of the most progressive laws in the territory of Bosnia–Herzegovina.

Now, I would like to say something about changes related to parole. Parole no longer signifies just being released from incarceration; it now includes the continuance of serving a sentence, but under different circumstances. As for the cooperation, we have very good cooperation with the Ministry of Justice of the Federation (FBiH) and the National (State) Ministry of Justice. I can generally say that we have good cooperation with all penal correctional institutions in the territory (State) of Bosnia and Herzegovina.

Q: Are there problems in interagency cooperation regarding the perpetrators of specific acts?

A: Cooperation exists, and we have tried to improve these exchange relationships since 2007 by enabling the transfer of convicts from one entity to another. At this time, we have convicts in the RS and in the FBiH who were transferred because they had problems with other prisoners.

Q: Do you think the problems may be caused by nationality, particularly prisoners of war crimes?

A: Exactly. That is why we introduced an article in the Law in 2007 that enables a person who is convicted, with his consent and the approval of the Ministry of Justice of the entity to which reference is made, to transfer to another entity. In 2008, a contract (treaty) was made between the Federation and the RS to accept such convicts, but it was stopped for some reason. I have information that the Office of Higher Representatives stopped it, because they fear that doing so would create ethnically pure prisons (prison populations segregated according to sectarian or ethnic origin). In the treaty proposal, it was stated that these transfers could only be done primarily for the protection of the safety of prisoners and not merely because they wanted to be with their own people. We implemented these changes in the new law, in which these out-of-entity transfers can occur only with the written consent of the convict. If the Federal Minister agrees to the transfer request, we issue a decision on his transfer to another entity. To my knowledge, today, in Bosnia (State), including both the RS and the FBiH, there are about 10 such prisoners for which it would be advisable to move them to another entity not only for their safety but also for easier contact with their families.

Q: Can a prisoner be transferred for the sake of his safety without his or her consent?

A: To another entity? (*Yes.*)

No, because we have introduced a provision that controls political interference.

Q: Can you tell us something about the cooperation with neighboring countries and with other Member States of the European Council?

Cooperation has been achieved primarily with Serbia, Croatia, and Slovenia. As for other countries, we have achieved cooperation with the countries where our representatives have been to, such as Sweden. Recently, we have made a proposal of cooperation between the RS and Finland, and their experts should come to the RS and visit the prison facilities to provide certain suggestions and implement specific training programs and training of our staff. After that, we will go to Finland to eventually offer the same if there is a chance for it.

Q: Can the RS make bilateral agreements with other states when it comes to prisoner exchange?

A: No. When it comes to other countries, everything must go through the Bosnia–Herzegovina (State) Ministry of Justice.

Q: Do you have a prisoner exchange with other countries, and can a foreign prisoner receive visits from his family?

A: A citizen of BiH who is serving a prison sentence in Germany, for example, may submit a request for extradition. As far as the courts in the RS are concerned, if there are equivalent provisions in the Criminal Code, then the court will recognize that country's verdict. As far as foreigners are concerned, we have only one institution where they can serve their sentence, and that is the penal correctional facility at Banja Luka. This is also the largest city in the RS, and therefore, the conditions of imprisonment are the best in that institution. They have rights even greater than those for Bosnia–Herzegovina nationals. We are obliged to notify the prisoner of his rights as soon as he arrives, immediately familiarize him with all his rights and obligations, allow him to make arrangements for family visits, and notify his country's ambassador of his incarceration. The main problem exists with weekend passes outside the institution. It is very risky to allow an out-of-country prisoner to leave the institution for a weekend. First of all, where would he go?

Q: How many employees do you have within the RS correctional system? How many women and men?

A: As of the 31st of December 2009, we had a total of 758 employees working on the execution of sanctions (correctional administration) employed in our six penal correctional institutions. Of these, approximately 56% work in the security section, 10% in the service of treatment, 2% in the health service, 18% work in the economic-instructor service, and 13% in supporting universal service. I do not have exact information on the breakdown by gender, but there are about 100 women employed within all services, legal, financial, etc.

Q: What kind of education have these workers completed?

A: It all depends on in which service they operate. A member of the security services must have at least a secondary education, fourth degree. The commander of the guard must have a college degree (includes associate degrees), whereas the head guard and department chief must have a university degree (bachelor's degree). Those personnel working within correctional treatment must have a university education. This includes teachers, psychologists, special educators, therapists, sociologists, sports educators, and social workers. When it comes to the health service, we attempt to have a full-time medical doctorate for each facility. We now have medical doctors as full-time members of the permanent staff at four of our facilities in addition to our nursing staff. The vocational instructors represent a number of occupations, including locksmiths and plumbers. Here, each department supervisory chief-of-staff must have a university degree, and they all need to pass a professional exam.

Depending on the education level, workers with secondary education have to take the professional exam after 6 months of work in front of the commission designated by the Minister of Justice of the RS. All persons who have a higher degree must pass a professional exam after 1 year of work, again in front of the commission. You can fail the exam only once—you lose your position upon a second failure. As for training, every employee is obliged to familiarize himself with the regulations of penology, penological andragogy, penal correctional institutions, the Law on the Execution (administration) of Criminal Sanctions, psychology, the basis of psychopathology, office management, and the Constitution.

Q: Are there libraries within the penal institutions, and do you acquire the most recent literature for your employees?

A: In addition to passing the professional exam, after that, there are two articles in the law that refer to the continued training of personnel. So, each facility is obliged to devise a training plan for its professional staff.

Q: Can the workers themselves make suggestions as to what educational training should be available?

A: Sure, but there is also a group of people in the government involved in the training of workers of penal correctional institutions, composed of doctors of science and other experts who organize the training schedule. In 2 years, we have conducted additional training in the fields of prisoner's rights, criminal law, criminal procedural law, penology, basic penology with penological andragogy, and basic psychology with psychopathology. We also have a training schedule for all personnel in all departments, from guards to treatment services. You asked about the library: each institution has its own specialized library, and this applies especially to security service and treatment, but again, everyone is vying to get the most recent releases in their field. We have excellent cooperation with the Institute for Penealogical Research in Belgrade (Serbia) and are using their literature. We also have access to the Police Academy's library in Banja Luka.

Q: Is there a minimum age requirement for employment in the correctional system?

A: The minimum requirement is 18 years for a guard or security service officer, and they cannot be older than 27 years to start their career, although consideration is given for years used in obtaining higher educational degrees.

Q: Are the guards or other officers armed, and if so, what kind of training do they go through when it comes to handling weapons?

A: They receive special training, which is highly regulated by law and training standards, including regulations on the use of force. Overall,
they undergo 6 months of intensive training and must pass an
exam. Every year, we also have practice shooting from automatic
rifles and pistols.

Q: What kind of weapons are we talking about?

A: Weapons for watchtowers and patrols are the M70 assault rifle and pistols that are manufactured mostly by Crvena Zastava (Red Flag
Industries, producer of the Yugo automobile, Kraguijevac, Serbia).

Q: Can you tell me about the structure of the System for Execution (administration) of Criminal Sanctions (corrections) in RS? How many
institutions, where are they located, and what is the size of the
inmate population?

A: There are six institutions, each under the jurisdiction of a district court:
Banja Luka, Doboj, Bijeljina, Eastern Sarajevo, Foca, and Trebinje.
Of these six institutions, we have three that are closed and three
that are open. The closed facilities are located in Banja Luka, Foca,
and Bijeljina, whereas the open facilities are in Doboj, Eastern
Sarajevo, and Trebinje. Based on new legislation, which came into
effect in February 2010, the district prisons were abolished, and
now, all penal correctional institutions fall under one authority
with three open and three closed facilities.

Q: What about the demographics of the inmate population?

A: Year after year, the situation becomes more difficult because we have more
and more convicts who are returnees and persons who have committed serious crimes and criminal acts with elements of violence,
war crimes, traffic of narcotic drugs, robbery, and so forth. There
are 192 inmates serving sentences for murder, aggravated murder,
manslaughter, and negligent homicide, followed by those convicted
of larceny–theft, robbery, drug abuse, theft, and war crimes. When
it comes to the imposition of sentences, most of the inmates (155)
are serving a prison sentence of between 5 and 10 years, followed
by those (143) serving a sentence of 3–5 years, with the remaining
inmates serving sentences of 1–2 years. Regarding the age structure
of the convicted persons, the majority are between 25 and 30 years,
followed by those between the ages of 20 and 25. The average age
is 30. As for the women convicts, we have one division within the
penal correctional institution of East Sarajevo, where women are
serving their sentence. On the average, their population is composed of about 15 incarcerated women at any given time.

Q: What is the total number of convicted persons serving time within the
RS Correctional system?

A: The number ranges roughly between 920 and 970, including both those convicted and serving their sentences and those being held (detained persons) awaiting trial or sentencing. This latter group consists of about 160–180 persons who are being held in custody awaiting further adjudication.

Q: Does your correctional system have the capacity to handle all these people?

A: Yes, there is enough capacity. We performed measurements on the basis of certain standards approximately 7 years ago and found that the optimum number of inmates we can handle is 1085, with space for 200 slots for those being held without sentencing and the rest for convicted persons serving their sentences. The total of 1085 has already been revised due to the renovation of the correctional facilities. Our renovation program has intensified within the last 3 years so that, now, our capacity has substantially increased, including the construction of a special section in Foca and another one in East Sarajevo. In Doboj, we have built an entire new floor, which has increased the capacity for 60 more prisoners. So, I would say that today, overall, we have the capacity to hold from 1200 to 1300 inmates within our correctional system.

Q: Is there any fluxation in the number of convicted persons within your facilities?

A: Well, as far as I know, no. We had an initial increase in the number of persons serving sentences during the period from 2006 to 2007; however, since 2008, the inmate population has varied by about 30 or so inmates, bringing the total number of people incarcerated to roughly between 920 and 970.

Q: What are the rights of convicted persons, and how are their complaints handled?

A: Of course, the basic law on which the complete execution (administration) of criminal sanctions is based, the Law on Execution of Criminal Sanctions, required us to adopt bylaws of which we have 18 regarding the administration of criminal sanctions. For the convicted person (inmate), the most important one pertains to the regulation on house rules. The law specifies their (inmate's) rights, duties, and obligations, and in the Regulation on house rules, those rights, duties, and responsibilities are outlined in detail, and one knows what is respected. Any person that comes to the Corrections and Penal agency KP institution, at first, stays in the reception department, and it is obliged, as well as by the institution, to be acquainted with the Law on Criminal Sanctions and Regulations. These regulations are useful for the convicted person, and he should study them with the help from pedagogues (teachers and legal assistants). However, if that person chooses his own method of becoming familiar with his rights and obligations, it must be done in some other way (through some seminars), because regardless of how they address this issue, they have to be familiar with these regulations. As for complaints, the laws and regulations clearly state that all convicted persons have the right to an appeal, and this right cannot be disputed.

Q: Is there a possibility that someone can deny or conceal the appeal of a convict? If so, what are the mechanisms to reveal that?

A: There is no possibility at all, because we went a step further since 1996 when the system was being organized. Then, you had a great number of organizations such as the International Police Task Force (IPTF), Stabilization Force in Bosnia-Herzegovina (SFOR), and others, which had a mandate to visit prisons, whenever they wanted, to make sure that there is full compliance with the prisoner's rights. I have been working in the state system for the administration of sanctions for years, and I can responsibly claim that there is nothing hidden in this field not only in the RS but also in the FBiH, because there is no advantage in concealing things. The convicted person has the right to write a complaint; he even has the right to legal assistance. This is his fundamental right, and every institution has a person assigned to provide legal assistance to prisoners. Legal aid also provides advice on other legal issues, such as, for example, the question of his property. When disciplinary proceedings are conducted, he is entitled to his lawyer, his right cannot be denied, and we hold out the hardest disciplinary penalties for correctional workers who deny the prisoner his rights.

Q: Do you have a lot of unfounded complaints?

A: As for complaints, when the representatives of some international organizations come to a penal correctional institution, many directors of correctional institutions mistakenly think that the fewer the complaints, the better, but I would argue the opposite—where there are no complaints, repression exists, and there is work for these representatives of international organizations to look more closely at that institution. I'm not sure what kind of complaints exist most, but each complaint is considered valid and is investigated regarding its merit.

Q: What if a convicted person commits a crime while serving the sentence? What is the procedure?

A: If it is done in prison, the institution is obliged to take action and process it as any other offense committed outside the prison. Correctional officials are required to refer the case to the local prosecutor. Moreover, if probable cause is found, the convict is automatically denied his benefits until the criminal proceedings are complete. If the accusations against him are rejected, he can continue to use his benefits. However, if found guilty and again convicted, it is absurd to talk about his benefits; he loses these benefits.

Q: If the penalties for a new criminal offense are greater than his current sentence, will they consume the previous sentence?

A: There is the possibility that the sentences will run concurrently, but I'm not sure that this is the rule, because for some, the rest of his first sentence can be added to the new sentence. If they are not united (running concurrently) while he is serving the first sentence, he will have to serve the second or subsequent sentence(s) following the completion of his original sentence. These decisions are determined by the courts and not by our correctional administrators.

Q: What about conjugal visits?

A: Conjugal visits are not a right in itself; it is determined based on good behavior during imprisonment. A convicted person, after serving a certain portion of their sentence, depending on the crime for which he was sentenced, can request conjugal visits. For crimes like robbery, rape, war crimes, drugs, and those sentenced to at least 10 years of more, they must complete at least half of their sentence before they can petition for conjugal visitations. For some crimes, if a person is serving a sentence of up to 10 years and has not been convicted before, he must serve a quarter of the sentence before requesting conjugal visits.

Q: What are some of the other benefits available to inmates?

A: There are several kinds of benefits, divided into internal and external. Internal benefits are such that the convicted person is allowed by prison authorities to have a laptop or radio or to move to a better room or better section of the institution. These are examples of internal benefits. External benefits means they can go home for the weekend to the town and use part of their holiday.

Q: Holiday?

A: Anyone who works has the right to holiday (vacation days), and that is a right that no one can dispute. They are entitled to a minimum of 18 days of holiday annually, and each institution has specific facilities, specifically for this purpose. So, they can use their external benefits in our sponsored facilities and programs, or they can spend part or all of holiday at home.

Q: Are these decisions at the discretion of the warden?

A: Yes. As for visits, visits from family members are a basic right that cannot be disputed, unless it is proved that the visit represents a criminal offense or that such visits may adversely affect the flow of administration of criminal sanctions. Then, the director of the institution can make a decision to suspend that right for a limited time. When it comes to visits from a spouse, there are common and intimate visits, as we say "room for intimate visits." This is a privilege that must be earned and is not a basic right. There were some abuses of this privilege, with inmates serving their sentences in the FBiH, and to prevent this from happening here, we now allow inmates to use conjugal visits only if they are married or living in a common-law relationship with that person. Regarding the latter, they must possess a certificate from the Centre for Social Welfare or municipal administrative bodies on the status of the common-law marriage. In the case of common-law marriages, we ask the Center for Social Welfare or the police to go to the address and make sure that the person actually lives at that address. A girlfriend is out of the question, because you have no evidence to confirm who is a girlfriend and who is not. In Zenica, there were many cases in which the prisoners paid for sexual services, which in itself makes it a criminal offense.

Q: What does the average day of the prisoners look like?

A: Each institution is obliged to issue a schedule of daily activities, which includes the schedule of activities in working days and the schedule of activities for holidays and vacation days. The activities are not the same on Sunday as it is on weekdays. Usually, the inmate population gets up at 06:00, washing, brushing their teeth, and lining up for breakfast. Then, those with work assignments go to work, whereas those who do not have jobs remain in their living rooms until 15:00 (3:00 p.m., lunch time). After lunch, they have free time. Free time does not mean you get to do what you want. We call it "organized free time," with planned activities organized during this time under the supervision of educational professionals, including sports directors. These activities range from sports, art, and so on. However, another option for some is to sleep in the afternoon in his room. Even then, he must respect the house rules if he wants to sleep—no noise, and so on. After that comes dinner, and after dinner, depending on the facilities and space at their disposal and the time of the year (season), there are other scheduled activities. For example, in winter, they do not go outside, because it gets dark earlier. In areas that are designed for common rooms, they have a TV room, reading room, library, and various studios where they can spend their time until 22:00 (10:00 p.m.). At 22:00, the lights go out, but it is possible to allow them to watch TV if there are some movies or sport matches, but only for those persons who have expressed a desire to watch them. And then, they are required to clean up that room.

Q: Is there a difference between closed and open types of institutions regarding conjugal visitation?

A: Yes. Logically, if you compare East Sarajevo (open institutions) and Foca (closed institution), the difference is in the number of guards required for surveillance, which influences the time and freedom available to convicted persons, and so on. Those are the differences.

Q: Are there any external organizations working within the prisons?

A: If you are thinking of nongovernmental organizations (NGOs), well then, there are a few. There is a provision allowing this type of cooperation, but it seems to me that there is not sufficient interest in most of these NGOs in this region for our penal–correctional facilities. Recently, well, for the past 2 years, the NGO *Victoriais* was involved. It is an organization that deals with drug addicts. They asked for approval from us, and we approved their entering our facilities in the RS. As for the other organizations, for example, religious organizations, I have personally sought the engagement of such organizations, given that the practice of religion is one of the prisoner's basic rights. One day, an Orthodox priest will come; another day, a Catholic or Muslim priest—everyone has his day. Inmates can even request certain religious officials, and we try to get them to come to the facility. Usually, these visits are most frequent during religious holidays such as Christmas, Easter, and Eid.

Q: Can the Bosniaks, who pray five times a day, do this while incarcerated?

A: A true believer, at least the way I understand it, does not need any special preparation or any specific room, but any area and the right direction of world. In the case of Muslims, it is enough to turn toward the east and to pray. Of course, each institution has the facilities for religious purposes, and usually, there are three such areas or three rooms available (one for Catholics, one for Orthodox Christians, and one for Muslims—the three major sectarian groups within BiH), and if someone wants to exercise their faith, nobody will deny it.

Q: Are the inmates allowed to leave their work duties to perform a religious ceremony and then return to their posts?

A: Yes. I have to admit we do not have many such cases, but if someone expresses the desire to pray five times a day, it will not be denied.

Q: Are there educational programs available for the prisoners?

A: It depends on the classification of prisoners. There are educational–correctional measures at our educational–reformatory institution, where education is mandatory, especially when minors are concerned. For example, someone who has not completed primary school is bound to finish school at the institution. We have a person who is a permanent employee and engaged in their education. That person makes contracts with schools in the community and external collaborators to provide instructive classes and organizes exams for these inmates.

Q: They go to the school facility?

A: Yes. They are enrolled at the schools in the city and not in jail, and they receive a degree from the school, and on this degree, you cannot see that they finished school while they were serving their sentence. When it comes to juveniles, prison schooling is obligatory, but when it comes to adults, it is not mandatory. But, any convicted person can express the wish to study for some kind of exam, crafts, even in colleges. Actually, we have a large number of inmates who, while in prison, went to college to take exams.

Q: Must the faculty be in the same town as the prison, or can it be located in another city?

A: We try to accommodate these needs locally, where the prison facility is located, but there are some exceptions.

Q: Are these inmate/students accompanied by prison staff when they leave the institution?

A: It depends if they have the right to use external benefits. Even then, if the institution determines that there is little danger for escape or the commission of an offense, then usually, we allow the administrator for education to accompany that person to university for the first few times. When it is determined that there will be no escape or security problems, then that inmate is allowed to attend unescorted.

Q: Do you receive any assistance from the Ministry, from various organizations such as the International Criminal Investigative Training Assistance Program (ICITAP), European Union, the European Commission, and the like?

A: No, never.

Q: Do they organize any training for your employees?

A: Assistance in terms of grants, no. But, our staff can benefit from programs offered by the Council of Europe, the OSCE, and the EUPM that are also extended to a larger population of professionals.

Q: What would you like to see happen within the penitentiary system of the RS in the future, and what would you like to see happen with the penitentiary system of Bosnia and Herzegovina?

A: I will start with the RS. My livelihood comes from the administration of criminal sanctions, and that's my main and only source of income. I would like for all my colleagues and myself to go to work with a smile on our faces, with fewer problems. How is that accomplished? We strived for the establishment of an independent prison (correctional) administration in 2009, but our efforts have failed so far. We want to organize and establish a Prison Authority in the RS to replace the current Department for Prisons within the Ministry of Justice. It would still be an independent Ministry, with its own director, and the directors of the prison would be his assistants. This plan would make it far easier to manage our facilities, to maintain control over these institutions, and to organize the work of these institutions.

Q: Because it would not be a domain of the Ministry, but a separate, independent organization?

A: Yes, exactly so. The Prison Authority would have its own economic sector for all our facilities, and we would not be held to standards that hinder our own economic products. Now, we buy more expensive meat while struggling to sell our meat to someone else, or some other of our articles, and so on. This would be the right solution in an era of economic crisis, when we all are struggling to find some profit, in terms of employment of convicted persons. And, the Prison Authority, according to its regulations, could allow the industry to finance itself and become a source of income throughout the prison administration such as allowing the correctional institution in East Sarajevo to produce meat and eggs and to ensure the placement of its products in the other six penal facilities. This way of thinking provides the opportunity for the Prison Authority to be a force in the economy, allowing them to sell their products on the open market.

Q: Do you see any major problems in the system of administration of criminal sanctions of the RS, the Federation, and Bosnia and Herzegovina?

A: In relation to previous years, our budget has increased. Even then, prisons seem to be bottomless pits, given an ever-increasing number of convicted persons from high-risk groups and the increasing problem of drugs in prisons. Currently, our institution does not possess adequate technical tools to detect drugs (so-called secondary crime). Another problem is getting funding for new personnel, especially for our educated staff. If we cannot afford adequate compensation and without sufficient incentives, most teachers would rather work in an elementary school instead of a prison. As for the FBiH, they are now working on drafting a new law on the administration of criminal sanctions based mainly on our laws on the administration of criminal sanctions. The goal here is for the harmonization of the laws so that they are the same throughout BiH, allowing for the transfer of persons from one entity to another. As for the Ministry of Justice, they have a bigger problem in that their administration authority is applicable only to persons convicted by their Court, and although it would be advantageous to have a single, nationwide Ministry of Justice, the current political situation makes that unlikely. Nonetheless, in my opinion, people who are good at their work, regardless of the organization, are able to easily agree about everything.

Q: Implying that these problems exist more among sectarian politicians than among correctional professionals?

A: Yes. Everything that concerns the execution (administration) of criminal sanctions such as correctional treatment is similar in both the FBiH and the RS. The main problem is when the politicians get involved regarding establishing a state (national) level agency.

Q: What is your view regarding the case of Stanković, who was convicted by the Court of Bosnia and Herzegovina for war crimes and then sentenced to the facility in Foca, from which he escaped? Here in the Federation, the opinion is that it was a political move, that someone let him go.

A: Concerning this case, Stanković escaped on May 25, 2007. I was appointed a day later as the acting director of the penal–correctional institution in Foca on May 26, 2007. Because the Government of RS automatically relieved the former managers of the institution (as well as the shift chiefs) of their duties, I'm not sure who organized the escape. There certainly was a failure within the penal facility, especially regarding the manner in which he was escorted to the hospital. To me, it is unbelievable that they did not have a plan of escort, because no matter who is concerned, they must have a plan of escort to know exactly who is responsible for what, especially when it comes to a high-risk escort. They had no such plan, and that is the reason why I fired them. There were 10 of them, even though Stanković did not escape from the prison but left while being escorted to the hospital. To this day, I do not know who was involved in his escape.

Q: Can we conclude that positive changes were made following the Stanković case?

A: Absolutely. The RS is no longer the same as before Stanković. I say, the one who organized the escape of Stankovic or Stankovic himself is unaware of how much damage was done by this event to himself, his family, the institution where he was serving his sentence, and all these people who lost their jobs. It was the event that transformed corrections in RS.

I'd like to thank you for such detailed answers and the fact that you took the time to do this interview.

You're welcome.

Conclusion

The RS is the most homogeneous portion of Bosnia–Herzegovina, composed mainly of Bosnian Serbs. Dusko Sain is the head of the RS correctional facilities, which is the most progressive penal institution within the divided state of Bosnia–Herzegovina. Not only was Sain cooperative, open, and frank in our interactions but he also came back to clarify issues that may have arrived during the initial interview. The authors/interviewers/interpreters also had the benefit of visiting the "open" facility in East Sarajevo on a number of occasions, given that it is a well-known restaurant located a few kilometers from Sarajevo and the FBiH/RS border.

Interview with Dr. Antal Kökényesi, Lieutenant General, Commander of the Hungarian National Prison Service

4

JÓZSEF BODA
ZSOLT MOLNÁR

This interview was done at the office of the Hungarian National Prison Headquarters, in the heart of the capitol of Budapest. The office is situated in the Fifth District, which is exactly at the center of the town, close to the Parliament building and to other ministerial offices. The office is the administrative center of the Hungarian Prison Service and is the liaison body for the superior Ministry of Interior.

As we learned from the Commander, the history of Hungarian prisons started in the Middle Ages. In the beginning, there was almost no regulation for prisons. The first institutes or prisons were only some manorial or county jails. The first legal instrument entered into enforced in 1878 was called the *Csemegi Code.** This act contained many modern prison rules and was considered a modern law. During the Hasbro–Hungarian monarchy, significant developments were started on the facilities and buildings in the administration. Large prisons were established as judicial centers together with the offices of the judges and prosecutors. Some of these buildings are still operating as prisons.

The prison service is legally defined as the armed law enforcement organization that carries out measures and sentences of imprisonment and criminal procedure enforcement, and also executes confinements of fine defaulters. The prison service is subordinated to the Ministry of Interior. The minister of the interior is responsible for the prison service and also controls the employment of inmates in the limited companies operated by the prison service.

The supervision of lawful operation is exercised by the Prosecutors' Office.

The Hungarian Prison Service is directed by the National Prison Administration Headquarters, which manages 31 prisons (two of them operate within the framework of the Public–Private Partnership), five auxiliary

---

* Károly Csemegi was the codificator of the Act on Penal Code.

facilities, and 12 limited companies created for the employment of the prisoners. The annual budget of the service is approximately 161.4 million euro.

The overall number of staff employed by the Hungarian Prison Service is 7808; of these, 6714 are uniformed (1249 commissioned officers and 5465 noncommissioned officers), whereas 1005 are nonuniformed civil servants, and an additional 89 employees in this category work part-time.

The total number of prisoners is currently at 16,537; of these, 15,445 are males and 1092 are females.

The legally classified detainees are grouped into four categories:

1: Pretrial detainees before the first instance of trial (4832)
2: Convicted prisoners (11,409)
3: Prisoners in confinement for noncriminal offenses (119)
4: Prisoners in forced psychiatric treatment (177)

There are currently 618 foreign national detainees and 571 juveniles in the correctional system.

In compliance with the effective legal regulations, the overall capacity of the 31 penal institutes is 12,335 persons; therefore, penal institutions are characterized by overcrowding. At the end of December 2010, the average national rate of overcrowding totaled 134%. In some regions of the country (where the crime rate is higher or accommodation capacity is smaller), prison overcrowding can be higher than the average national level (180%–220%).

In 2008, the Hungarian Prison Service launched a new strategic development program. The aim of the so-called Responsible and Prepared Program is to examine the strengths and weaknesses of the organization using the Strengths, Weaknesses/Limitations, Opportunities, and Threats (SWOT) analysis by forming indicators on which the short-, medium-, and long-term development programs are based. This new strategic program has modernized the future objectives and mission of the prison service. The development objectives of the professional work are based on five pillars. Within this framework, several individual projects are continuously monitored by the responsible branches.

The first pillar, called "security and safety," covers the improvement of circumstances of prisoners' accommodations, programs, and the security aspects. A new security and suicide prevention strategy has been established, and security regulations were also updated.

The "integration and reintegration" pillar aims at strengthening the acknowledgment of the prison service, especially its social and institutional connections. Our main objective is to facilitate the reintegration of the detainees into society and the labor market; therefore, local partnerships were established with various social partners. An expansion of the education and training opportunities for the prisoners was also started. The goal was to increase the number of working inmates and to widen the scale of free-time activities.

The third pillar, called the European standard—high-quality personnel, focuses on various staff-related issues. The working and living conditions and the uniforms are gradually improved and modernized. Efforts have been made to keep the colleagues within the organization, to reinforce the well-prepared and dedicated personnel, and to improve their education and training. Personal allowances received by the prison guards have been increased to the same level broadly accepted in other law enforcement agencies in Hungary.

The fourth tenet of the development program is called consolidation, and aims at modernizing the transportation system. Transportation vehicles have been replaced or renewed to facilitate the security conditions. The basis of the information technology in the registry system was also a high-priority issue.

Besides safeguarding the values and principles of the organization, the last pillar, rationalizing, takes aim at using the funds available to the prison service as efficiently as possible. This is a complex reform for streamlining the financial management of the whole body to maintain sustainability.

Molnár (hereafter, M.): Thank you very much for hosting us, as well as for your commitment to the interview. As you have already been informed, this is going to be a part of an international project on interviewing senior leaders who are connected to the correctional system. In addition to this, we would like to emphasize that the focus will be on your personal opinions, impressions, and thoughts just because we would like to learn your views based on your professional experiences. Each interview will be a book chapter that should be usable to teach students in a university class. It should be a source of knowledge and information to readers interested in legal systems, including judges, lawyers, prosecutors, and related professionals.

This was considered important, because the prison itself is always judged and "torn to pieces" by outsiders. Therefore, it is necessary to let the representatives of this field express their views. To this end, it is a reflection from the inside out and to reach toward the audience. Before we go into the details of the professional issues, please give us a short briefing of your career: length, organizations worked in, etc.

Kökényesi (hereafter, K.): After graduation, I now have 32 years of service in law enforcement. It was almost 30 years in the Police Service. Mostly, I was working at criminal agencies. I climbed the ladder and reached all the positions step by step. I began in a district police station, then in the Budapest Metropolitan Police Headquarters; after that, in the Hungarian National Police Headquarters. One year after the political system changed in Hungary (in 1991), reforms started in the whole administration. A new leadership was created at that time. I applied for a station commander position, and I succeeded. At that time, I had other higher qualifications already, for example, a university degree on the faculty of law, as well as a bachelor's degree from the Police College. So, I ran into a successful career. I became the station commander of a so-called "priority police station."* Later on, I was redeployed to another priority police station in a different district of the Budapest capitol. From 1998 to 2003, I was the chief of the Metropolitan Police of Budapest; thereafter, I worked in the Ministry of Interior as a head of the department (in the crime prevention field). I served a few years as a chief of Borsod County Police Headquarters and as the deputy head of the National Police Force. I have been working in this current position for almost 3 years.

Boda (hereafter, B.): Please tell us something more about the beginning. How did you grow up, and why did you choose to be a police officer?

K: It is a little bit romantic or nostalgic. I grew up in a small village, very far away from Budapest. First, I listened to the radio, and later, when we got our first television, I watched the films and movies about policing, crime-themed programs, and criminal investigation. So, I wanted to be a criminal investigator, because it seemed to be a successful thing. First, I got a degree in a university, and later on, I came to the police. It was a degree from the Horticultural University. This was my basic course. I performed the faculty of law in an evening university besides doing my regular job.

B: What was your first position in the police?

K: I started my career as a detective in a district police station on February 1, 1979. It was District No. 3 of the Budapest Metropolitan Police. I had no professional qualifications at that time, but I could sign up with my *civilian* degree. I shortly completed the course of the Police College that was designed for those who already had a diploma or higher qualification.

B: What was your first rank in the police?

K: As far as I remember, I was a chief petty officer after the recruitment procedure, just because I had a degree, but to be honest, it had no particular significance at that time.

B: What was your first managerial position later on?

---

* Priority police station: Some of the police stations were qualified as priority police stations, because the crime rate was high in their area of responsibility.

K: Actually, my first serious leadership position came in 1991. I became a station commander of the District No. 15 Police Station of the Budapest Metropolitan Police. I mentioned it was a priority police station, which means the station had some difficulties at that time; that is why the position had been opened up. I made lots of developments in this area, and because of this, I was relocated to District No. 8, also as a station commander of a priority police station. It was probably the most challenging district from a professional perspective at that time, in the middle of the 1990s. For example, this district was the base of prostitution, and organized crime and other antisocial circumstances were present.

B: What positions have you held before that, and why did you apply for the position?

K: I worked in the National Police Headquarters in the 1980s, also on criminal matters, as an investigator. Answering the second part of the question, there were many determinative factors for my decision to apply my knowledge, professional background, and university degree, as well as my rural origin or social background. Helping others was always present in my education. So, I decided to apply. I feel that this was my mission even in those days, because I grew up in quite difficult circumstances, and I felt that there was a substantial need to help people. I remember there were seven applicants who competed for the position. We were almost the same on the qualifications and on the background. The only difference was that I was the youngest among us.

M: Was it a real benefit at that time?

K: Yes, definitely it was. I was a bit more than 30 years old. Before the transition, there were people in the managerial positions for decades, just like in other areas of the state or the administration. So, it was an important issue to find new leaders with new *energies*. For example, the position was tendered; it was not like that before. People were simply appointed without any competition or transparency. It was not previously common. It was also something new that, after our application, we had to defend and explain our future perspective security program at a local committee. So, I got selected from among the seven people.

B: Who were the members of the committee, only police officers?

K: No, it was quite a comprehensive company. There was a local government representative, the representative from the leadership of Budapest Metropolitan Police Headquarters, and a police officer from the station, who represented his fellow officers' interests. Other areas were also represented. I think there were five or six people on the committee.

In 1991, the month of June, I took over the leadership of the station. There was a strong need for changes, because the police and the neighborhood were faced with a deteriorating security situation. As far as I remember, they were only able to explore 10% of the reported crime cases. Anyway, it was a similar situation in the other districts and in the bigger towns too. Even the position was not filled for some time, so I thought it was exactly a place where a young man had the possibility to show his ambitions. As a result, I was asked to move to a much larger district (the 8th) to do the same thing, improve the performance and the local security years after. It was the greatest experience of my life, and perhaps also, I got the most experience from there. In 1998, I became the chief of the Budapest Metropolitan Police. I think these previous successful years in the stations played an important role in appointing me for the higher position.

M: What methods or approach did you use for improving efficiency in the police stations?

K: First, I considered that the setting of a personal example was important, as well as result-centeredness, empathy to the people, and strict discipline were my principles from the beginning. I proclaimed these aspects to my people and asked my colleagues to follow it.

M: Did you find these principles missing in your predecessors' actions?

K: I've never been a man who said anything about his ancestors. I arrived at every place always by myself. I started to work on the methods, and I formed the environment in which my work has helped. I tried to make people recognize their own interests and to make them meet the requirements set out by me at the same time.

M: How did working in the correctional system come into your life and career?

K: I defined it exactly at my inauguration in mid-April of 2008. I said that my previous experience with the police was nearly 30 years. I learned the path to the prison. In other words, I knew how crime happened—how an innocent child became deviant, obviously not on his/her own account but mainly influenced by his/her environment, even family. I saw how a juvenile or teenager became a criminal. I was aware of the impact of the environment and other adult offenders. But, I knew much less about these people after they were sentenced and imprisoned. I did not really know what was happening in the correctional system or what they did after getting released from prison.

It is probably interesting that, when I was asked to do this job, I was the deputy chief of the Hungarian National Police. I just said that my previous positions were also highly regarded. Before

I accepted it, I thought that it was an excellent opportunity to broaden my knowledge and learn more about the prisons and the correctional system as well. I also found it a great challenge. From an organizational perspective, it should be added that the Hungarian Prison Service belonged to the Home Affairs Sector (Ministry of Interior) in the 1960s in Hungary. Later on, it had been transferred to the Ministry of Justice as part of the judiciary. In 2006, the government and ministries were reconstructed. The police and the prison service came under the supervision of the newly established Ministry of Justice and Law Enforcement. This created a relatively new situation in the life of these two organizations. Anyway, the transition from my previous position to this new one did not seem to be a big deal then.

M: Did the request (to be the commander) surprise you?

K: I have had so many things happen in my life that probably I do not even know this word: *surprise*. I worked in many places in many high positions or different levels of the management. It might be the recognition of that. As I told you, I worked as a chief of County Police Headquarters in Borsod County, the head of Department in the Ministry of Interior. I think the decision makers took my experiences into consideration and the successful actions I took in crisis situations. The chance to learn more about a specific area that I did not know in detail just challenged me.

M: Did you have any preconception concerning the organization (prison service)? Did you change these ideas later on?

K: Yes and no. Not more than others who had or are having a professional relationship with this organization. The former minister told me at my inauguration that he expected me and the newly appointed leaders to modernize the Hungarian Prison Service. He wanted us to make a more open organization that was human oriented and ready to go through an evolution process. We just started to implement the program on the first days of the planning process. The program itself was under preparation for approximately more than half a year. The program or this strategy had been accepted or entered into force at the end of that year 2008. This was called "Prepared and Responsible." The whole document has nearly 100 pages, starting with a summary of the current situation found in the Hungarian prison system. After the state analysis, we were looking for a way out of the problems. It was also outlined in the material as a strategic plan. We worked out what would lead to a better, more modern, cost-efficient, and reputable prison service in Hungary. This is an ambitious program that did not exist before as such. Feeling the support of the Ministry and the staff, we found it was necessary. Therefore, we have been making the most out of it. Not hiding away that the prison service was in an unfairly difficult situation from technical, organizational, and training perspectives, as well as in terms of eligibility, these were the basic and main facts we needed to make everyone face, including the leaders of the Ministry. We made our people accept it too. We made them understand that significant steps will be taken in their interest as well.

Just let me give you some concrete examples. The bonus system of the prison workers was less rewarding than other law enforcement employees' were. We promised to increase it, and we managed. Previously, the basic training was only a 4-week course; we found that this was not enough. Shortly thereafter, the course period was increased to 15 weeks, more than triple. It turned out that the technical condition of our vehicles was more than bad. The cars and the vans were 10.5 years old, on the average. We said it was unsafe and unacceptable, both for the officers and for the prisoners too. So, it was a significant problem in the everyday operation. We renewed our vehicles very shortly thereafter with governmental support. We put into the spotlight a more modern way of thinking and a project-oriented paradigm. To this end, we created a function in the headquarters, a strategic and coordinating function that is called Coordinating and Strategic Deputy Commander.

We started to take into consideration the country's carrying capacity, which is finite. So, we had to learn to apply for grants. Let me say that one of the biggest successes that we were able to launch was our IT development, which was aiming at renewing the more than decade-old information technology in our system. That was a more than 1.3 billion HUF* investment built on European Union fund support.

We submitted 82 applications to various trends and won six of them. We found that the *load-bearing capacity* of the country or the state budget is not something endless, so we cannot expect to receive everything immediately. We cannot only demand and consume, but rather, we have to give and produce. We want to take the central budget's help only in matters where we cannot finance from other sources. We made long-term programs in many areas. Of course, we have short, medium, and longer term plans included in the strategy. The implementation is constantly being followed by a group that also directs this project, and they report regularly on what has been achieved or done.

* 1 USD = 200 HUF; 1 EURO = 270 HUF.

M: Wherever you put your feet in, revolutionary changes or fundamental interventions are always being made. What were the external factors that contributed to the changes and developments? What support did you get for the reforms?

K: I think we needed and still need to do things in order to be known by society. We accomplished a lot in this field too, which had not been previously done. We created a lot of presentations introducing the prison service in Hungary. In the main broadcasting time, TV series were launched, showing prison life. We definitely opened up communication. We wanted to be very proactive in this field, so we did not want to wait for negative news or incidents that are mainly of interest in the mass and commercial media. We learned that people do not know too much about us, and they are not particularly interested in this subject. Nevertheless, opening communication was important in order to make others aware of our problems and our situation. After they had learned more about us and the circumstances we were working in, we could turn to them and ask for cooperation, so these facts were not unprecedented to those who could be our potential partners.

There have been changes in the government in recent years that also played an important role in this progress. The prison service and the police came to be directed by the same ministry—the Ministry of Justice and Law Enforcement. At the same time, some other law enforcement bodies and organizations were removed. The Ministry of Interior was closed up from 2006 to 2010. Being under the supervision of the Ministry of Justice and Law Enforcement helped us create a closer relationship with one of the largest law enforcement agencies (the police). The most important change has occurred this year when, once again, the structure of government was changed. The reestablishment of the Ministry of Interior created a new situation in the security sector. Almost all law enforcement agencies were placed under the supervision of the Ministry of Interior. Thus, cooperation was established between the police, disaster management, civil security services, internal relief, and many other bodies. These organizations have the opportunity for daily, operationally realistic, and good cooperation. I feel it is very important. It is obvious that the country's security problems lead to the reinforcement of the police. There are places in the country where the retail demands are elementary on this field. This is connected to the correctional system as well. For example, just in this year, the number of the prisoners increased by more than 1000. So, it means that these factors are interconnected, and if you change or develop one of them, it will create the need to change or develop others too.

M: Did it create any difficulties for the people who were working in the correctional system when their organization and their activities came
under the same supervision and consideration of the police?

K: To me, obviously, not as the head of the organization, only because I
brought another organizational culture with me. You know, the
prison service was within the Ministry of Justice alone as a law
enforcement body long before. Thanks to my previous professional experiences in various organizations in my career, I could
make the prison service benefit from the new situation being in the
Ministry of Interior. I had the opportunity for a direct comparison.
On that basis, I can say that the things we previously did not have
in the prison service, we have them now. We even have them on a
higher level than in other areas of the administration. The prison
service could not manage such a development previously because
it operated in a close environment. Joint activities led to this result.
Collaborating with others created the opportunities to compensate
those differences that had been previously formed between us.

M: Have you experienced any resistance in the prison service in connection
to working together or being together with other law enforcement
agencies?

K: I think not in our body. Everyone has come to the conclusion that things
got opened all around us. It was also very important to learn from
other areas how benefits, bonuses, or other technical areas have
been developed in recent years. People in our organization realized
that this was more beneficial than a disadvantage.

M: What do you think people who are working in different organizations
can learn from each other (e.g., those who are working in the
prison service and police officers)?

K: As I told you, I have seen this phenomenon in my previous positions, so it
was not unusual for me. Quite a few years ago, detention was mainly
centered at the police. Currently, they prefer to place detainees in
prisons. During my police work, I knew how police performed
detention, how custody is delivered by the police, and other things
like that. I was in a close connection with the whole system before
and saw the process from the beginning. Perhaps, the daily cooperation is more flexible and *can be more active* by taking part. There
is interoperability among the various law enforcement agencies. I
feel a stronger professional recognition of each other's activities.
Sometimes, it is not favorable, because our people wish to join the
police, who have certain benefits we do not have currently. We have
to admit that this is part of interoperability. Anyway, we experience much more operational cooperation.

For example, if we are conducting a long rural transportation of prisoners that have higher security concerns, the police can monitor the whole progress, since we have the same telecommunication system. So, they can follow us via radio, and they provide immediate assistance in case of need. Our colleagues are doing similarly in case of a flexible inclusion or even when the police want to contact the inmates. We cooperate according to the rules and regulations, of course. Improved cooperation is mutually important. Openness was necessary to improve relationships with the prosecution, the courts, and the probation supervisors. Prison service seems to be a very *self-contained world*; however, our relationships are extremely broad. In addition to this, the prison service is a highly structured system. It is very complex, having different services just like hospitals or medical services, etc.

M: You mentioned that cooperation can be more active between agencies. Is it more active or less active cooperation now than it was before?

K: I think it is more active now. It must be like that, because we have common supervisors and common goals.

M: Has legislation helped your work in recent years?

K: Hungary joined all those international conventions, and legislative tools were important from the perspective of the European Union. We are not only a member state; we are part of the EU. Some decisions connected to prison regulation are directly enforceable here in Hungary too. There are prison controls conducted by international bodies regularly, and we also participate in these measures, just like other countries do. On the other hand, I think Hungary is having an EU conform legislation system, and all our legislative tools exist in other EU countries as well. The problem is that the basic act is rather old; it is the 1979 Legislative Decree on Prisons that was modified many times. Creating a code is part of the legislation program in recent years, but it has not been completed yet. We feel that it is very much the time for finalization. Besides all of this, I believe that those ministerial decrees or government decrees that determine our activities can provide safety in the everyday service and are good guidance.

M: What should be amended or changed in the regulation?

K: I think a comprehensive legal instrument, what I earlier called a prison code, should be important. I would not amend or change anything; I would rather feel the importance of one consistent law, which could accumulate all the regulations. This is quite an urgent task of the legislation, creating a common platform of different legal interventions.

M: What is the current and future role of the prison service? What are the
main directions of the prison service?

K: There was almost a non–state regulation in the Middle Ages in Hungary
for a long period of time. There were only manorial or county
jails. The first regulation was the Csemegi Code, which was first
enforced in 1878, and contained the modern prison rules. The
whole code was a very modern act. It is well known in our history
that there were significant improvements in all areas of life during the Hasbro–Hungarian Monarchy. Large prison facilities were
built, together with offices of courts and prosecutors as judicial
centers. These facilities, with their significances, are still the main
characteristics of the current prison system. Some of them are still
there. They were built in the cities just in the middle of town as
modern buildings. Of course, these are outdated nowadays.

After the world wars, in the 1950s, there were also lots of changes
in the prison structure. The liberal paradigms, detainee-oriented
approach, or multistage recognized prison systems had been completely changed together with the regulations. The prison system
had a significantly political function in those decades. There were
other changes in 1961 and in 1978 as well.

The next modifications were mainly based on the adaption of rules
from the European Union. I have to add that, from the 1980s, prisons
were overcrowded. For example, in 1986, there were 25,000 prisoners in Hungary. Comparing it with the 1970s, the average was 20,000
inmates, which is a huge difference. Then, the transition came, when
the number of prison inmates had been increasing again. The changes
we had after 1990 increased security problems in Hungary, but the
prison system did not really receive structural or other support. So,
it resulted in some difficulties in our service too. The alternative sentences appeared afterward; those could decrease the number of prisoners. Also, some newly built prisons and facilities could improve our
performance. New PPP prisons* were established in Szombathely for
the first time and, then, later in another town, which brought a significant difference and gave a new direction to the system. These institutions were constructed in a modern and more specific way. They
have prison cells or guard houses for a few persons only, and they also
use modern operational solutions. Thanks to them, capacity has been
increased by 1500 spaces.

To this end, we are now operating in a relatively normal saturation and circumstances. We currently face new challenges and,

---

* PPP prison: Prison operating under a Public–Private Partnership contract.

again, an increasing number of inmates and congestion. The current ratio is more negative than positive to be seen. We made an international comparison on this issue. We found that, in many Western European countries or, for example, in the Scandinavian states, the statistical ratio is better than ours. The comparison also deals with the data concerning the inhabitants of the country (projected to 100,000 people). There are countries that have a similar situation as we do. This can be considered as a reply to the public safety problem. We think that the problem is very comprehensive. It is related to society in general, migration, population, and demograpics, as well as alternative sentencing practices and the prison culture. There are many factors that are influencing this rate. We believe that these determining factors are very much taken into consideration not only by us but also by other decision makers and legislators. There is going to be an urgent need regarding the problem of increasing levels of saturation.

M: Did you bring a new approach to the prison service?

K: I'm sure, yes. When I got here, we started to launch a new program that had never before been seen in the organization. I found this approach was new in our service. The main principles of the program were the following: manager orientation, project-centeredness, openness to society, and factual thinking. I wanted to make people and the organization face the problems bravely and see what situation we were in. We defined our mission according to the following sentence: "We keep our tradition and will do all necessary changes in the same time." I would not say that all these things are only because of one person or because of my personal contribution. As a matter of fact, together with the new leaders and with 8000 very active employees, we have managed to do a lot of new things and were able to make many changes.

B: Did you look for the opinion of the former prison commanders?

K: I met with them in the beginning. I invited all of them for an informal meeting, and I spent one day together with them. We talked a lot about everything. I sensed that we had to step over their 10- or 20-year-old practices. The meeting was important, but to be honest, we were looking for newer things. I frankly say that I respect all of them because of their professionalism and dedication. It was very important for me indeed.

M: What existing methods do you see that should urgently be changed or improved?

K: We have not reached this topic yet during this interview. It is also an important principle that we must be active internationally as well. A forum for prison commanders of Central European countries had been established in order to bring them together once a year for some discussions. Currently, this informal platform is represented mainly by our surrounding countries. It also has members from Lithuania and from non-EU countries as well, such as Croatia. This year, nine countries, including eight national commanders, were hosted for a 2-day roundtable meeting in Hungary. This process started 2 years ago in Austria. We meet in a different country every single year. This is a good opportunity to learn about the situation of other countries. Good practices can be followed within this framework too.

Let me share a concrete example with you. My deputy will lead a delegation of our experts to a study tour to Austria. They will learn more about the electronic surveillance systems and about the devices and methods there. As you might know, our Austrian colleagues have more experiences with these alternative methods. I think that, in this respect, the openness to the international area, which is validated from concrete and practical experiences, can also bring benefits.

Continued on December 6, 2010, 14:00 at the same point.

M: Let us continue with the correction philosophies. What prison or correction philosophies should be developed in Hungary?

K: I think we talked about this already. I do not want to go back to how the system evolved over the centuries or decades. Our current legislative background is able to direct our activities. The program we have launched recently that I described as openness, modernization, upgrading, etc., is aiming at strengthening the prison service in order to make it better able to maintain the system.

M: How are prisons currently operating?

K: This is a philosophical question again. I read the official publications on how other correctional institutions are operating. There are countries where it is run completely by the government or by the state. There are some places where it is shared with the private sector. Also, we know about the countries and practices where it is completely passed over to the private sector, even the management of it. We have mainly and basically a single state operating system, with the exception of the two PPP prisons, where the operations are undertaken by the private sector. So, we have a little bit of a mixed picture to that extent. It is considered to be a modern thing. At least, many people seem to think so. My personal point of view is that the capabilities of our countries should be in proportion to our possibilities. So, an internal operation is obviously cheaper, but the external one carries other benefits. We share others' opinion on that. We have to admit that the external operation required a lot of new things for us. We learned a lot about technical novelties from the business sector that were not previously known. Also, it was sort of a paradigm shift, because additional methods were learned on the fields of expenditure, etc. So, it was very useful for us.

M: How could a different or better operational system contribute to the correction of inmates? How could it serve the utilization of free time?

K: Dealing with the inmates or detainees is a state monopoly. The operation cannot influence the enforcement of these professional interests. We have unified the health care delivery, education, and training systems. These figures are quite a lot, so I would say that it has not typically been a breakthrough in this area. On the other hand, there are greater abilities to conduct better training courses with the contribution of external collaborators in these new PPP prisons, which are proportionally greater than an average institution like ours. They have more than a hundred people on staff, so either they can organize high school or other levels of trainings.

M: What other services should also be introduced?

K: Our current services are varied, even for those working only inside the walls of the prison. The supervision patrons are working separately, but in very close collaboration with us. There is also a very significant role played by churches. We have 33 pastors, employed by the prisons. They provide peace of mind to the prisoners and are integrally involved in educational and other correction programs. There are 12 limited companies that employ the inmates. It is important for them to get public orders that are currently provided by the new government, so they also function as an integral part of the prison. The producing structure of these four agricultural and eight industrial limited companies is very diverse. Similarly, I see the expansion of hospitals and health services, ranging from therapeutic occupations to medicine and other concerns.

There is a very large topic we have not really detailed yet, that is, education and spending leisure time usefully. This service is implemented by different professional groups, such as cultural groups ranging from different faculties, for example, literary, artistic groups, etc. The full range is demonstrated in the system, which is typically performed by civilian actors. This assistance may also be important.

M: What services should be eliminated?

K: I do not see the possibility for this now. Regarding our financial and legal situation, and other frameworks, we can provide sufficient service. It is clear that there can be changes in this field too, but every service needs to be replaced instead of eliminated.

M: How is your relationship with the supervisory mentors or supervising patrons?

K: Actually, they are being reorganized. Some of them are located in the newly established Ministry of Justice and Administration. Previously, we were directed by the same ministry, the Ministry of Justice. The new situation does not really impact our good cooperation. Each and every correctional institute of ours is in very close cooperation with the judicial offices and with the supervising mentors, who are sometimes working in the prisons too. They participate in the preparatory process before the release of prisoners and organize their life in the postliberation period. They are important factors for reintegration, an activity that is crucial for corrections. The reoffending rate is reportedly around 40%. This means that there is a lot to do in this field too.

M: How do intermediate sanctions serve your actions?

K: They partly serve. This includes house arrest. If this is imposed on a larger number of inmates, logically, there will be fewer pretrial detentions. We want this to be developed in the future. Although Hungary has no long tradition of electronic detention or electronic monitoring, my colleagues will go to Austria this week to learn about their more extensive experience. I see that progress is needed in this area. It will be a sort of seminar in Austria, and other countries also delegate colleagues. The conference we organized 2 weeks ago created the platform for such cooperation. We are literally proud of that event, because nine countries , including eight national commanders, were present. So, this study visit to Austria is the result of that meeting.

M: What is the biggest problem or challenge in the prison service system?

K: It is clear that many problems could be listed. First, I have mentioned the saturation level. It is higher than 2 years ago. However, it is significantly lower than in 2002, because there were more prisoners for fewer seats. So, one is the saturation. Second, the current financial situation requires a very conscious economy. There is austerity in the central budget that is concerned about the prison service too. It is a positive that we can pay for all the needed allowances of my colleagues, so the budget will provide the basic conditions of operation. Many of our facilities that were built in the nineteenth century are to be modernized or reconstructed. As I just mentioned, some of these facilities are still working as prisons. They are no longer adequate for today's requirements. Their location or equipments are no longer sufficient. These are serious problems. We have to move along the path on which we have already taken significant steps, for example, the development of vehicles. Development is also needed on the number of staff, which has never followed the changes. The ratio between the inmates and the employees has become unfavorable compared with other European Union countries. It is also an important issue as to how we can further the education of all prisoners and staff.

We have achieved a significant increase due to the high school for inmates. In 2000, there were barely 100 inmates who participated in some kind of schooling. Now, we have around 1000 inmates involved in secondary level courses. The number of primary school graduates is also increasing. An additional major task is to increase the number of trainees. These things depend on us not partly because they are very serious fiscal issues and financial resources are obtained through applications.

M: You mentioned mainly external factors that lead to the problems. How about those that are coming from the organization (e.g., corruption)?

K: According to some public surveys, prison service is not more corrupt than other law enforcement agencies. It is probably because our activities are closer or perhaps because of the permanent presence of the leaders or superiors. Maybe, the corruption rate is even better than anywhere else. I am always mentioning the importance of education and training. Now, it is also under development not only for the prison services but also for the entire law enforcement sector. The focus is on the modular nature and also to ensure interoperability. Our training was working independently of others so far. This was manifested in the duration of the training courses, in the training institutes, and in other factors as well. Of course, efforts should be made on the specificities too, since this work is incomparably different from other services. This work is incomparably different from some other public services, those that have much more publicity, such as the police. There are many specialties that should be approached differently. The load level is different. The fact that our employees are permanently working in a closed environment together with the prisoners is a huge physical demand. It must also appear during the recruitment.

We have created a brand new organizational chart. The audit activity was raised to a higher level. We transformed the communications of the organization, outside and inside as well. We also delivered new press and media products. We have completely changed our image to the public. We have started new developments, became more open. These reforms made the prison service respond as well. A specific department with a minimum required staff is working on various tenders and applications, and they also deal with the project management. It is also something new that was not done previously.

The program, Responsible and Prepared, is a long-term modernization program. It has a separate governing body with appointed members. One of my deputies is the leader of this group. These did not previously exist. So, we have created an institutionalized background to provide additional resources. These resources are to promote our reforms and developments and not for the basic or minimum level of performance.

M: Is there any element or part of your strategic program that has already been completed or succeeded?

K: The minister, who accepted the program, said that the administration had not seen such a thing. It was a great experience, because the minister is well known in the public sector as one of the most experienced bureaucrats. I can say that we had been working out this program for more than a semester, and a lot of people were involved. We also involved the professionals; we organized presentations for the Ministry leaders. We asked the scientific community too. For example, one of the most popular social scientists, Prof. Katalin Gönczöl, also commented on this material. These are very much the first indicators or results that show a smashing change in the organization.

M: What is the relationship between theory and practice regarding the prison service? How can you utilize the different research?

K: We pay attention in this regard too. The deputy position I have detailed previously was created in order to ensure the communication and development of scientific activities, including research and international relations. Actually, we have institutionalized the input points of the science to prison work. My colleagues regularly participate in various surveys or scientific researches together with the OKRI.* Hungarian universities and a nongovernmental organization, the Prison Affairs Company, also often organize such activities in which we are involved. We have a magazine regularly published, *Prison Affairs*, which is an open platform for experts and professionals to interpret and to explain their views on related topics. We feel the importance of following international progress in order to provide our development. As I already mentioned, we have launched new training courses, which are based on very serious results of surveys, for example, training for mediation or negotiation techniques in crisis situations. These innovations never existed before. They can be considered as the utilization of the scientific results or as some reactions to these achievements. It led

---

* OKRI, National Institute of Criminology, located in Budapest.

to a new security perception of the prison service that is over the static security conception. It has become obvious that the task of prison service is not only to "preserve." We are now discussing conflict resolution, improving the personality of the inmate, and new methods together with new contributors. These are the part of the incorporation of scientific results day by day.

M: To what extent can you adapt the good practices?

K: Exactly due to these international conferences and bilateral relations, we have the chance to scrutinize and learn these new methods. Compared with other countries, we have a different legal environment in many aspects. For example, we know that personal data protection of the inmates is diverse. We have a very strict regulation in this regard compared with those countries where the name or other personal data of the inmates can be written on the door of the cell. We also know about other forms of sanctions, just like when the person is imprisoned only on the weekends and whether, during weekdays, he/she lives a normal life. We learned about more stringent and more lenient probation supervision from others too. We know about distinct practices of imposing penalty by the courts compared with ours, for example, various conditional salvations or other controlled solutions. We closely monitor these things. We defined many things from these examples, and these are very utilizable in the Hungarian environment during the preparation of the new penalty code. Of course, we are fully aware that the prison service is not creating the law; nevertheless, we receive different inquiries of that regard daily, where we can express our opinion.

M: Would you mention some specific examples?

K: This is based on foreign examples such as that of resolving conflicts among staff and inmates and becoming the explicit object of education. We are working on these issues very proactively. For example, having a hostage in the prison has not yet been a problem in Hungary. However, we noticed that it is a real thing in some other countries, so we decided to take some preventive measures for this. We collected and utilized the foreign experiences in this regard. There are lots of examples that previously were not a practice in Hungary and became a model after analyzing international experiences in order to respond accordingly.

M: We have already talked about the subject of international relationships. Would you detail a bit how international cooperation affects your everyday duties?

K: The full-fledged EU membership of Hungary allowed us to develop a close, daily relationship among other things, with all member states. For example, Penal Procedural Code (CPP) checks regularly on Hungary. This committee opposes torture and inhumane treatment. They had an examination recently in Hungary. They affect us, such as by formulating international standards: those we can meet, or want to meet sooner or later. The European Commission sets out recommendations in relation to the prison; these are also relevant for our work. There are glaring cases when the detainees appeal to the European Court of Justice. Thus, the EU's relation with the completely remodeled prison service is getting stronger. There is a lot of historical change in the region: for example, Croatia, Slovenia, and Serbia have formed a new country, whereas the Czech Republic and Slovakia also suggest the need for much closer bilateral relations. The number of foreign prisoners is not that much higher in Hungary, but those 500–600 people are especially from those countries. There are some countries where a higher proportion of prisoners are here. Therefore, it is necessary for cooperation. We are fully engaged to provide contact between the foreign inmate and his/her representative from the embassy or consulate. We also have this reporting obligation and fulfill all requests. We are increasingly part of a process, which is also increasing international respect.

M: Are these international relations useful?

K: Certainly. It is very important to see how things are going on outside. We need this information as well. For example, the question of saturation, which I always emphasized. We have pointed out that Hungary belongs to midrange countries in this regard. To this end, this is a developmental opportunity. The change is partly up to us. This is also the part of the legislation and the question of penalty-shaping practices. This also depends on how the state power approaches the issue, furthermore, how the whole system favors the correctional system and how the intermediate sanctions are used and imposed by the judgments. There is a very strong connection with the crime rate, the other legal solutions, and the tendencies of building and constructing prisons or correctional facilities. If we put it into a whole system matrix, we can simply realize how to utilize these international experiences.

M: Was this "whole-system thinking" significant to the former leadership as well?

K: I brought this from the police service. I liked to speak in any environment where people were curious about what I was saying. I was usually successful in these events. I think it is important to not get stuck on a topic, especially when it is needed to go further on. It can happen when your knowledge is not that deep, so you should not be very detailed. In these cases, I was trying to put all things together and to see what was important and what was not or what was related to the topic and what was not. I mentioned that I once worked in the Ministry in the crime prevention field. To be honest, I did not like that post, but it was a good place to learn about complexity.

M: What is going to be next? How do you predict the future of the prison service?

K: There is an increasing pressure and demand for better public security in Hungary and in Europe as well. Logically, the police and the law enforcement agencies are strengthening. It will also lead to a more effective correctional system, because the traditional ways and methods will no longer be sustainable. There is a governmental decree under review that will be enforced soon that aims at overviewing the correctional system. It is going to be a huge assessment that will look for strengths and weaknesses. It will also aim at seeing if we can comply with international requirements and standards. I am sure that the number of staff will be increased too. Technical developments are also to be continued. Cooperation among different fields is also important. Thus, both qualitative and quantitative improvements are needed.

Interview with John Rougier, Commissioner of Prisons of Trinidad and Tobago

5

DIANNE WILLIAMS

Contents

Introduction

The Trinidad and Tobago Prison Service is an arm of the Criminal Justice System and a division of the Ministry of National Security. It has at its head the commissioner of prisons, who has delegated powers under the Constitution of the Republic of Trinidad and Tobago and is ultimately responsible to the Ministry of National Security.*

There are currently eight prisons and institutions under the authority of the Trinidad and Tobago Prison Service. As of January 26, 2010, these eight prisons and institutions housed 2292 incarcerated men and 133 incarcerated women in Trinidad and Tobago prisons, 180 juveniles in the Youth Training Center, and 986 in the Remand Prison. The mission of the Trinidad and Tobago Prison Service is to protect the society and to reduce crime through the reduction in reoffending by facilitating opportunities for the rehabilitation of offenders while maintaining control under safe, secure, and humane conditions.* The strategic objectives of the Trinidad and Tobago Prison Service are to

1. Protect—Protect the public.
2. Correct—Improve educational, work, and social life skills of offenders.
3. Relate—Improve community relations.

* http://ttprisons.com.

4. Reintegrate—Promote law-abiding behavior in custody and after release.
5. Restore—Reduce crime by addressing offending behavior.

One of the earliest records of a prison in Trinidad and Tobago was in the late 1700s, during a time of public executions. In 1808, this structure was destroyed by fire, and a new one was rebuilt in 1812. The Prison Service Act was enacted in 1838 and revised in 1950. The first women's prison was built in 1854, with a second one being built in 1886. In 1937, due to a labor dispute, the number of arrests skyrocketed, causing overcrowding in the existing prisons. As a result, Nelson Island, one of the small islands of the country's northwest coast, was used as a prison camp. In 1949, the Young Offenders Detention Institute was relocated.

In 2002, the Government of Trinidad and Tobago appointed a task force to evaluate the country's Penal Reform System. One of the main recommendations of the resulting report was the need to implement a Restorative Justice Philosophy. One of the pioneers of the implementation of the Restorative Justice Philosophy within the Criminal Justice System of Trinidad and Tobago is the current commissioner of prisons John Rougier.

Interview

Dr. W: Let me begin by asking you to introduce yourself and state your official title.

Com. R: My name is John Rougier. I am the commissioner of prisons of Trinidad and Tobago.* I have been in the prison service for 38 years. I was appointed commissioner of prisons in 2005 and have remained in this position up to today and I am coming up for retirement in the latter part of 2011. (Mr. Rougier retired on October 7th, 2011)

Dr. W: You obviously worked your way up through the ranks. Can you tell me a bit about this?

Com. R: Yes, I worked my way up through the ranks. I actually entered the prison service as a trainee and worked from prisons officer 1 right up the ranks to commissioner of prisons.

Dr. W: Did you have any specializations while you were in the prison service, any special training that you felt made you more qualified to become the commissioner compared to, say, someone else with the same qualifications?

Com. R: There were a number of opportunities to which I was exposed. I was placed in a Specialist Unit early in my career. I was a training officer

* http://ttprisons.com.

for a number of years. I had a good academic base, i.e., BSc and MSc, and I was fortunate to attend a number of international training programs. Very early in the service, I had the opportunity to be placed in one of the special units that is now called our Emergency Response Unit.* At that time, it was referred to as the Reserve Unit. At the end of that tour of duty, I was moved to the Training Department. I was a training officer for a number of years. While at this department, I continued my academic studies. I obtained my A Levels and then attended The University of the West Indies, St. Augustine in 1979 and completed my BSc degree in sociology in 2008. I think that was critical as far as the direction my career took. It was critical in both positive and negative ways. Positively, it gave me confidence. My experience, coupled with my academic background, gave me a vision of what I felt the Service should have been, and therefore, I waited for the opportunity. When I got the opportunity, I was able to implement some of my ideas. For example, I was fortunate again to go to a 6-week training program in the training department in a Canadian prison. Again, that experience was tremendous for me, because on my return to Trinidad in the Prisons Training Department, I was able to implement some programs I saw in the Canadian training system. I was then fortunate again to go for another 6 weeks of training in Syracuse, where I looked at three or four juvenile facilities. Again, I was exposed to a wide range of experiences, and as a result, when I returned, I combined the practical application with the theory I learned from my studies. I was then fortunate to be placed with a mentor of mine in the prison service, who was, at that time, given the responsibility to occupy, for want of a better term, a new youth training center they had recently built. He took me on board and allowed me to do a lot of things and implement a lot of ideas. I'm seeing the results of that now as the commissioner of prisons where, to me, the Youth Training Centre is one of the best facilities in the region.

Dr. W: What motivated you to enter the field of corrections in the first place?

Com. R: Actually, my brother.

Dr. W: Is he a Corrections Officer as well?

Com. R: He was a corrections officer. As a matter of fact, we were fortunate to hold posts at the helm of the prison service. I was commissioner of prisons and he was deputy commissioner of prisons for a couple of years before he retired from the Service. The two of us worked our way up. He joined the Service in 1970, and I joined in 1973. Again, it was because he literally was my mentor, and I just

* http://www.newsday.co.tt/crime_and_court/0,143207.html.

followed, because I saw him doing well, and I wanted to be there as well. I remember him working in the Accounts Department of the prison service, and I worked in Training. I remember talking with my brother about how we would improve ourselves as we sought upward mobility in the Service. We were very young, and we felt that we needed a stronger academic foundation, so we did our A levels in Economics. I, however, got ahead of my brother in academia when he got married. I, at that time, went on to The University of the West Indies, St. Augustine. I took, for a year and a half, a no-pay study leave. Those were the sacrifices that were made to acquire our first degrees. What seemed unfortunate at that time was my being qualified so young. At that time, there were only three persons who were qualified within the prison service at the degree level.

Dr. W: How many officers were there overall?

Com. R: At that time, there could have been roughly between 1500 and 1800 persons, and there were only three of us with degree-level qualifications. Eventually, my brother earned his, making it four of us. The problem there is that we were targeted. Jealousy, envy, and negative comments were thrown at us. The job of a prison officer required no degree… a "turnkey" sort of thing.

Dr. W: How did that impact your performance? How did it impact the direction that your career ultimately took?

Com. R: I was determined, and I got the support from my instructor/supervisor who, it appeared, liked me. As a matter of fact, he brought me to the training department as a physical education instructor, and interestingly, up until my position of Ag. assistant superintendent, I operated under him until he was promoted as assistant commissioner. He supported me and encouraged me. I remember when I wanted to go to The University of the West Indies, St. Augustine, I spoke with him and he said, "Well, go ahead." He was close to the then commissioner of prisons, and therefore, I got that support and coverage from them, because they knew I worked well. I was a good and committed worker. I rarely applied for sick leave in the early days of my career, because I just wanted to move on in my career in the prison service. To be honest, I have always said this to my wife and even apologized to her. I neglected my family. I left home early and slaved long hours at work, returning home late. I always have to say that I have a good wife, because if she wasn't a good person, she would have left me, and I would have lost my children.

Dr. W: Did the way your career developed, the trajectory that your career took, did it surprise you?

Com. R: No, it didn't surprise me, because as far as I'm concerned, I have always been an ambitious person. My brother once recalled a young man saying, "You see that brother of yours, he's going to make your family proud." My brother said that, afterward, he was just watching and supporting. Although I made it to commissioner and he didn't, he remained supportive of me and my career. The support I received from my brother and other persons allowed me to also encourage others who were ambitious. It was never a case of me rising through the ranks and pulling others down. I was carrying people with me. This is one of the good things about it, because I remember the suffering my brother and I endured with no paid study leave, and I promised myself that, if I got the opportunity to assist, no one will have to suffer like I did.

Dr. W: So you changed that policy?

Com. R: I literally changed that policy, and this is why I feel hurt at times when I hear people who I supported in acquiring further education speaking the way they do.

Dr. W: Did your work prove to be as interesting or as rewarding as you thought it would have been before you joined the service? And even as a young rookie with expectations and anticipation, in hindsight, was it as rewarding as you thought it would have been?

Com. R: There was that level of reward, but there was always the negative side to it, because as a young person moving up too fast, I always had my problems and challenges. But with all of that, they knew I had a strong work ethic, not only from the prisons point of view but also operational and administrative. I was involved in football and cricket. I was part of the management committee of the Sports Club. I was very active. I think I enjoyed the work as a younger person in the job than when I became senior, because as I said, I felt that a lot of people were envious, and therefore, in some cases, when I assumed senior rank, the support was not there. I didn't bother about that, because I was so confident in myself, and I was the type of person who, if I didn't know something, I would have asked and when given information, I would learn. There was that satisfaction in continuous learning even as I completed my postgraduate degree in human resource management. I just continued learning and developing.

Dr. W: Were there any opportunities that came your way throughout those 38 years, and if so, do you have any regrets that you did not pursue those opportunities and that you stayed the course?

Com. R: No, I have no regrets. As a matter of fact, I was once thinking about leaving the Service, but I was thinking about leaving the Service very early in my career, because I felt that I wasn't being treated the way I should be, as far as movement is concerned. That was from prison officer II to the position of supervisor, but overall, I have no regrets. I'm commissioner of prisons now. If there is satisfaction in the senior rank, it is satisfaction because of the fact that not only do I feel confident in what I have done (other people may say otherwise, and they may have done their things and tried to pull me down), but I have impacted the things I've done in the prison service, and by extension, I have impacted the wider society. But more than that, I have impacted the region from a corrections point of view. Additionally, I helped to form and register the regional Association with a group of people here in Trinidad. We set up the bank account and have been moving on. This year was our fifth conference.

Dr. W: Let's talk a bit about the changes that you have experienced and changes that you have created within the region. What do you see as the most important change that has occurred in the field of corrections over the course of your career from the philosophical perspective—organizational arrangements, specializations, policies and programs, equipment, technology, rehabilitation which I know you will talk about, methods of community supervision, intermediate sanctions, personnel diversity, etc.?

Com. R: I had the opportunity to visit a number of correctional facilities worldwide. I visited facilities in countries like America, Canada, England, and Israel. I learned a lot from those visits. One of the most essential things I learned from those visits was the importance of training. So, I was instrumental in the acquisition of a training facility that the prison service could be proud of. For example, I have been to McCormick in Syracuse, and I was able to implement a number of things, structures, and programs and training within our facility training. I also helped with the development of the curriculum for the training facility. But, the most important impact that I have had is that of the Youth Training Centre.* I was given the opportunity to literally run that Youth Training Centre. One of the philosophies that I attempted to implement there was the Restorative Justice philosophy.† I was met with a lot of resistance for trying to implement that philosophy. But eventually, people started to see the benefit of it and they began to support it.

Dr. W: You are actually known as the head of the agency who has been most progressive in changing the tone of the criminal justice system from punitive to restorative. Tell me a little about this. Where did

---

* http://www.gov.tt/gortt/portal/ttconnect/Bus_jobseekerDetail/?WCM_GLOBAL_CONTEXT=/gortt/wcm/connect/gortt+web+content/TTConnect/Business/Role/AJobSeeker/EducationandTraining/YTEPP+-+The+Youth+Training+and+Employment+Partnership+Programme.

† http://missingtrinbagonians.wordpress.com/2009/10/27/2009-10-27-restorative-justice-a-farfetched-idea-for-the-caribbean/.

this come from? What drives it, and do you expect to see it implemented in the prison system before you retire?

Com. R: I think it has been implemented already. The foundation was laid
already at the Youth Training Centre, and maybe, that is what I
was required to do—to lay the foundation. I was supported in laying the foundation by my then superintendent and deputy commissioner. But, we were met with much resistance in this endeavor.
This resistance is being experienced today in the prison service as a
whole with respect to the implementation of the restorative justice
philosophy. I think there is a general lack of understanding of this
philosophy by many stakeholders, and this may be the cause of the
resistance being experienced. To some extent, I take some blame
for the perceived lack of understanding of the philosophy by others, because I might have been remiss in properly communicating
it to others. As a result, they resisted. It was always a case of "what's
in it for me?" Another change that I was instrumental in implementing was the use of religious leaders for all denominations. I
got the idea from one of my visits abroad, where they were using a
Catholic chaplain at a correctional facility. I expanded on the idea
to meet the religious diversity of the Trinidad and Tobago society.
But, some problems developed with that system. For example, too
much "poaching" was taking place. That is, Baptist leaders were
trying to convert Pentecostal prisoners, and Pentecostal ministers
were trying to convert Muslim and Hindu prisoners, etc. So, I said,
"Here's what. Let's come together. Let us form a council of chap-
lains." And that is what happened. Now, the council is responsible
for all religious and spiritual activities within the correctional system. Any decision from a spiritual point of view is made by the
council, and they simply bring it to me for administrative approval.

Dr. W: Tell me what changes in external conditions, for example, support
from the community, change in political administration, support
from legal and legislative powers, relations with minority communities, resource provision, political influence, or lack of influence,
have had a significant impact on the current correctional practices
and policies in Trinidad. What outside influences have had a significant impact on the current practices and policies?

Com. R: There were a number of external influences on the policies and
practices of the prisons service, for example, the United Nations
and Amnesty International. The prison service was under tremendous pressure from these international organizations at one point
in time, because the conditions in the prisons were really bad. The
government of the day then allowed Amnesty International to
come into the prison and have a look at the conditions with the

view of making suggestions and recommendations to move forward. That visit resulted in the Baptiste Task Force Report.* What was good about the report was the fact that the public got involved. The public was responsible for some changes taking place within the system, because the task force report went to all corners of the country, and the public made many recommendations. As a result of the Baptiste Report and the public input, we have seen many improvements in prison policy and practices, but we are still a far cry from where we want to be.

Furthermore, what was interesting about the task force report was that it was supported by the then existing government and, after elections, by the newly appointed government as well. In addition, members of the judiciary and all areas of the criminal justice system came together and supported the prison service. There was a lot of camaraderie and support that helped us to make many changes. They saw the importance of the prisons as far as crime fighting was concerned and their ability to see that was a crucial thing.

Dr. W: Overall, has the quality of prisons, jails, and community supervision in Trinidad changed? Has it improved, or has it worsened over the past 10 years?

Com. R: There has been improvement, but I am still not satisfied. I'm being honest. I'm still not satisfied, and it's probably a personal thing. I'm not satisfied, because I know much more could have been done. When I became commissioner, I had already decided on a number of things I wanted to do and the people who I could work with to achieve those things. But, a major problem for me was the Prison Association.† From the beginning of my tenure in 2005/2006, the Association literally started to attack me, so during my early tenure as commissioner and even now, I had to spend a lot of my time "putting out fires." This distracted me, and as a result of that, things that I could have done were not done.

Dr. W: How has that challenge of being constantly under attack impacted basic things like your ability to control the personnel to inmate ratio, for example, or provide a variety of training, a variety of programs to inmates, or additional rehabilitation strategies or even to source additional money? How has the constant attacking impacted your ability to do those things?

Com. R: I think it brought out the best in me, and as a result, I was able to get much more done than my predecessors. For example, when I was

---

* http://ttprisons.com/downloads/taskforcereport.pdf.
† http://www.poa.org.tt/.

occupying the lower ranks such as assistant superintendent and superintendent, the training vote was TT$300,000–TT$400,000 per year. When I became commissioner of prisons, I did my draft estimates for a lot more money than that. As a result, my training vote from then until now has always been in the vicinity of TT$2,000,000–TT$2,500,000. As a consequence of this large increase in training vote, training from 2005 to now has been at its highest level ever in the prison service.

In addition, I saw the need for the academic development of prison officers as a way of developing the prison service. This led me to approach the Director of Personnel Administration and the Service Commission* with a proposal for a merit-based promotion system. The existing promotion system, which was based on seniority, was outdated, and it led to a situation where officers were not working efficiently. They were just sitting around waiting on their "turn" to be promoted. So, I wanted to change that by advocating for a merit-based promotion system. However, this proposed change was met with resistance from the Association. As a consequence, officers were not being promoted within the system the way that they were supposed to be promoted, and this affected the service and morale but not just morale. In any case, it is the Association that tends to give the public the impression that morale is low as a result of promotion practices, but this is not so. There are people who are waiting for this merit-based system to be implemented. I have seen quite a large number of young people moving toward the tertiary level institution to develop themselves. There are four women that I know of who are on the verge of completing their master's degree, or they may have already acquired it, and they are at the rank of prison officer I. Some of them are acting in the capacity of prison officer II. Such officers should be considered for elevation, but they would not be so considered under the present seniority promotion system. As a result, I am fearful that these officers would leave the system to the detriment of the prison service.

Dr. W: Now, you talked about wanting to implement promotion based on merit and not seniority. How did that impact interagency relationships, because the other agencies would, I imagine, not have been happy with that direction?

Com. R: Interestingly, we are the only institution within the protective services that has retained the seniority-based promotion system. The

* http://unpan1.un.org/intradoc/groups/public/documents/un/unpan023205.pdf.

fire service, the police service, the army, customs, and immigration have all turned to the merit-based promotion system. So, it's hard for me to understand why some persons are still fighting the merit-based system in the prison service. The Prime Minister is talking about the merit-based system in a positive light, and many other persons in the country are doing the same, but sadly though, the seniority system in the prison system still exists. The problem is, with the seniority system, you are going to get a number of recalcitrant officers.

Dr. W: Tell me a bit about the effectiveness of top management and their ability to provide quality control and directing and managing line personnel, also their relationship with the inmates and their ability to foster staff safety, and I also want you to touch on inmate suicide rates.

Com. R: I am not satisfied with the performance of probably 75%–80% of my senior officers. They are not good. I'm being honest. They are not corrupt to the point where they are trafficking in drugs or anything like that. When I say that they are not good, I mean that they cannot take the prison service along the developmental path it needs to follow. I find that they are not ambitious and they seem to think that the retributive approach does not require any amount of intellectual growth and so they favor that approach over the restorative approach. I recall, very early in my service, I had started my master's degree at Leicester University distance learning in Security and Risk Management. After that, another officer applied successfully. During that time, another officer applied and complained that the then commissioner was not supportive. When I was appointed to the position of deputy commissioner, I went out of my way to secure approval for him to the tune of TT$60,000. I have been commissioner and acting commissioner since 2004, and to this day, that officer has failed to present evidence of his having earned his degree. Nor has he given any account of the funds he received.

Dr. W: How does that impact, though, the ability to effectively manage your people if you have senior administrators who lack, and I'll use the word, finesse, the administrative background, the academic background to move your organization into the twenty-first century like you want. How does that impact?

Com. R: The impact is so negative. For instance, it fosters difficulty with my family, because I have to spend most of my time at work, sickness, I've undergone an angioplasty because of stress, etc., I've been criticized for micromanaging, but I have to, because in the long run, I have to give account, and therefore, if I have to account and the work isn't being done, I have to ensure that it is being done in some way or the other. It sometimes entails "faces to the floor." This is usually done by a small group of people who are working, but they are burning out. They are burning out.

Dr. W: How does this manifest itself in inmate and staff safety?

Com. R: We have a situation within our system where we're on stations. The junior officers are the ones who are running the stations, because the seniors are not showing interest. I'm being honest. The senior officers have been looking for promotions for power, but they are not prepared to do the work. As a result, there's a complete change in approaches, in policies. Junior officers are changing the policies and, in some instances, creating their own policies and things like that.

Dr. W: In the direction that you want?

Com. R: No, this is it. For instance, look at what's happening as far as the use of force. The amount of monies in litigations we have to pay is astounding. In the long run, the attorney general asks, "What are you doing? You could cause our country to be blacklisted." This is what is happening, all because our senior officers are not showing interest. It isn't only about promotion; it doesn't seem as though they are capable of this new rehabilitative approach. They are not capable in this modern time to take the service forward.

Dr. W: Now, the junior officers, you're saying, are changing the rules. Are you thinking of training for them to change their method of operation if they are of the retributive mind to change it to the restorative approach?

Com. R: Of course. Now, this is one of the things that I started to do. The problem is, I don't think that I have enough time to complete that and there is also the question of whether the people who would be taking over will continue it. Again, I'm not trying to say that I am the best around and there wouldn't be any other person, but right now, if we go on the seniority system, the next person to take over, I may be wrong, and I'm hoping that I'm wrong. He's going to create havoc in our system and I'm not the only one saying that. I've heard a number of other people who have worked within our system talking about that, because the next senior person in line is retributive, and a number of other people under him are retributive, so you can well imagine what would take place. But, I'm hoping I'm wrong so that inmates will continue to benefit.

Dr. W: Do you have a high level of inmate suicide now?

Com. R: No, interestingly we don't. We have had suicides within our system but not a high level of suicide. We have had one or two persons committing suicide in the history of our system, whereas internationally, you will hear four, five, or six people commit suicide for the year. In our system, suicide is the result of human error, not doing what is supposed to be done and not supervising and monitoring inmates properly. As a result, some desperate inmates would take the opportunity. Our problem would be not monitoring and supervising to the point where you could recognize that there's a serious issue with this person. The people who are trained, like the health care officers, etc., also subscribe to the retributive approach, which is what I've been struggling to change. This problem doesn't lie with all prison workers, but with quite a few. It appears that most of our prison officers don't like prisoners, and I mean, that tells it all.

Dr. W: So why become prison officers?

Com. R: The money and the power.

Dr. W: Then, is it more or less difficult to become a correctional officer, a supervisor, or a warden/regional manager now than in the past?

Com. R: It is more difficult now, and it will be more difficult based on what I've been trying to implement as far as a merit-based system of promotion. In the past, some persons would have gotten promotions based on seniority, but they still had to be trained by junior officers and, in some instances, by prisoners. Those are things I can't verbalize in the public, but these are things happening. Thank God there is that group of officers, some seniors and a number of juniors, who understand the system and who, from an operational point of view, know what it's all about, and they are prepared to go the limit. The problem is they are suffering from burnout.

Dr. W: Let's talk a bit about your personal correctional philosophy. What do you think should be the role of prison, jail, and community supervision officer in the society? What should be the role of that entity in the society?

Com. R: Okay, in saying what that role should be, I'm looking at the people who come to us and why they come to us. Yes, they have committed an offense, they have been sentenced to be punished, and the punishment to me is deprivation of liberty and, outside of that, the punishment ends. If you look at all correctional facilities, correctional policies, and ideologies, you will notice that we are to take over, take control of their lives, and therefore attempt to get people back on track, to get people to become more law abiding, to get people to come to terms with themselves and relate with the wider community in a civil way, in a just way, in a humane way. Therefore, each of these facets has roles. The prisons have roles and community corrections also have roles. Prisons are made for people who cannot be controlled in the wider society. That is what they're there for. Therefore, people who can be controlled in the wider society should not come to prisons. They should not come to prisons.

Dr. W: Who determines who can be controlled and who cannot?

Com. R: The judiciary deals with that, and therefore, I am saying this is where we have fallen down. I have always been in agreement with a proper sentencing policy and that sentencing policy should not only be the remit of the judiciary. I'm of the view that a sentencing policy should also have a sentencing committee, and in some cases, the judge or the magistrate should not be passing down sentences.

Dr. W: Should that be based on the crime? For example, if it's murder, then should it be just the judge or should the sentencing committee adjudicate all?

Com. R: I'm still saying the sentencing committee should adjudicate all and the composition of the sentencing committee will determine their responsibility and the result we expect.

Dr. W: What are you recommending, then, for the composition of the sentencing committee?

Com. R: For instance, we need to have people like psychologists and psychiatrists, because we need to understand what's happening with their inmates' minds. You need to have that intellectual person who has a general understanding of those things. You need to have one or two of the ordinary people so that you would have a wide cross section of the people who better understand the individual so that, when you make a decision, you make a decision that benefits the persons and the whole society. I still have my doubts as far as capital punishment is concerned.

Dr. W: Do you believe that capital punishment is a deterrent to crime?

Com. R: It is, but to who? The person who is dead? It probably deters me also, because I wouldn't want to kill somebody and hang as a result. But generally, I don't think that it is causing a reduction in the murders from my 38 years of experience. I have seen the numbers of murders continue to rise. The thing is, they have not been carrying out the penalty, but it exists. If it exists, people should have some sort of fear that they could suffer that sentence, but people don't care about that because of weaknesses in the whole judicial system, and low arrest and detection rates. Offenders are aware that capital punishment, in the books, isn't happening, and therefore, when a murder is committed and witnesses are around, they attempt (and sometimes are successful) to kill the witnesses as well. Again, what we're talking about is the whole system; the justice system needs to be overhauled and overhauled fast, but it's not happening.

Dr. W: What is this phenomenon about prisoners behind bars having the ability to put hits out on people on the outside? Is that a reality, or is it just on TV?

Com. R: It's a reality. I have my doubts as to the extent of this occurrence, but it's happening. One of the things is that you know when police are under pressure, they will blame anybody to protect themselves, but it's happening, and it's happening as a result of this new phenomenon, cell phones within the prisons. That's the big problem, and it is a problem not just in the region but throughout the world. I have been to Israel, a country hip on security and monitoring. Listen, I have seen some ways in which people hide cell phones. I have been to Canada and America, and I've seen the same thing. The question is how do you deal with it? That is the problem. Now, the other thing too is that, from an intercept point of view, how do we handle this phenomenon? This is one of the ways intelligence agencies get the information they need from the inside. They want to get to the point where they legally intercept conversations from inside.

Dr. W: So they want cell phones on the inside, which defeats your purpose.

Com. R: Exactly! That's the whole thing. They won't tell the public that, so as a matter of fact, we're getting all the blame. Now, there are corrupt officers who are bringing it in and creating problems. But generally, intelligence would be able to really make a dent in crime if they intercept the calls. But, they have to then manage it properly. The whole issue is management. If you can manage it and you know of a killing going to take place, you could put a stop to it. My understanding, based on one of the agencies that was monitoring, is that they had prevented a lot of hits in the past, but the thing about it is some still happen. There is now talk about the whole issue of corruption or inefficiency, but there is some value in having cell phones within the system from the intelligence agency and law enforcement perspectives. This is not public information, so we have to take the blame while they're benefitting from it.

Dr. W: Tell me about postprison or postjail supervision or diversion, not sending someone to prison, and having them supervised outside. How do you see that impacting your organization as it stands? If that type of recommendation works, will it eventually make yours obsolete?

Com. R: No, no, it wouldn't. I don't think that prison would ever become obsolete. This is my view. The quality of prisons or the type of prisons will change definitely, but I don't think it will become obsolete. Diversion or postjail supervision is going to help with the overcrowding. A parole system could be one such thing. There comes a point in time when we need to look at the offenses. But, there also comes a point in time when an inmate is in prison for a long period of time and he would have developed himself, and having developed him, the authorities begin to use him by taking him outside to get

involved in schools and counseling other supposedly potential offenders. The whole family relationship also has to be taken into consideration such that the offender could be placed on parole, knowing that,
if he/she violated the conditions, it would be revoked. That to me is a
better control for some inmates, not for all, because some inmates will
use the opportunity to reoffend. Research has shown internationally
that 75% of inmates who use illegal cell phones just use it to maintain
contact with their family, and therefore, there are 25% who are using
it for nefarious reasons. Therefore, one of the things that we have been
trying to do, and we're having a lot of challenges with, is to have a public telephone system within the prison service so that inmates could
have access to call their relatives. These conversations will be monitored. But, the technology doesn't exist in Trinidad, so internationally, people are going to come in and work with Telecommunication
Services of Trinidad and Tobago Limited (TSTT) to establish it. That's
one of the things that we've been told, because, remember, for you to
make a call, you have to pay for it, or someone has to be paying for it.

Dr. W: What about your recidivism rate? How does the local procedure
impact the recidivism rate? How does the process, the current status quo, impact the recidivism rate?

Com. R: Years ago, the system impacted negatively on the recidivism rate.
Negatively, because very few activities and opportunities were made
available to people. I have seen, in recent times, some changes taking place as far as recidivism is concerned, and I'm going even further
than recidivism to reoffending, because the way I see it, reoffending
is the overall generic thing, and the recidivism is part of it. I'm saying, therefore, that I have seen a drop in reoffending, which includes
recidivism. Let me show you why. In the past, the total population in
the prison system was structured like this: two-thirds were convicted
prisoners, one-third remanded prisoners. Right now, it's almost 50/50,
so in other words, there's a drop in conviction. Now, there is the theory
that the older experienced ones are using the young people to commit
crimes, and therefore, there has been a drop in the whole recidivism
and the reoffending rate.

Dr. W: Do we have halfway houses here?

Com. R: We don't have halfway houses. Halfway houses are different; at that
facility you are able to complete your sentence. There are a number
of initiatives, for instance, the Ministry of Science, Technology and
Tertiary Education Retraining Program.* A number of inmates in

---

* http://www.gov.tt/gortt/portal/ttconnect/Cit_disableDetail/?WCM_GLOBAL_
CONTEXT=/gortt/wcm/connect/gortt+web+content/TTConnect/Citizen/Role/
APersonwithaDisability/FindAJob/Retraining+Programme.

the vocational skills training have been able to get small contracts in house construction, and therefore, they are able to earn money and maintain their homes.

Dr. W: Are there any other programs that you would like to see offered that you either cannot afford or won't get the support for?

Com. R: Well, one of the things that we want to get is the development of the prison industry, but it calls for some infrastructure, and this is what we don't have at this point in time. We also want to see the public assume their role in the prisons. People have to trust that a person who, having served a period of imprisonment and come out, would have done his time. If there is no acceptance and support by members of the public, the ex-offender may be forced to return to his "old way of life." Employers have to take risks and give people jobs, because there are more honest people who have gone through the system and don't want to come back again than people on the outside.

Dr. W: So, a lower level of reintegration would result in a higher level of recidivism.

Com. R: That's right! That's right! Additionally, when people leave the prison service, they also leave the treatment they would have received while on the inside, because we would have been maintaining their health problems. When they go outside, they need to link up with the hospitals, and somebody needs to monitor them as we would have been monitoring them inside. But, it doesn't happen, and therefore, once they start to get health problems, as simple as it may seem, they commit crimes and come back inside.

Dr. W: You're talking about the prisoners who cannot get the quality of support they got inside the prison when they get out they reoffend simply to get back in.

Com. R: And these are the recidivists.

Dr. W: In first-world countries, the intermediate sanctions are common. Is that something you see happening here?

Com. R: It's going to happen, because the Ministry of Justice* and Ministry of National Security,† have held discussions with us as it regards parole, electronic monitoring, and house arrest to reduce the overcrowding in the prison population. They are even considering reduced sentences; for instance, if a person's sentence is for a year and under, they may get half off.

Dr. W: Are intermediate sanctions the type of treatment programs that are suitable for this culture? Bear in mind, as you answer, the other

---

* http://www.moj.gov.tt/node.
† http://www.nationalsecurity.gov.tt/.

sanctions like intensive supervision (you mentioned electronic monitoring), and how will they impact recidivism? Should the community be worried about being safe when offenders are being released early? And what about cultural idiosyncrasies? Things like ankle monitors and house arrest work wonderfully well in first-world countries, but Trinidad has some traits that are specific to Trinidad.

Com. R: I think one of the things within the system here is the whole concept of risk management. Therefore, there has to be trust in the prison administration that we would have done the homework, done our checks inside, and monitored the individual inside. Not only that, there must be monitoring on the outside as well, because one of the things we have started to do in our system is to bring families inside. If we effectively monitor the interaction, we will be able to determine which inmate should be discharged or is ready to be discharged.

Dr. W: Let's talk about the problems and the successes that you've experienced. What policies and programs have worked well and which ones have not, and can you say why they have or have not worked well?

Com. R: One of the policies, and not just policy but also the structure, that we're actually trying to put in place that hasn't worked well is that of a senior officers management model, where senior officers take control of their stations (taking full responsibility). In the developed countries, a facility has its budget and manages its budget. At this point, we can't do that in our system, and it isn't for want of trying. I recall when we started the drive toward this Restorative Justice philosophical approach, I and a number of other people were given the okay to start training with our seniors. I recall, once a week for 3 years, we held training sessions with our senior officers, where we would have brought internationals in to conduct the training. We also had training in human resource management. One of the things that we told the officers was, "Look, you know your needs at the station. What we want at budget times or just months before budget time is for you to do an assessment and evaluation and determine what you need and let us know. You will then meet with the executive and we'll review it and determine yes or no. That is how we're going to develop our budget." Another issue is performance management. That, to me, has been a failure as well, and I feel really hurt about it, because a lot of work has gone in, and we've not seen the benefits materializing at all. I consider it to be a failure.

Dr. W: Can you speculate on why it's a failure?

Com. R: The whole mentality and culture of our senior staff is to be popular rather than be effective at their job.

Dr. W: Popular with whom?

Com. R: With the juniors, and therefore, you can't be effective and popular; you can't be. You have to take some decisions, tough decisions, and they're not prepared to do that.

Dr. W: What would you consider to be the greatest problem facing the Trinidad and Tobago correctional system at this point in time?

Com. R: The greatest problem, as far as I'm concerned, is the staff. I'm being honest. If we are to move forward, we really have to get to the members of staff and change their mindset. The bulk of the inmates, 75%–80% of the inmates are ready and are changing. They see the benefit in what we're doing, but some of our staff don't seem to be on board. For example, we have volunteers coming in, and our staff at the lower level are of the view that the volunteers are an inconvenience to them. As a result, most days, they arrive at their stations late without reason, simply because they are sitting around and not going to their assigned stations. It would mean, then, that a good senior officer would be required to ensure that they are at their posts on time. This will be the action of an officer who doesn't seek the favor of the junior staff. Is it that they don't care about the prisoner, they don't like prisoners, or they don't care about anything at all? All I can say is taking responsibility and commitment are two of our biggest problems. The mentality in the prison service now is one of "Whatever we're doing, let's see how much money we could get."

Dr. W: Is that going to be easy to change?

Com. R: It is not going to be easy, but it has to change, and for change to occur, someone has to take the bull by the horn and bite the bullet. That is what is required to take the prison service forward. No one says you're not to be rewarded for whatever you're doing, but the Police Association* feels that it should be paid for everything they do, even negotiations. It appears they don't understand that getting money impacts taxes and therefore has an impact on lifestyles.

Dr. W: So you've talked about internal problems like the culture of the organization, managerial deficiencies, even, perhaps, some allegations of corruption. You didn't mention gender-related problems.

Com. R: There are gender-related problems. As a matter of fact, our administration, meaning our Ministry, doesn't understand that this has been one of our biggest problems over time. One persistent

---

* http://ttpsswa.org/index.htm.

problem I have found is that the people at the Ministry of National Security feel they know everything in the prisons, in the police, etc., and are not allowing people who work in these agencies to do their work. Their responsibility is for policy. Having developed the policy, allow us to do it, implement it, and assess and evaluate it as well. But, it seems persons in the Ministry want to implement the policies as well without the kind of experience that is required. A good example of that is where we want to have gender training to allow male and female officers to be dispersed at different stations. As it stands, females are working in the male institutions, but we want to introduce it in the female institution to combat the lack of female officers and to have proper coverage of the prisons. Persons at the Ministry insist that, instead of sending male officers for gender training, we should first develop a policy before they could consider "doing something new." The thing is, this approach is not new. This has been taking place in developed countries from time immemorial. The men won't, at any time, be in direct contact with female inmates, but it is absolutely necessary to get them properly trained and gender sensitized before sending them in. The university* developed a program for us, but the Ministry insists they know what's best with regard to this problem. This is the problem.

Dr. W: Now, if we talk about externally generated problems—resources, community support, parole and probation procedures, or the lack thereof—how would you sum the problems up?

Com. R: The problems are many, but it has been reduced from what it was in the past. We've gotten a lot of financial support from our governments. We have gotten, to some extent negative and in some cases positive, recognition from the public. Because of the media, the public has a better understanding of the system, and the public makes demands on us. Nothing is wrong with that, because in the long run, the public is who we are working for. They are our stakeholders, and therefore, what they want is what we have to give.

This is another thing with our prison staff. They think the prison is theirs, not realizing that we are actually servants of the public. Therefore, demands are made. As a result, we're seeing improvement in certain things. In 2008/2009/2010, I did an analysis, looking at statistical data on our budget, and it was evident that in 2008, 84% of our budget went to salary. Do you understand what's going on? This, then, explains what is happening to other initiatives, for example, managing, running, and developing. In 2009,

* http://sta.uwi.edu/.

it was 76%. In 2010, it was 74%. This budget indicates the recurrent small budgetary allocation that is expected to deal with initiatives in the prison service. Therefore, we have to go to the public who has been supportive. The private sector has been supportive. Governmental agencies have been supportive, and that is what has been helping us really.

Dr. W: What is the most successful program you've worked with within corrections?

Com. R: There are quite a few. One of the successful programs is the program run by the Ministry of Science, Technology and Tertiary Education. It is a program that has been implemented in four or five of our facilities: retraining of inmates. I've seen the benefits of that. There have been some negatives, but more positive than negative. I've seen people come in, go through training, exit the system, be employed, and get back on track. Another successful program is at the Youth Training Centre.* Again, their academic program is amazing. As a matter of fact, as a program, the Youth Training Centre has been a success. I have seen at the Youth Training Centre boys coming to the institution not caring about themselves, their appearance, or how they smelled. But, after having gone through programs, the boys changed their outlook. I've seen at the Youth Training Centre boys and their families united or reunited because of the kind of visitation programs that takes place there. I've seen boys participate in apprenticeship programs on the outside and leave the institution with TT$40,000.00 and TT$50,000.00 established in accounts. Those are success stories. I have seen boys who had no knowledge of certain sporting activities yet, after 2 years, were able to represent Trinidad and Tobago in boxing, in rugby, and I'm talking about going abroad, and within the region. Those are some of the successes I saw at the Youth Training Centre. We continue to see it developing, because more people are getting involved, because they want to help. What is good about it is that, even though there may be some level of corruption there, the corruption level is very low, because people are coming there with an interest in helping these boys. This assistance is to prevent that movement from the Youth Training Centre to the adult jail.

Dr. W: What is the most successful policy with regard to the positive improvements that have been made to the prisons?

Com. R: I'm saying the policy has to do with the restorative justice philosophical approach. We have opened up our system in ways that,

---

* http://ttprisons.com/index.html.

in the past, people could not even dream about. We have opened up our system to the media. We have opened up our system to the public, to volunteers, to researchers, to international people, and it's only to our benefit, because we're receiving academic support, spiritual support, vocational support, sporting support. You name it, they are there and helping.

Dr. W: In your view, what should be the relationship between theory and practice, particularly as it relates to corrections?

Com. R: It definitely has to go hand in hand, because no longer are we operating in an *ad hoc* way within our system. We need to be guided, because we are interfering with people's lives. We are impacting people's lives, and therefore, we need to be on the ball and not operate just off the cuff. In the past, working in an *ad hoc* system may have been successful, but now, we need to look at the theory and blend the theory with what you're doing from a practical, operational point of view.

Dr. W: What can practitioners learn from studying and applying theories, and what can those who create theories of punishment gain from practitioners?

Com. R: As a practitioner, from a theoretical point of view, I have developed myself, and I've been able to contribute and impact. From a theoretical point of view, the theorists can observe and experience and learn, which helps their understanding, and therefore better, more applicable theories can be built.

Dr. W: What kind of research, in what form, and on which questions would you find most useful for practice?

Com. R: One of the burning topics I feel must be researched in our system is the issue of homosexuality, because there is the feeling, publicly, that there is widespread homosexuality within the system, and I am not of that view. I can't explicitly doubt it, because I don't have the research data to show. Neither can the public make comments, because they don't have any research. It's just an "old folk's tale" at this point. It doesn't mean that there isn't homosexuality within the system. There are also other areas of research that will help us develop our system. For instance, research in the area of drugs and the use of drugs and even drug traffickers. Researching to find out why, for instance, criminality exists, why someone would become a criminal, and the findings can help us build theories and, in some instances, develop initiatives and interventions. Working on research as it relates to "at-risk" persons and special populations, such as women in prisons and juveniles. We need to do that, because we have to stop juveniles at the juvenile level, because they become the (adult) criminals. In the case of women, women have families, especially in our country, where there are many one-parent families. When the mother leaves, a void is created in the family. Women who give birth while serving sentences have always been a pet peeve of mine, since no tactile relationship is created between the mother and the baby, as family members take away the infant as soon as it is born.

Dr. W: Where do you find your theory-based information? Where do you look, journals, professional magazines, books, publications, reports?

Com. R: All of the above. We have also looked at international associations like the American Correctional Association and the International Prisons and Corrections Association. The university is a valuable medium from a theoretical point of view. Observation as it relates to visits to prisons in developed countries. I always say that America tends to be very retributive, but they have a system (structure and documentation) that we can benefit from. When a system carries out proper documentation techniques, proper reports can be done and analyzed. This is what America is good at. Also, regarding observation as a medium, conferences, workshops, etc., help because at these forums qualified people from a practical point of view, as well as from a theoretical point of view, meet with you and share ideas and information.

Dr. W: Would it be fair to say that your department or your agency conducts research on its own?

Com. R: Yes, there is a research unit. But, I am not satisfied with the work that is done in that unit (because more can be done). What we have worked on so far includes, as I mentioned earlier, the research on our annual estimates so that we were able to highlight the financial status of the prisons when we met with the Ministry of Finance.* It is my view that researchers from the university can come in to the prisons and conduct research; members of staff within the prison can do the same. For instance, in recent times, our Penal Reform and Transformation Unit, which is located at the Ministry of Justice, did research based on a request from the Prime Minister on recidivism and reoffending. Based on their research, we found that there was a drop in our reoffending rate by 3%. That percentage decline, to us, is significant. Our staff can take the initiative and conduct research, without it being the response from a request made by someone in authority.

Dr. W: What is your recidivism rate now?

---

* http://www.finance.gov.tt/.

Com. R: It fluctuates between 55% and 56%. Calculating the recidivism rate was based on a pilot project that was done at Carrera* some years ago. Five hundred persons participated in a program and were released. Checks done years later revealed that there were only three returns. From that moment, we implemented those programs throughout the system and monitored them to determine effectiveness.

Dr. W: Let's talk about evidence-based corrections. In your experience, has your agency made use of the various evidence-based programs that exist?

Com. R: Yes, but not sufficiently. To some extent, it may be the fault of the administration. Evidence-based corrections for me is not simply reading research from a document but actually visiting, observing, and experiencing other situations so that, when you experience it, you can return and suggest changes to our system and ensure that documentation is done to evaluate effectiveness. For instance, I see cleanliness as one the most significant of all evidence-based approaches. I am always amazed when I visit prison facilities in some of the developed countries and their level of cleanliness surpasses ours. I keep wondering why our facility can't be clean. I always tell people, "A clean prison is a good prison is a safe prison." There are other solid evidence-based practices that I have seen, for instance, the House Mast System, which was developed in Britain and an extension of which occurs in Canada. Trained officers being responsible for a dormitory is something we have tried at the Youth Training Centre and which we are also trying to implement at the adult institutions. The Programs Unit† can also be assessed as evidence based. The Programs Unit must, however, now be tighter and better structured to effect better documentation for future reports, for better evaluation and monitoring, since this information is what the courts have recently been requesting.

Dr. W: Do you feel that it is best to use evidence-based practices, or what works, or is this focus not important?

Com. R: That is most important. This is what I have thrived on. Whenever I get the opportunity to visit other prisons, I don't simply attend for enjoyment and entertainment. I ask questions about their operations and programs and documents. My interest in their operations most times ends with them shipping their information (in the form of documents) to me. I go through and use what I read and

---

* http://ttprisons.com/about.html.
† http://www.nationalsecurity.gov.tt/MediaCenter/Speeches/PrisonServicePassingOut CeremonyforIntake343/tabid/119/Default.aspx.

experience to develop our training system and implement initiatives in our prison. I've always been telling officers that they need to go and experience other prison facilities. It is only when they do that they can truly merge the theory with the practical.

Dr. W: Which evidence-based practices do you use?

Com. R: I would look at my Programs Unit, because they have made a difference in our system. When I mentioned earlier that there are some people who are burning out, these are some of the people I was referring to, because their heart is in it. I have been able to engender their passion and get further training for them, but it is simply too much work for that small group of people.

Dr. W: So do you feel that using more evidence-based practices would benefit the system?

Com. R: Definitely! To do that would entail what is referred to as Study Tours. The problem is our Ministry will not give us the kind of finances we require to send people abroad in groups.

Dr. W: Where did you get your information? How were you able to implement the process with respect to the programs unit?

Com. R: My information was retrieved from three territories: America, Canada, and Israel. Evidence-based practices are a crucial process in those territories. One such practice is a drug treatment unit that we in Trinidad are still trying to establish. In the aforementioned territories, the drug treatment units within the prison system house individuals separately from other persons who are convicted for other crimes. These persons are tested every day, and if, at any time, they are found with drugs in their possession while at the institution, they are thrown out of the facility. No one wants to be thrown out, because there is the benefit of recovering from drug addiction while at the institution, forcing them to stay clean. On those visits, we have spoken to experts and requested their documentation to evaluate the effectiveness of their program. Therefore, with that information, we are able to implement these programs (the ones that make sense to Trinidad of course).

Dr. W: Let's talk about transnational relations. How have you been affected by the following in your organizations work and the following would-be developments outside of the country: human rights demands, the universal code of ethics, practical interactions with correctional officers from other countries, personal experiences outside the country, programs developed by other countries that you are assimilating here, new sentencing laws, and political strife or war in Trinidad or neighboring countries (we may not have war here, but we may have political strife)?

Com. R: What is interesting is that I have never observed any political strife in any of the places that I have been to. It may be as a result of my short stay in the country. However, one thing I always rave about is interactions with corrections officers abroad. They are always willing to help, but that seems to be their culture. That's the kind of attitude they have (willingness to assist prisoners and visitors), and this may be a result of development and ethics and human rights. What is demanded of them ensures they act accordingly. Perhaps it is easier for those officers to be dismissed than it is for our officers in Trinidad. In Trinidad and Tobago, any attempt at dismissal must go through a Service Commission tribunal. The process takes years. We have also had an exchange of personnel from America and Canada through several associations. The ideas that are exchanged in those interactions (we are gaining from them and they are gaining from us) are unique. As a matter of fact, three of our officers were sponsored to go up to Israel from an IT point of view, and when they returned, they told us that these people were monitoring our system. Additionally, they said there's a unit that is responsible everyday to take reports to their leaders, that's the Head of Corrections there, as to what's happening in corrections throughout the world. Conversely, when one of our officers was killed, they were able to tell some of my officers they had already known about it as a result of their monitoring our system. They also maintain contact from an alumni point of view. We get a different level of support from officers in these various territories. This is one of the weaknesses of Trinidadians: we don't maintain contact. These people maintain contact and send tons of information and magazines to us.

Dr. W: General assessments. Are you basically satisfied or dissatisfied with developments in the field of corrections locally and internationally?

Com. R: Locally, if I have to gauge it and give a percentage, I would have to say that I am probably satisfied with above 50%, but I'm making that judgment, because there's still much more to be done, although I have seen changes. I have seen changes and also plans for changes, which is different from the way corrections was run in the past. When I joined the service, there were no plans; we weren't hearing about any plans. As a matter of fact, I always remember the former commissioner of prisons when he said that, when he joined the Service, there were verbal plans for the government to move the inmates and officers from the Port of Spain Prison to Golden Grove.* He has left the service. He is now approximately 80 years

---

* http://ttprisons.com/index.html.

of age, and the Port of Spain prison remains in its place. Another development is that, in the past, officers were not recognized at all for their efforts; not that they are fully recognized at this point in time, but at least, they are being recognized, and they are called on to give their two cents in committees. All of these things I'm saying are changes, and I'm satisfied with that, and I can only see it improving.

Internationally, I'm dissatisfied with some of the retrograde steps some of these areas continue to implement. The United States continues to be retributive with the introduction of supermax prisons. I thought, for example, that England was always well ahead, but from what I'm hearing (I've never been to or visited any facilities in England), they're behind. Canada is well advanced. I understand Holland and other places like New Zealand are well advanced as far as the restorative justice approach. Even though there are some negatives in America, I understand Ohio is well ahead as far as the restorative justice philosophical approach is concerned. I am also not satisfied with the development of the prison system within the region. Infrastructure doesn't exist for the type of initiatives that must be implemented for the prison system to stand the test of time in the twenty-first century. Would you believe I went to Dominica last year, and upon my arrival I realized that there was only one computer? I sat back and watched, and I said "If my officers only know what's taking place… Almost every desk at our administration building for each facility has a computer." There are recently built prisons in Barbados, St. Vincent, and St. Lucia, but when you look at these facilities, they're terrible; they're frightening. This is the kind of change I had hoped I would have impacted. I'm not going to give up, because I'm prepared to offer myself as an advisor or consultant when I retire from the Service, because as a head of prisons, it's difficult to balance administrative work, outreach, and consultancy at the same time, especially in my case, where I have to ward off the constant attacks by the Prison Association. If we have someone handling or just advising other prisons in the region (and I'm prepared to handle that), then we would really have a greater impact, especially where there is interest expressed by America and Canada to help with respect to funding. We need to capitalize on that.

Dr. W: What do you think of the relationship between sentencing laws and public opinion to the functioning of jails and prisons and community supervision?

Com. R: I don't know, but let me look at our region. There is the phenomenon of an increase in horrendous types of crime. The people in the region are "calling for blood," and it doesn't appear as though they are satisfied with the sentencing laws and the sentences that are handed down to some people. When we look at Trinidad, we must take into consideration the fact that some new good laws are being debated, but there are also a set of draconian laws this government wants to put in place. I do hope that, in the midst of this, the government addresses new laws as it relates to the release of the inmate. There is a strained relationship between the existing sentencing policies and public opinion. The public has to understand, as difficult as it is, that initiatives are being implemented not in the hope of fixing the situation at this moment but, rather, in the hope of effecting positive change in the crime situation years into the future. In the long run, we all will benefit. That's a difficult thing for members of the public to swallow, but it's something we have to do. In the meantime, structures have to be put in place in conjunction with more social initiatives. Law enforcement is important, because you have some criminals who must be treated in a certain way, but generally, when you look at some of the people who are coming into the system because of arrest for a drug device or a piece of marijuana and the nature of police response to those crimes, it makes you wonder, "*Why prison?*" What these people need is a drug rehab center, not harsh prison sentences. We must look at what exists and see what really is required and what is relevant and get rid of the policies and initiatives that are not working. This is a huge job for anyone. Who's going to do it?

Dr. W: How do you view the release procedures in Trinidad and Tobago, and do they contribute to or inhibit recidivism?

Com. R: To some extent, they contribute to recidivism or reoffending. I am the first to say we still have a long way to go. There needs to be more initiatives if we are to reduce the recidivism and reoffending rate.

Dr. W: And they're focused more on rehabilitating now?

Com. R: That's right, that's right; rehabilitation and reintegration. However, there is the continued need for those initiatives and for support from persons who are on the outside of the prison service, like more NGOs and community-based organizations. Involvement by the public in the reintegration of ex-offenders is necessary. Government's intervention as well in this venture is needed. Let me explain why more of these community-based reintegration programs are imperative. A lot of times, people leave the prison system with health problems because of the closeness of it and the airborne diseases, and their treatment is seldom continued when they return to society. There must be holistic support and treatment for inmates and ex-inmates. This is what is required. There are some people who started academic programs; would the tertiary institutions or other types of academic institutions register them to continue their education once they are made aware that the person registering is an ex-offender? There are academic programs going on inside, but there must be continuity for the ex-offender.

Dr. W: You mentioned that use of intermediate sanctions such as house arrest and ankle bracelets, etc., is still being discussed?

Com. R: Yes.

Dr. W: How could changing the balance between intermediate sanctions affect prison and jail environments? How could the introduction of more intermediate sanctions affect the environment in the prison?

Com. R: It's going to reduce the overcrowding within the system. There are some people who, I think, could be supervised in the community as can happen with intermediate sanctions such as monitoring, remaining in the home, curfew, etc. People could be managed there, even community-type corrections where you do a 40-hour workweek (community service) and leave the prisons for the hardened people who cannot be supervised within the community setting. That means there will be more room so that you can better work with these people. This initiative may reduce the number of violent episodes within the prisons.

Dr. W: What are the developments that you see as most likely to happen in the next years, and which developments would you prefer to see happening?

Com. R: I see an increase in the prison population because of the current crime situation and the initiatives that are being put in place to try to deter would-be offenders. There's going to be longer sentences, and as a result of that, there's going to be more violence in prisons. What I want to see happening is that of a holistic approach to corrections, meaning community sentencing, retrofitting, rebuilding, or building of more facilities.

Also, at this point, within the prisons, we must build and creatively develop a psychiatric unit for mentally unstable persons who are handed a prison sentence upon conviction. We must also think about attaining better health care facilities to deal with the people who come to our facility.

I'm looking for changes in laws as well, the prison rules that will give formality and legality to some of the initiatives that need to be implemented in the system.

Dr. W: Finally, what is most needed now to improve prisons, jails, community supervision, and the overall punishment process in Trinidad and Tobago?

Com. R: Laws. Changing the laws or addressing the archaic laws that still exist in our law books. When you look at the region, especially Trinidad and Tobago, the laws that we have written in 1838 have only been changed minimally over the years. This must be addressed to evaluate whether the laws that were passed in colonial times are still relevant today. We must also have a mandate to uphold high ethical standards within the prison service. Change the laws to see prisoners as people. Change the laws to increase some of the rights of the prison officers. The new laws should ensure that people understand that the entitlements of these persons exist. New laws are as important as improvements in infrastructure. For example, in three or four facilities, you still use this old pail system, not toilet facilities, and this speaks to the humane treatment of inmates. Those are some of the things we want to see taking place.

Dr. W: Commissioner, thank you so much.

Com. R: The pleasure is mine, my dear.

Interview with John Pastorek, Warden at North Fraser Pretrial Centre in British Columbia*

6

DANIELLE MURDOCH

Contents

Introduction

This interview describes the views of John Pastorek, warden at North Fraser Pretrial Centre (NFPC), a remand facility opened in British Columbia (BC) in 2001. The NFPC incarcerates offenders who have been remanded in custody pending trial or sentencing as well as individuals on immigration detention,

---

* This interview describes the views and opinions of John Pastorek, warden at North Fraser Pretrial Centre, and does not necessarily reflect the views of British Columbia Corrections.

and conducts the assessment and classification of offenders who receive a term of imprisonment of 30 days or more from a Lower Mainland court (BC Corrections 2010a). The NFPC is one of two pretrial centers operating in the Lower Mainland of BC and is situated in Port Coquitlam, one of the 22 municipalities in Metro Vancouver, a regional district composed of 2.1 million people (BC Corrections 2010a; Greater Vancouver Regional District 2010).*

John Pastorek started his career with BC Corrections in 1976 and became the warden at NFPC in 2006 after 30 years of working in both male and female correctional facilities throughout the province.† John Pastorek generously donated 3 h of his time on April 20, 2010 to participate in this interview, conducted in his office at the NFPC.

Background Information

Canada is a nation of approximately 34 million people with a unique system of corrections, wherein Canadian correctional responsibilities are divided based on the 2-year rule. The 2-year rule, legislated at Confederation in 1867, requires provincial or territorial jurisdiction for offenders sentenced to 2 years less a day and federal jurisdiction (Correctional Service of Canada; CSC) for offenders sentenced to 2 years or more (Griffiths 2010a; Milhorean and Kong 2008).‡

Canada spends approximately $13 billion operating and maintaining their criminal justice system, of which $3 billion is spent on federal and provincial or territorial correctional systems (Griffiths 2010a). Most of the corrections budget is spent on the operation of correctional institutions, although only 5% of all of the individuals who become involved with the Canadian criminal justice system are sentenced to a term of imprisonment (Griffiths 2010a).§ Most offenders sentenced to a term of imprisonment in Canada fall under the jurisdiction of provincial or territorial correctional systems, with 55% receiving custodial sentences of less than 1 month (Landry and Sinha 2008; Kong and Peters 2008).

In this interview, Warden Pastorek reflects on his 34-year career with BC Corrections, providing a unique insight into two primary issues: 1) the

---

* The other is Surrey Pretrial Services Centre, originally built in 1991 and redeveloped in 2004 to create a separate women's remand facility (BC Corrections 2010a). It is located in Surrey, the second largest city in BC and is also one of the 22 municipalities comprising Metro Vancouver.

† Warden Pastorek has held management positions since 1987, including his previous role as deputy warden of programming at NFPC and deputy of operations at Alouette Correctional Center for Women.

‡ Provincial or territorial governments are also responsible for offenders serving community-based sanctions such as probation and offenders sanctioned to custodial remand and other forms of temporary detention such as immigration holds (Landry and Sinha 2008).

§ The remainder of the corrections budget is spent on programs, service, infrastructure, and personnel costs (Griffiths 2010a).

changes BC Corrections has seen throughout the past 30 years and 2) the challenges BC Corrections is currently experiencing in providing provincial correctional services.

Correctional Philosophy

Correctional systems pursue conflicting goals; they are expected to protect society by housing offenders who pose a serious risk to the community while simultaneously preparing these offenders for their eventual release into the community as both law-abiding and contributing societal members (Griffiths 2010a).* Warden Pastorek discusses his correctional philosophy in achieving these conflicting goals:

> Being rehabilitation-based in terms of providing skills to the offenders has always been my personal philosophy of what corrections should be, because I have seen it work over the years. Because of where I've been and worked— maybe not in this remand environment so much—but in other environments, I've always viewed at us as educators, looking for opportunities for "teachable moments" to effect change, and I really believe that, at our core, that's what we do best—if you watch correctional officers that have been around for a long time, that you know are really good correctional officers—if you sit back and you watch that's exactly what they do. They develop a relationship with the offender, they're respectful, they use humor, and they use opportunities to get people to look at the world in a different way. It's not really a program; it's a philosophy and an approach, and I think that is probably the most positive kind of work we can do in corrections. Although I'm rehabilitative in my approach, I'm also a realist in knowing that it doesn't work for everybody and that there are some bad people in the world who are never going to change, so we just have to manage them, including placing some really restrictive controls on. Our primary responsibility will always be to contribute to public safety by providing secure custody for those entrusted to our care.

Canada's acceptance of various international human rights agreements and conventions such as the United Nations Standard Minimum Rules for the Treatment of Prisoners and the United Nations Standard Minimum Rules for Noncustodial Measures is reflected in Canadian legislation and the Canadian Charter of Rights and Freedoms (Griffiths 2010a). The Charter protects the fundamental rights and freedoms of Canadian citizens, including those who are imprisoned. However, as the former commissioner of CSC explained, "No amount of policy, legislation or oversight mechanisms can

---

* All provincial/territorial offenders and approximately 95% of all federal offenders in Canada will eventually be released back into the community (Griffiths 2010a).

ever ensure in, and of themselves, respect for the rule of law and for human decency. That responsibility rests with each of us (working in corrections) individually" (McClung cf. Miller 2008, 172). This principle is reflected in Warden Pastorek's correctional philosophy:

> I'm not at all punishment oriented; punishment is not part of our correctional mandate. The court imposes sanctions including custodial sentences, and I think that, by keeping people apart from society, that is punishment enough. And so, If I hear correctional officers or others start talking about how we should punish people, I get a little concerned, because that sounds to me like they're looking for ways to make it hard for people when they're in our care. And, we're entrusted with their care and keep them away from society, and we do have lots of rules and restrictions on what their freedom and rights are while they're in here. Those are all defined by law, and that's what we do; we enforce the law and follow the regulations that flow from them. Over and above that, we have an obligation to treat people with respect and dignity. It's important for the staff, the front-line staff, the ones with daily contact, to have this philosophy and value, because I think things start to go sideways when they don't.

The importance of taking a "throughcare," systemwide approach to preparing offenders for their reintegration back into the community has been recognized (Griffiths et al. 2007; Borzycki 2005; Borzycki and Makkai 2007). This approach is based on the premise that reintegration efforts should begin before offenders are released from correctional institutions. Thus, interventions are offered to offenders both upon entry into custodial institutions as well as upon release to support and reinforce gains achieved from participation in custodial treatment programs (Fox 2002). This reflects a continuity of care in the provision of services and assistance offered to offenders throughout the correctional process.

Given that most offenders sentenced to a term of imprisonment in Canada are sentenced to 1 month or less (Kong and Peters 2008), provincial or territorial correctional systems may experience significant difficulty in providing throughcare to both sentenced offenders and those in custodial remand, an issue corroborated by Warden Pastorek.

> Provincial in terms of transitioning people from custody to the community, we don't do as good of a job (as CSC). We haven't given that a lot of focus until now. This is changing—we are piloting an integrated offender management program that focuses on providing continuing care—but that is only for those that have a longer sentence followed by a period of community supervision via probation order. The short prison terms people receive impacts our ability to provide throughcare. Instead, it is about managing risks. It's about introducing new notions to the offenders—that change is possible—and to get people motivated about the possibility of change. It's also about having

some programs and activities available to support that—some of the programming initiatives at sentenced facilities do a good job of that. But, short prison sentences, say, of 3 months, means you're not going to be able to do a lot; you won't have time to set up supports in the community.

Changes and Challenges

As Warden Pastorek relates, "The one thing about corrections is that, if you stick around long enough, change is always occurring, and so sometimes, it's not so much the choices that you make; it's the choices that are made for you because of circumstance."

Correctional systems are dynamic and ever-changing agencies, where personnel are required to manage and work with a diverse clientele brought into their care through the decision-making activities of other criminal justice agencies, particularly the police through enforcement activities and the judiciary through sentencing. Changes to the legislative and policy framework within which correctional systems operate also affect the day-to-day activities and decision making of correctional personnel (Griffiths 2010a).

These external factors and the unique features of correctional systems—for example, the fact that correctional systems are asked to pursue conflicting goals—create numerous challenges that affect the operation and management of correctional agencies. As Warden Pastorek reflects in the previous and subsequent statements, correctional systems operate in a continual state of change, often resulting in the emergence of new challenges.

> You find that you always have challenges in operating and managing correctional facilities; it's merely a matter of learning how to address them. I talked about change being the constant state throughout my career in corrections. You become pretty adept at adapting to whatever you're handed. Is it frustrating? Sometimes, yes, because you can't accomplish all of the things you want to do. But, it is our reality, and I think that people who work in corrections are very pragmatic. I think that we're kind of forced into being flexible, reacting and adapting to the changes and challenges. So, reacting to change presents challenges, but it's always been challenging, so we've learned to be flexible, reacting and adapting the work we do to the environment and realities we're operating within.

Offender Population

One of the most significant challenges affecting the correctional systems in Canada in the twenty-first century is the hardening of the offender population with respect to the risks and needs offenders pose. The federal system, CSC, has seen an increase in the number of offenders with mental health and substance abuse issues, the rates of infectious diseases, and the number of offenders imprisoned for homicide and classified as maximum security at admission (Griffiths 2010a). A similar trend exists in provincial or territorial systems despite the decrease in the number of adults admitted to sentenced custody; these systems have experienced an increase in the number of adults admitted for violent crimes and property offenses (Babooram 2008).* Warden Pastorek identifies the hardening of the offender population as the most significant change he has seen throughout his 30 years of working for BC Corrections.

> Well, probably the biggest change I've seen is the people that are in the system, in the custody facilities now. With having more conditional custody options, I think that what's happened is that the number and type of people who may have previously been incarcerated in our care now end up under community supervision. So, I think we've seen a hardening of the profile of people that we deal with in adult corrections on the custody side. Some of the options we once had aren't there anymore. For example, one of my first open custody experiences as a correctional officer was in the Outward Bound program run for young offenders. I saw how putting people through as a structured program—maybe people who hadn't ever learned how to cooperate and work with others—and how that environment forced them to do that allowing for skill development and an improvement in self-esteem. I saw some significant change that people made from the start of the program until it was finished. I don't think any of it was ever really measured, and it probably couldn't be replicated, and the skills that they were taught didn't teach them how to get a better job, but those kinds of things—basic skill development and self-esteem—made a positive impact on people's lives. I saw it firsthand, and I know that it worked. And, that's going back 30 years ago. But it focused on a group of low-risk offenders that aren't even in custody today.
>
> Another long-standing program that probably doesn't have a lot of research or evidence behind it is at Fraser Regional Correctional Center (FRCC) in Maple Ridge, where they send work crews performing community service work under supervision, providing a benefit to the local community in lots of different ways. I've worked on those crews before, and you can see it; the offenders know they've done something beneficial for the community, and they just feel better about themselves. There's less of that generally in corrections than there used to be, so that's a bit of a program trend that I'd like to see turn around. But the reason we've seen a reduction in this type of activity is

---

* Between 2003/2004 and 2006/2007, the number of adults admitted to provincial or territorial correctional systems for violent crimes increased by 5%, whereas the number admitted for property crimes increased by 6% (Babooram 2008).

the hardening of the people we're dealing with. The numbers of people that are appropriate to put in that environment have just dwindled, so that's a dynamic at play, and it's obviously a resource issue too, because you need to send them out under supervision, and so, there's a staffing component to it too. In communities where that still happens, I think that there's probably people that recognize that there is a great benefit from it. It will continue if we're smart about the kinds of things we do, where it doesn't impact on other people's ability to access work. It's doing the work people don't want to do, or that won't get done otherwise.

Prison administrators in Canada at both federal and provincial or territorial levels have seen the proliferation of inmate gangs in recent years because of new tough-on-crime legislation and police enforcement efforts. Gang members will often assault, intimidate, and exploit others to obtain power, status, and influence in the prison environment, resulting in instability and creating challenges with respect to managing and separating feuding gang members (Griffiths 2010a).

When I say there's been a hardening of the offender profile, that includes the proliferation of gangs. Dealing with that population also poses some challenges for us.

Evidence-Based Corrections

BC Corrections has an evidence-based best practices approach to rehabilitative programming and has followed this approach for over a decade. We offer programs that are complimentary to our rehabilitative intentions—and these are proven effective. In addition, we provide a host of program activities which assist offenders in dealing with the effect of incarceration. There are many examples of this within the Branch.

Overcrowding

The most pressing challenge would be the overcrowding issue, because it just gets in the way of good corrections, of best practices.
Prison overcrowding occurs when "the numbers of persons confined in a prison are greater than the capacity of the prison to provide adequately for the physical and psychological needs of the confined persons" (Griffiths and Murdoch 2009, 1). Correctional systems throughout the world are experiencing overcrowding, resulting in significant consequences, including increased supervision and transportation costs, increased tensions both

among inmates and between inmates and staff, increased vulnerability to violence and exploitation in prison, and, in some jurisdictions, poor physical and mental health conditions (Griffiths 2010a; Johnson 2003; Kong and Peters 2008). Overcrowding may also hinder management's ability to effectively manage prisons with respect to addressing offender risks and needs, placing the community at risk if offenders are not given adequate programming opportunities (Griffiths and Murdoch 2009). Warden Pastorek states his views:

> There are lots of ways that overcrowding manifests itself. I think that the number of inmate-on-inmate assaults is probably related to the fact that you're sharing close accommodation with somebody that you're not compatible with. I think that's a reality. It's become more difficult for line-level staff over the course of the years because of overcrowding... just in terms of the number of people that they have to deal with, with all of their concerns and needs; it's become more challenging for the staff. There's less time for staff to get to know who they're dealing with, so the opportunities to do things, like prosocial modeling, supporting people, listening to other people—that's part of what we ought to be doing—is hearing people's stories; that ability is impacted by the numbers of people we have to deal with.
>
> A growing concern in this remand center is the inmates ability to adequately prepare for trial—I think that with the amount of disclosure of evidence that lawyers are expecting their clients to know about the case against them—that more and more, electronic disclosure material comes to us, and a lot of it's obviously very sensitive. And so, how do you allow someone to have enough privacy? How do you balance the need for privacy and time to prepare versus the reality of having to put two people in every single cell? That's a problem that comes with overcrowding.
>
> Building more correctional facilities is necessary, especially if the remand wcount continues to grow, because we simply don't have any place to put them. It is needed to respond to the growth in population and certainly in the Vancouver Metro area, considering the number of people being charged with serious offenses because of the enforcement focus on organized crime and gangs. So, is building more capacity the answer? It's needed, so yes, that's part of it. Effecting change on people is certainly more achievable when people are not merely surviving, and we've been in survival mode for a period of time because of the overcrowding. So, to be effective as an organization, we cannot sustain this level of overcrowding. The more significant solution involves things like having adequate supports in school and other preventative measures in place, putting resources at the front end so you have appropriate contacts and interventions with kids, before they start going down the wrong path. I mean, we see the end product of it every day. If we don't invest front-end supports we need to continue development of appropriate corrections programs that are evidence-based. That is driving a lot of the program development that we're moving forward with.

Remand

Concern exists worldwide regarding the use of pretrial detention and its impact on prison overcrowding. As indicated by Shaw (2008, 2), who states in the foreword of a special issue of *Justice Initiative*, "At any given moment, an estimated three million people worldwide are in pretrial detention… a practice that undermines the rule of law and endangers public health." In Canada, this practice of pretrial detention is known as remand custody, wherein the accused individual is held in custody while awaiting trial or sentencing (Kong and Peters 2008).

The remand custody population in Canada has increased during the past decade and a half, as has the length of time adults accused spend in remand custody (Landry and Sinha 2008).* These increases have the greatest impact on provincial or territorial correctional systems, as they are responsible for remanded individuals.

> Overcrowding is a major issue, specifically, with the remand population (which is) a national trend. We don't always necessarily, have the opportunity to keep sentenced inmates separate from other people awaiting trial for criminal offenses. That's a challenge because of our numbers; we don't keep them totally separate, although we try as best we can.

This is problematic, given that the lack of separation of custodial remand offenders from their sentenced offender counterparts violates Article 10 of the International Covenant on Civil and Political Rights, which states that, "Accused persons shall, save in exceptional circumstances, be segregated from convicted persons and shall be subject to separate treatment appropriate to their status as unconvicted persons." (U.N. General Assembly, 1966, 176).

Various factors contribute to the increasing number of remand prisoners: legislative changes in 1997 and 1999 expanded the situations in which individuals can be remanded; there has been an increase in bail order violations in some jurisdictions resulting in remand of the accused; there has been an increase in incidents of serious crimes, and remand is typically given to individuals accused of more serious offenses; and last, accused individuals who are remanded are spending longer periods of time in remand custody because of longer court processing times for more serious offenses (Landry and Sinha 2008). Warden Pastorek provides his insight into other factors that contribute to the increasing remand population within the BC Corrections system.

---

* From 1996/1997 to 2005/2006, there was a decrease in the number of individuals sentenced to provincial or territorial custody (28%), with a simultaneous increase in the remand population (22%; Landry and Sinha 2008).

Some of the remand population, the people settling in to get the two-for-one credit, it's compounded the overcrowding problem.* I think that judges are responding to public pressure too. I think they're not immune to it. When they read in the paper criticism regarding decisions that were made on granting bail or not, I think that has an impact on sitting judges, whether or not they ever admit it. Another factor is the increased police activity to get gang members off the street in the Lower Mainland, because the level of violence among gang members is abhorrent, and I think the reality of it is that the public gets fed up and puts pressure on the politicians, which leads to increased police resources and enforcement. I think that has also played a part in some respects, in getting additional resources in terms of building capacity. The reality is that the public expects, and deservedly so, to feel safe, and that means putting the bad guys in jail.

The increasing remand population has numerous implications for correctional systems, primarily because it contributes to prison overcrowding, the consequences of which were previously discussed. A consequence of particular concern for remanded individuals is that overcrowding generally prevents correctional systems from providing programming opportunities for these accused (Griffiths 2010a).

Although data are not available for BC, data from Saskatchewan suggest that remanded individuals have a greater number of assessed needs than their nonremanded counterparts, identifying the need for programming opportunities for this population. Warden Pastorek acknowledges the absence of adequate programming for remanded individuals in BC Corrections, in addition to discussing the new programming initiatives being developed to address this inadequacy.

I don't think that we've ever really, as a provincial system, addressed programming needs for remanded individuals; there really hasn't been much, I mean we've tried, and we have a few things going on. There's a school program and a workshop—where people are assessed for suitability and can work and be productive—we use these remand individuals to do maintenance and painting and that sort of thing.

Although we've talked about trying to move forward with the programming for remand people, realistically, until we get their numbers down, it's going to be difficult to do. We do, however, do some offender programming

---

* It has been suggested that, before the implementation of Bill C-25 (February 2010), accused individuals would intentionally extend their pretrial detention period, because Section 719(3) of the Criminal Code provided that time spent in pretrial custody could be a factor in sentencing. In addition, Canadian case law dictated that an offender could receive 2 months credit for every 1 month spent in pretrial custody and that this credit could be adjusted to reflect the circumstances of remand custody (Kong and Peters 2008). When Bill C-25 came into effect in February 2010, two-for-one sentencing practices were abolished in the Canadian criminal justice system.

that we've adopted from sentence facilities. Some of the research shows that it's not effective, because we're not targeting the right people for that, and so right now, in our branch, we're really changing. We have an iniative called Advancing Offender Programming as an initiative, and there is a set of programs being developed specifically for remanded inmates; they're more skills based and short term, they'll build on one another, so that, if someone goes to a sentence facility, they've got some of the fundamentals that can be built on. We've reached the point in recognizing that people cycle through, so you strive to try to increase those periods of time when they're not in custody. And so, the programs ought to be able to build on each other and be short enough in duration that it may take the person three incarcerations to complete the program fully. But, I don't think that their basic needs change much over that time, so you know what the underlying issues are, so you establish a baseline and peck away at it over time. A lot of that programming is still under development, and we're probably maybe a year into the process, and it's probably going to take another 2–3 years before it's all fully implemented. So, I think that's a good trend and direction that we're moving in, although there are challenges in terms of getting staffing resources to do that. But, we're in the midst of doing that, and a major addition to this facility will be the addition of program space, so we're heading in a good direction.

Lack of Resources*

Although Canadian correctional systems receive $3 billion of the $13 billion criminal justice system budget (Griffiths 2010a), Warden Pastorek argues BC Corrections could use further resources to address the challenges the system is currently experiencing, in particular, prison overcrowding and the absence of programming opportunities for custodial remand populations.

The biggest challenge in improving prisons and community supervision in BC is, well, it's dependent on funding really, and the government's commitment to at least maintain the *status quo* and, hopefully, improve what we're trying to do, because we can't do it without the right resources. Getting money for corrections is a bit of a challenge when you're competing for health care and education dollars. It's been that way ever since I started, and it'll probably continue that way long after I retire.

---

* Subsequent to the timing of this interview, BC Corrections received funding approval for a 216 cell expansion to Surrey Pretrial Services Centre—currently under construction—in addition to funding approval for planning a new 360 cell correctional centre in Oliver, BC. These initiatives represent the largest capital expenditure in Branch history and will significantly address capacity issues.

We work in a highly political environment, and we're competing for resources with other ministries and government priorities, and that's always been a challenge and will be a challenge. But, I think there's been recognition lately, at least provincially, that overcrowding has reached the point where something has to be done. In fact, two capital expansion projects are underway right now valued over 50 million dollars that will add 124 cells and planning is underway for a further 216-bed expansion. Nine correctional centers closed around 2000 or 2001 because of budget pressures, and that put a lot of strain on the remaining facilities, and we've been operating this facility at 200% capacity for a long time. The downsizing that was forced on us in 2000 has made the conditions less than desirable because of overcrowding; this facility has 300 regular cells, and our average count this past year has been over 600. Double bunking is the norm. Does the public care about that? Probably not, but it is more challenging and more difficult for us to manage with that kind of environment, so with regard to quality, if we are going to focus on change and rehabilitating people, then we need to pay attention to the environment that we keep people in.

Funding has been an issue for us in terms of building facilities then and also in rolling out the Advancing Offender Programming Initiative sooner than later. We know where we want to go; we'd just like to get there quicker. And, there are other initiatives, like introducing technology for offenders, for instance. We've got a plan, wherein we'd put an inmate network in place, so they can access e-mail instead of having to rely on the traditional way of communicating with family members and accessing their trust account fund information. The network would give them the opportunity to put in requests to see the doctor, launch a grievance of complaint, or access their disclosure material and online reading material, right from their cells. I think that we've got a pretty good strategy and plan in place; it's just that these initiatives take time to implement. Funding is in place over the next four years.

Disconnect between Public Perceptions and Reality

There is a considerable gap between the Canadian public's beliefs and perceptions of crime and the criminal justice system in Canada and the reality of how the system operates (Roberts 2008). This gap is often attributed to the public's overreliance on the media to provide them with information on crime and criminal justice issues (Griffiths 2010a). The Canadian public consistently thinks crime rates are increasing, regardless of whether they are going up, down, or remaining stable; they think sentences are too lenient because of sensationalized media reports, and most underestimate the Canadian incarceration rate—which is the focus of considerable concern, given Canada's overreliance in using this sanction (Roberts 2008). The public lacks confidence in the Canadian criminal justice system in general; however, correctional systems receive the lowest levels of public support.*

> It's challenging for an organization to have a mandate to try to provide opportunities for change and to support change when that's out of sync with the public's expectation that we just lock people up and not do anything with them. Public policymakers are not immune to pressure from the public; I think the Mandatory Minimum Sentences that the Conservative government is introducing are a response to public perceptions and pressure. And really, I don't know how useful that is in making things safer in the community, having that kind of an attitude of wanting to harden things up. Even CSC releases just about everyone who comes through their doors, and you don't want to make them worse when you put them back out, and that's not understood enough by the general public and, sometimes, by politicians as well.

As a result of public concern regarding increasing gun crime in Canada and concerns regarding serious offenses resulting from gang violence and organized crime, the federal government is moving in the direction of implementing legislation to increase the number and severity of mandatory minimum sentences (MMS) of imprisonment (Griffiths 2010a; Roberts 2008).† Although there is considerable public and political support for the implementation and use of MMS, there is an absence of research evidence supporting their use. Considerable concern exists, as research evidence demonstrates that MMS limit judicial discretion, contribute to unfair sentencing practices, have little or no deterrent value, and result in increased costs for the system because of increased "not guilty" pleas and prison overcrowding (Griffiths 2010a,b).

Despite low levels of public support for correctional services, community volunteers work with offenders in both community and institutional correctional facilities, demonstrating their interest in delivering programs and services for offenders (Griffiths 2010a).

> We've always had a strong base in whatever center I've been involved with in terms of the community coming in and being involved in the delivery of services and what we're trying to do. So, I think that, although it's not out in the mainstream as much, there has always been a dedicated group of people who come in and provide service, contact, and support for people in custody. Organizations like John Howard and Elizabeth Fry and MAM and just individuals who come in through the work of the chaplains.

---

* Police services continually receive high overall public approval rates of roughly 80% (Griffiths 2010b).

† Subsequent to the timing of this interview, in March 2012, the Conservative Party of Canada passed Bill C-10: The Safe Streets and Communities Act, which increases the number and duration of mandatory minimum sentences of imprisonment in Canada.

Mentally Disordered Offenders

Mental health disorders are much more prevalent in correctional populations than among the general Canadian population, including disorders such as schizophrenia, bipolar disorder, and major depression (Public Safety Canada Portfolio Corrections Statistics Committee 2007). Research findings suggest that roughly 56% of individuals entering BC Corrections are diagnosed with a mental health, substance abuse disorder, or both, although this does not account for those offenders who are admitted and who are undiagnosed (BC Corrections 2010b). Warden Pastorek discusses the issues offenders with mental health issues present and the available resources within BC Corrections.

> The closing of Riverview has impacted our prison populations, and we have the Downtown Eastside in our catchment area, so we see a lot of people who cycle through who are clearly battling mental health issues with addiction issues.* You know, that's been a real challenge for us, and it's really quite tragic in a lot of respects that we're not really trained to deal with that population to the same level as healthcare practitioners. I think we've had to deal with them out of necessity, and we've done some pretty good work with some people. But for me, knowing that, maybe, there's a floridly psychotic person in a segregation cell, it's just wrong. You know, someone that's certifiable, and that because there's no bed space at FPH, we have to keep them here without the benefit of being able to medicate them against their will.† You watch people decompensate, and it's really a shame.
>
> We have dedicated staff that have specialized training as mental health liaison officers who work closely with our psychologists, and there's a staff member in our Health Care Department who has some expertise in that area as well. They work well as a team in working with that population. We also have a unit that we tend to classify that group of people to because there are additional resources to deal with them. And so, for people who can manage in an environment living with other people, with other supports, we put them in that unit. But, at the other extreme are the ones who just can't live in the unit; they're in a psychotic state and ought to be in a hospital. So, what do we do? We try to maintain contact with FPH, and we have some successes in moving

---

* The Downtown Eastside is commonly called "Canada's poorest postal code," with high rates of crime, drug use, and poverty. Many offenders in this neighborhood exhibit both health and social problems, including mental health illnesses, poverty, homelessness, and substance abuse (alcohol and/or drugs; http://www.criminaljusticereform.gov.bc.ca/en/justice_reform_projects/community_court/).

† The Forensic Psychiatric Hospital (FPH) is a mental health facility that is located in Port Coquitlam, BC, and provides rehabilitative and vocational training, as well as clinical services for patients, including those who are involuntarily admitted for treatment (BC Mental Health and Addictions Services 2010; http://www.bcmhas.ca/ForensicService/ForensicHospital/default.htm).

people, or we do things like trading someone, maybe someone who's been there awhile, who's more stable, and bring them back into this environment and send off the one who needs to be there right now. So, there are resources in place to deal with it, and that's kind of what we're doing; we make do, and we've put some resources to it.

The issue is that many of their needs are so complex, and by the time they hit here, they'll have run the gamut of resources available in the community, and so, I think what's needed is better interagency communication where individuals are being dealt with by multiple parts of government and health authorities. It also comes down to addressing some very basic needs, like finding housing for people, as there's a major homelessness issue in Vancouver. It's out there, and it's real, and although there's been some social policy decisions made to reduce homelessness—I mean, they've got a lot of facilities in the Vancouver area for supportive housing and all—at the end of the day, we need more. There are people who leave here without a roof over their head, and we're not going to have much luck with them. Although we're sensitive to the homelessness issue, I know the sentence facilities I've been at before, and when I worked as a correctional officer, you're aware of that, and if you can, you try to make referrals. You try, if you can, not to just put someone out the door. And even for the remand population from here, some of the work of the Mental Heath Liaison officers too is that, if they know someone has a court date upcoming and there's a chance they might be released, they work with them to try to find housing even before they go to court; or they make contact engaging in dialogue and communication, if they're involved with the community court.

Unfortunately, the future impact of mentally disordered offenders is a great unknown, because a lot of that is dependent on strategies, decisions, and events that happen outside corrections, things like housing availability together with whether regional facilities and mental health facilities will be expanded.

Substance Abuse Issues

Offenders admitted to correctional institutions often share the common attribute of high rates of substance abuse, both before and during incarceration, and for most offenders, substance abuse (drugs or alcohol) is directly or indirectly involved in their criminal behavior (Griffiths et al. 2007; Griffiths 2010a). To address substance abuse issues related to criminal behavior, most federal and provincial or territorial facilities in Canada offer substance abuse interventions for offenders (Griffiths 2010a).

We offer Substance Abuse Treatment Programming here, and it's one of those programs that's being revamped and changed. We've always had some form of substance abuse programming, and it's currently being condensed, being rolled out. In addition, we contract two individuals here who help make referrals and get people lined up for treatment. So, even with the remand population, even if they may be getting out or they're looking for a place to land, they can tell their defense counsel that they have treatment lined up. We have a list of facilities that have been approved, that we work with. I think there are a lot more facilities out there that, maybe, don't have the same reputation as these ones, and my experience is that some of them operate to run as many people through in a month as they can; more in it for the buck. And, we try to stay away from those facilities.

We also use methadone as a harm-reduction strategy, and I personally think it's a good one. Is it flawed? Yes it is. Do inmates attempt to divert it despite our best efforts? Yes they do. It's really run here in the right context though, in that it's a medical decision. So, our doctors make the decisions on whether to initiate or not, and they manage the program. Sometimes, it's frustrating for correctional staff to wrap their head around it; there's probably a fairly even split if you ask the correctional officers if they think it's a good idea or not. It's a good idea in that, as a harm-reduction strategy, it's good and sound. For people who've been established on a program in the community, it keeps them from using heroin. There's a benefit to that for everybody. Some staff get that, whereas some staff see it as, they wonder, why should they—as do many people in the public—why should offenders get a drug while they're incarcerated? And sometimes, when they see people abusing the program and not facing an immediate sanction of being kicked off of it, or whatever—because it's a medical decision that's made, and it's confidential—they make their own assumptions, so sometimes, that doesn't endear the program to them. So, it's a bit tricky managing it, but I think overall, it's a good program.

Women with Histories of Abuse

Correctional systems have long recognized that females require different correctional programs and policies tailored to their unique needs to facilitate their successful treatment and reintegration (Griffiths 2010a; Babooram 2008). Although data are not available for BC, data from Saskatchewan provincial facilities indicate that women exhibit a greater number of needs than men; personal or emotional challenges create some of the greatest differences in the need profiles of women versus men (Babooram 2008). This is not surprising, given that a large number of female offenders have histories characterized by physical and sexual victimization (Brzozowski et al. 2006; cf., Griffiths 2010a, 25).

Women have always represented a smaller proportion of custodial populations in provincial or territorial correctional systems in Canada; however, during the past 5 years, the number of female offenders admitted to both provincial and territorial remand, and sentenced custody has increased (Babooram 2008). Warden Pastorek discusses BC Corrections' position on providing correctional services for women offenders.

Well, I think that we, under our branch, have done a pretty good job with managing female offenders generally and recognizing that there are differences in their histories and in what their needs are. Even going back to Lakeside and BCCW days, a lot of the programs were unique for the women and supported, and even eventually in the Branch philosophical statement, there was recognition that there's a difference. And so, the programs evolved differently, because their needs are different. Their needs have always been recognized as being unique, maybe not always in a formalized or articulated way. But, from being around the Branch long enough, I know that there's always been recognition that there are differences, and I guess that, more formally, in later years, when we started making statements at a high level about it, they were really reflecting the practice and what the attitudes were all along. I think that's probably what happened, and I, to this day, think it's recognized.

Moving Forward

Correctional systems are dynamic, ever-changing agencies, so Warden Pastorek was asked to predict potential changes that BC Corrections may experience in the future based on his more than 30 years of experience working in the system.

There will be a possible shift with remand populations because of Bill C-25—remand populations will likely go down, and there may be an increase on the sentenced side. We'll also have more capacity, so the level of overcrowding should be reduced. We'll continue to see an expansion of evidence-based programming to remand facilities. And then, there's the issue of the aging workforce, as there will be a fair turnover of more senior managers and supervisory staff over the next 5 years. So, there are good career opportunities for people, but there will be a loss of a knowledge base that's pretty significant too, and sometimes without having people around that you share those previous experiences with, people may have to learn from their experiences, and there's a chance they'll make mistakes.

Maybe, it boils down to personal philosophy and being around long enough that I think back to some of the things like the Oakalla Prison Farm. When you think back to its roots, what it was, it kind of goes along with the initiative of being self-sufficient in things, and I think what will happen is that eventually again things will go full circle. And maybe, an opportunity for people to be involved in raising their own produce, trying to be more self-sufficient, will arise. I mean, I know there's been a move away from that kind of programming, but you know, I still think that there's value in that kind of thing. I think that, at the end of the day, if (offenders) just have something to work at, it gives them an opportunity to maybe think about other things and to see that they're doing something productive.

You know, if you stay around long enough, you see things go full circle quite often, so getting back to where the future goes, if I was going to have any say in that, it might be along those lines.

Conclusion

BC Corrections has seen a significant change with respect to the hardening of their offender population and is experiencing numerous challenges in both managing and administering correctional services. Warden Pastorek's insight reflects academic literature documenting what is known about correctional systems throughout North America, that is, many institutions are operating at overcapacity because of overcrowding and they are managing an increasingly challenging population of offenders. Of further relevance is his insight into the issues relating to the increasing number of offenders with substance abuse and mental health issues, as well as the unique needs female offenders' present to the correctional systems.

References

Babooram, A. 2008. The changing profile of adults in custody, 2006/2007. *Juristat* 28(10). Cat. no. 85-002-X. Ottawa: Minister of Industry. http://www.statcan.gc .ca/pub/85-002-x/2008010/article/10732-eng.htm.

BC Corrections. 2010a. *Pretrial and Regional Correctional Centres*. Victoria: Ministry of Public Safety and Solicitor General, Corrections Branch. http://www.pssg .gov.bc.ca/corrections/centres/regional/index.htm.

BC Corrections. 2010b. *Strategic Plan: BC Corrections 2010–2013*. Victoria: Ministry of Public Safety and Solicitor General, Corrections Branch. http://www.pssg .gov.bc.ca/corrections/pdf/strategic-plan-2010-2013.pdf.

BC Mental Health and Addictions Services. 2010. *Forensic Psychiatric Hospital*. Provincial Health Services Authority.

Borzycki, M. 2005. *Interventions for Prisoners Returning to the Community*. Canberra: Australian Institute of Criminology. http://www.aic.gov.au/documents/F/6/E/ %7BF6E2B190-2C21-4C7D-B45F-2C7D6FA3DE45%7D2005-03-prisoners.pdf.

Borzycki, M., and T. Makkai. 2007. *Prisoner Reintegration Post-release*. Canberra: Australian Institute of Criminology.

Brzozowski, J., A. Taylor-Butts, and S. Johnson. 2006. Victimization and offending among the aboriginal population in Canada. *Juristat* 26(3). Cat. no. 85-002-XIE. Ottawa: Minister of Industry. http://www.statcan.gc.ca/pub/85-002-x/85-002-x2006003-eng.pdf.

Criminal Justice Reform Projects. 2010. *Vancouver's Downtown Community Court*. Province of BC. http://www.criminaljusticereform.gov.bc.ca/en/justice_reform_ projects/community_court/.

Fox, A. 2002. Aftercare for drug-using prisoners: Lessons from an international study. *The Probation Journal*, 49: 120–129.

Greater Vancouver Regional District. 2010. *Metro Vancouver.* Vancouver, British Columbia. http://www.metrovancouver.org/.

Griffiths, C. T. 2010a. *Canadian Corrections.* 3rd ed. Toronto, ON: Thomson Nelson.

Griffiths, C. T. 2010b. *Canadian Criminal Justice in Canada: A Primer.* 4th ed. Scarborough, ON: Thomson Nelson.

Griffiths, C. T., and D. Murdoch. 2009. *Strategies and Best Practices against Overcrowding in Correctional Institutions.* Vancouver: International Centre for Criminal Law Reform and Criminal Justice Policy. http://www.icclr.law.ubc.ca/files/2009/Overcrowding.pdf.

Griffiths, C. T., Y. Dandurand, and D. Murdoch. 2007. *The Social Reintegration of Offenders and Crime Prevention.* Ottawa: National Crime Prevention Centre. http://www.publicsafety.gc.ca/res/cp/res/_fl/soc-reint-eng.pdf.

Johnson, S. 2003. Custodial remand in Canada, 1986/1987 to 2000/2001. *Juristat* 23(7). Cat no. 85-002-X. Ottawa: Minister of Industry.

Kong, R., and V. Peters. 2008. Remand in adult corrections and sentencing patterns. *Juristat* 28(9). Cat. no. 85-002-X. Ottawa: Minister of Industry. http://www.statcan.gc.ca/pub/85-002-x/2008009/article/10706-eng.htm.

Landry, L., and M. Sinha. 2008. Adult correctional services in Canada, 2005/2006. *Juristat* 28(6). Cat. no. 85-002-XIE. Ottawa: Minister of Industry. http://dsp-psd.pwgsc.gc.ca/collection_2008/statcan/85-002-X/85-002-XIE2008006.pdf.

Milhorean, K., and R. Kong. 2008. Criminal justice trends in Canada. In *Criminal Justice in Canada: A Reader,* edited by J. Roberts and M. Grossman, 17–34. Toronto, ON: Thomson Nelson.

Miller, S. 2008. The treatment of prisoners in Canada. In *Criminal Justice in Canada: A Reader,* edited by J. Roberts and M. Grossman, 167–178. Toronto, ON: Thomson Nelson.

Public Safety Canada Portfolio Corrections Statistics Committee. 2007. *Corrections and Conditional Release Statistical Overview.* Ottawa: Public Works and Government Services Canada. http://www.publicsafety.gc.ca/res/cor/rep/_fl/CCRSO_2007-eng.pdf.

Roberts, J. 2008. Criminal justice in Canada: An overview. In *Criminal Justice in Canada: A Reader,* edited by J. Roberts and M. Grossman, 2–16. Toronto, ON: Thomson Nelson.

Shaw, M. 2008. Foreword. In *Justice Initiatives: Pretrial Detention,* 1–3. New York: Open Society Justice Initiative. http://www.soros.org/initiatives/justice/focus/criminal_justice/articles_publications/publications/pretrial_20080513/Justice_Initiati.pdf.

U.N. General Assembly. 1966. *International Covenant on Political and Civil Rights.* Entry into force: 23 March 1976.

Interview with Michael Boileau, Warden of Matsqui Institution, Correctional Service Canada, Vancouver, British Columbia

7

RICHARD PARENT

This interview explores the views of Michael Boileau, warden of Matsqui Institution, a federal prison that is part of the Correctional Service of Canada. Matsqui Institution is located in the town of Abbotsford, an eastern suburb of the city of Vancouver, British Columbia.

Canada is a nation of approximately 34 million people with two main prison systems: 1) federal and 2) provincial. Individuals convicted of criminal offenses that result in the judicial sentencing of incarceration for 2 years or more are placed within the federal system operated by Correctional Service Canada (CSC). Individuals convicted of lesser criminal offenses that result in the judicial sentencing of incarceration for less than 2 years are placed within one of Canada's 10 provincial prison systems. Michael Boileau began his career with the federal-based CSC in 1987 and rose through the ranks to the position of warden. In this interview, Michael Boileau discusses the various positions that he has held during his professional career, his insight into corrections, and the challenges faced by the federal correction system within Canada.

The interview took place on April 7, 2010, at Matsqui Institution, Abbotsford, British Columbia, Canada.

The Interview

RP: Warden Michael Boileau, to start this interview and to better situate our readers, please describe your professional experience that led you from being a correctional officer to being the warden of a federal Canadian prison.

MB: Well, I was born and raised in Langley (a suburb of Vancouver), joining Correctional Service Canada (CSC) at a young age in 1987. I
started off like most individuals, as a correctional officer, working
at a medium security prison. I did this for approximately 2 years
and was later promoted to the position of a second-level correctional officer, which resulted in my transfer to the correctional
institution of Matsqui, the one that I am now the warden of, some
20 years later. I've come full circle in my career, from a correctional
officer to being the warden of the same institution.

Back in the early 1990s, I worked as a correctional officer, and
then, I became a parole officer (1991–1993). It was during this
period that I became the victim of a pretty serious assault while
working as a parole officer. The injuries that I sustained resulted in
me being off work for 6 months. When I returned to work, I was
given the opportunity to transfer into our preventative security
department, which is our security intelligence section. I held this
position from roughly 1993 to 1998.

I then had an opportunity to go to our regional headquarters
and became the project officer for security. In essence, I became
the "jack of all trades," working in security on various projects.
A couple of years after that, I moved on to becoming the regional
administrator for security (2001). Around that same time, I entered
a university program being offered at the Justice Institute of British
Columbia and successfully completed my Bachelor of General
Studies degree, with the plan to become a Deputy Warden. A university degree was a requirement for this position.

I also completed several assignments at the National Headquarters
located in Ottawa, Canada's capital city, located in eastern Canada.
There was a period, around 2001–2002, when I was back and forth
between Ottawa and Vancouver. I learned a great deal in our
National Headquarters by revamping national policies and commissioner's directives pertaining to security. Then, in 2004, I transferred to Kent Institution, a nearby maximum correctional facility,
where I was promoted to the position of assistant warden of security
for 6 months. I then became the deputy warden at another nearby
correctional facility (Mountain Institution) for roughly 2 years and
later assumed the position of warden. Since then, I have held the
position of warden at three different federal correctional facilities
located in the eastern Vancouver area.

I would say that I very much like the job of being the warden. I have had a fantastic career with the Correctional Service
of Canada. They have been very supportive, and they are a good
organization to work for. I firmly believe that what goes around

comes around. The way people treated me and supported me over the years, I certainly have made that my model as well. I continue to support and develop people and to help them with their career.

I have been fortunate to spend most of my time with the service (CSC) here in the eastern suburb area of Vancouver, where most of our larger federal correctional institutions are located. However, I did spend some significant time in eastern Canada, and over the years, I have been fortunate to learn more about our national projects and administration, as well as being exposed to the Canadian Correctional Service national agenda.

RP: Your correctional institute is one of the largest federal correctional institutions in the Vancouver area, which has a population of roughly two million people. Could you please discuss the setting of this correctional institution and some of the main issues that you are dealing with from an institutional perspective?

MB: This particular institution is considered to be a high–medium level facility. We have 280 staff at Matsqui Institution. The staff positions range from correctional staff to clerical to institutional services, which includes plumbing personnel, kitchen workers, and gate workers. Of this group of individuals, there are roughly 180 correctional officers. With regard to inmates, there are currently 270 inmates in custody. This number is down significantly due to construction and redevelopment of the institution. These facilities were built in the 1960s. We were actually scheduled for closure and to be torn down. However, a decision was made to keep the institution open, and now, the federal government is spending $20 million in upgrades that will result in things like the provision of toilets and running water in each cell.

One of the challenges that I am faced with is the major plumbing operation currently going on inside the institution. The current situation is not a good thing during lockdowns, and as such, individual cells do not have a toilet. If a problem arises, we have to compromise the scene of an incident. For example, if an individual needs to go to the toilet, we have got to open his cell, and let him go into our communal washrooms. This can be a security problem.

In addition to the major construction program that is occurring, I am also dealing with labor management meetings. There are three main labor contracts that I deal with. There are the correctional officers, the clerical staff/parole officers, and finally nurses and informatics. I have a deputy warden and three assistant wardens to help me with my day-to-day running of the institution. One assistant warden is in charge of "management service," which deals with all support services in the institution. A second assistant warden is in charge of operations, leaving him to deal with all aspects of correctional operations. The third is the assistant warden of intervention, who is in charge of all parole officers, all programs, the chaplaincy, psychology issues, as well as elder services and mental health programs. There are numerous things going on within the institution that require management on a day-to-day basis.

RP: As a warden within the Canadian federal correctional system, could you please explain to our readers the jurisdictional and program differences that exist between the national correctional system and those of the smaller provincial correctional systems?

MB: In Canada, judicial sentencing is a key factor, as the provincial system is mandated with managing offenders doing 2 years or less in prison. The province is also mandated to manage individuals who are being held "pretrial" and have not been convicted. These individuals are waiting to go to court and, for various security reasons, must be held in custody until their day in court. To some degree, the provincial correctional system is focused more on warehousing offenders and, as a result, does not have the same level of programming as we do for inmates.

In contrast, our federal system is focused more on preparing the individual for a safe reentry into the community. Again, our federal correctional system is much more structured and well funded and well resourced, with emphasis placed on preparing offenders for eventual release into the community, in a safe manner. Public safety is our primary mandate with the Correctional Service of Canada. Any time I make a decision as a warden with regard to an offender, public safety is the paramount concern that I have. It is written right into law, and I follow it closely. We also realize that most of the individuals that come into our federal system will eventually be released and placed back in the community.

RP: One of the issues that tend to be somewhat controversial in Canada is that of "prisoner rights." As you know, there is a segment of the public that feels inmates in Canada have too many rights and too many privileges, even though they have been convicted of crimes against society. How do you, as a warden, manage this issue? What is your perspective on prisoner rights?

MB: Prisoner rights and those of the general public, at times, can be separated by a fine line, sometimes resulting in very difficult situations. Inmates do have rights, and this is clearly mandated under the law in Canada. Importantly, one of the laws in Canada is that inmates are to be managed and housed in the least restrictive environment. For example, if I have an offender that meets the criteria and components of minimum security, then the law says

I must manage him in a least restricted environment, which is minimum security.

However, because of the media attention, high-profile offenders such as gang members are frequently in the news. As you know, we have had a great deal of gang shootings in the Vancouver area, where several individuals have been murdered. This has resulted in a large amount of media attention and public opinion regarding gang violence and gang activities such as drug trafficking.

With regard to prisoner rights, there are three main criteria that are measured in Canada's Correctional Service, from low to moderate to high. The first criterion that is measured is institutional adjustment. How well does the inmate get along in the institutional environment? Does he engage well with staff? Does he engage well with other inmates? Is he following the goals and objectives that have been set for him? Has he been a problem? Once these questions are asked, we will rate the inmate from low to high. If an inmate rates high to institutional adjustment, he automatically goes to maximum security, where his rights are clearly limited.

The second key area that we examine concerns escape. Does the inmate have a history of escapes? Has the inmate committed a breach of trust? Once again, we will ask these questions and rate the inmate from low to high in these areas.

Finally, the third area is with regard to public safety. If someone comes into the correctional service with a history of entrenched crimes, what has he done to address those criminal values? Has the inmate successfully completed institution programs? Has the individual changed his criminal values? We use psychological assessments to address and measure this area.

For example, there is this particular inmate that has been here for all of 1 year, out of a 7-year sentence. He has a young child at home. The inmate is a pretty clean guy. He is a low-escape risk. He is respectful to staff and generally rates low in the criteria pertaining to institutional adjustment. There has been no violence. As a result, the issue of public safety concern is probably low. However, this individual has pretty entrenched criminal values, as he belongs to an organized criminal gang. As we discussed, organized gangs are a serious problem in Canada and are responsible for many of the violent crimes and murders that occur. As a result of this inmates' values, we now have a public safety concern.

Although this inmate appears to meet the criteria for low security, he is being housed here at Matsqui Institution, which is considered to be one of high–medium security. The reason why he has been sent here is because he has been involved in the high trafficking of large amounts of cocaine. Police surveillance and undercover cops were involved in an extensive investigation regarding his activities. They nailed him. This individual has real entrenched criminal and gang values. When questioned about gangs and his history of gangs, he still has not taken the jump to let go or disassociate himself from gang values. This inmate fails to recognize that the group he is associated with and values is an organized criminal gang. These individuals focus on committing crimes that often result in violence and death.

Nonetheless, this individual has expressed a desire to be transferred from our high–medium security institution to a much lower level of security, where he would have more freedom, less restrictions, and access to more visits from outside. As I noted, in most areas, this particular inmate rates low in the criteria that we use to determine the level of security that we impose and that ultimately impact on individual prisoner rights.

There are many other cases where inmates are clearly not ready to go to minimum security. They have been involved in numerous things and have not done well in our programs. They may have been violent toward other inmates or disrespectful toward staff and may have been involved in drug use. These cases are clear and easy to deal with. However, the more difficult cases are ones like this real example.

This example presents a dilemma for me as a warden of this institution. The inmate has been initially sent to a high–medium security institution for assessment and is now requesting a transfer to a low security institution. From a public safety perspective, I must first consider if I am meeting the needs of Canadians by placing him in a low security environment, where he could potentially walk away, and his incarceration time would be easier. This is a good example of how I get caught between laws, policies, and how the Canadian public expects that public safety is maintained. There are human rights issues, individual prisoner rights, and societal rights that come into play. One of the things I must also consider as a warden is the Corrections Service Canada mandate and that of the Public Safety Minister.

RP: Can you also comment on recent public opinion polls that have indicated that the majority of Canadians feel that the prison system is "soft" on prisoners? Specifically, there has been a great deal of media attention and public debate concerning the practice of most inmates being released after completing only two-thirds of their imposed judicial sentence. Although this has resulted in some public outcry toward judges and the initial sentencing that they impose, has this issue also impacted on Correctional Service Canada?

MB: This is somewhat of an issue for us within the prison system. For example, I have often been asked to speak at criminal justice workshops about the approach taken by Correctional Services Canada with regard to how inmates are handled. Typically, most of the individuals in the audience would be law enforcement personnel who would often provide negative feedback with regard to early release provisions. Law enforcement individuals, at times, see correctional services as the agency that lets inmates out of jail too soon. My response is that these provisions and the resulting practices of dealing with inmates are encased in federal law. The law is very specific in that an inmate must only complete two-thirds of their sentence in Canada. Federal law states that you must release the inmate after completing two-thirds of the sentence, unless you can demonstrate that the individual will commit another violent offense, in which case you may detain him.

However, if it can be demonstrated that the inmate will reoffend, then the decision to detain the inmate further is not made by Correctional Services Canada or the warden but by the Federal Parole Board. I have no say in this process. How it works is that my correctional staff will make a referral for detention. They will bring the case to me, where I will make a final decision on whether or not it is compelling and should go to the Parole Board. Basically, I have the power to refer or not to refer the case, but once I refer it, it is ultimately the Parole Board's decision on what occurs next and whether the inmate will ultimately serve his entire judicially imposed prison sentence.

The law enforcement community does not always understand this, even though the federal laws of Canada clearly lay out this process. It's a real fine line in these cases and, sometimes, a difficult situation. However, it is a good example of the different mandates that we have in Canada when dealing with law enforcement versus correctional services. At times, it appears that the two systems are at odds with each other, but ultimately, both are following the laws that are in place, and that have been passed by government.

RP: We live in an ever-changing society. There have been many recent changes and trends in the Canadian society. For example, the general crime rate has continued to fall over the past 10 years. The homicide rate in Canada is relatively low, with roughly 600 homicides occurring each year in a nation of approximately 34 million. However, organized criminal gangs and resulting violent crimes are a real concern for the public. What are your thoughts on these issues, and have you also seen a change in the profile of the typical inmate in a Canadian prison?

MB: There certainly has been a changing trend/profile among our inmate population. It's very much changed from those inmates that are now in their 40s and 50s and were considered to be career criminals. In the past, our population was typically composed of inmates that committed individual crimes in a discrete manner. Once detected and apprehended, these individuals went through our courts and often received a lengthy sentence.

The inmates that we see today who are coming into the system are now typically younger and being sentenced to shorter sentences. Usually, there is more violence involved and a younger "punk" type of mentality. These individuals typically use no discretion in public. Violent murders and attempted murders are committed in public places like restaurants and shopping centers. This is something new. These individuals are harder to manage within the prison population. They have no respect for authority.

The other profile are those inmates from an "organized crime perspective" who are often very easy to deal with inside the prison system. However, since they come from an "organized crime perspective," they are often difficult cases to make decisions on, as I discussed earlier with the example that I presented. So, there are two new trends that we see in Correctional Services Canada: the younger violent "punk" type of individual, and inmates who are here because of their organized criminal gang background.

With regard to gang members, these individuals have the ability to make changes. They often have the life skills and attributes to avoid criminal activities. However, they know that, for them, crime pays, and nothing is going to change that. You see these guys when they come in here wearing brand name clothing and wearing lots of jewelry. We do not issue prisoner uniforms, so they are allowed to wear their own clothes, but they must be within certain value limits. These inmates know the limits and work within them, but you still cannot help but notice the obvious wealth that is a result of their gang activities and associations. You also notice the visitors that come into the institution to visit them. I don't know whether they are hookers, escorts, or girlfriends, but they have very attractive women coming into the institution for visits.

In Canada, inmates are entitled to apply for "private family visits," but there has to be evidence that there was a common-law relationship or that they lived with the individual for some time prior to their incarceration. It is a program that the inmate must apply for and then pass certain criteria before they are eligible. However, yes, a lot of these individuals take advantage of "private family visits," which does ultimately allow them to have sexual relations with the individual that comes to visit them. In fact, many inmates over the years have conceived many children while incarcerated.

So, as I have noted, these newer types of inmates that are from organized criminal gangs tend to be the hardest to make decisions on, because they are often "model prisoners." They tend to have the best behavior in the correctional setting. They have good social skills and typically are not drug addicts. The previous old traditional inmate who may have been a serial killer or a drug addict was far easier to deal with regarding decision making.

From the prisoners' rights perspective, these individuals have a desire to do their time in a minimum security facility, where there is more freedom, more access to visitation rights, and more access to passes. Also, because these individuals are typically nonviolent, they will probably be allowed to apply for "accelerated parole review," where they can be released sooner. If these individuals remain in a medium or maximum institution, their chances of getting paroled are slimmer than if they are in a minimum security institution.

So, there is a degree of "strategy" used by these inmates in using the correctional system, the way it currently operates, to better their position in a variety of ways. However, the public and the law enforcement community have been vocal and watchful that these individuals fully serve their sentence in a secure institution and within the parameters established by law.

RP: Could you please comment on some of the safety and security issues that you have had to confront and deal with as the warden of a large federal institution? Have these issues impacted on prisoner rights?

MB: We always joke that the inmates are the easy part of the business. Managing the various staff within the correctional institution can be the biggest challenge for management. For example, historically, it was always known that, to work within a prison setting, there was an inherent risk associated with the job. You knew and accepted as a prison guard that there was some level of real risk associated with your job, and you accepted that risk and dealt with it accordingly by way of training, equipment, etc. However, today and over the years, our staff has focused on several provisions of the Canada Labour Code to deal with safety issues, which has resulted in some real challenges for institutional management.

I will give you an example of a challenge that occurred at another federal institution, a maximum security institution housing the most violent and most dangerous offenders. In this other institution, the unionized prison staff issued a formal labor code "safety work stoppage," because the inmates were being served pork chops. As you know, the bones of a pork chop are sharp and could be made into knives or weapons. When the staff heard about the pork chops being served, they immediately issued their formal "safety notice" under federal labor law, stating that a danger had been identified. As a result, the entire institution needed to immediately be shut down. The inmates were quickly locked into their cells, and the managers were required to do nonmanagerial things. The inmates became unhappy with the situation, which resulted in even more tension and stress.

A safety issue that has occurred within this particular institution was staff concern regarding communicable diseases such as HIV, AIDS, TB, and even H1N1. In fact, recently, there was 4-week period when we had seven guys that had H1N1. Although these individuals were quarantined, I expected that the staff were going to issue a formal safety notice, but fortunately, they did not. The management team and I were able to work with the staff to address their concerns and avoid a formal labor code safety notice.

As a manager, I have been very lucky and have had only a few formal safety notices served by the prison staff. I've grown up in this business and observed wardens that say that they are right and you will do what they say. I have also learned from those who tended to communicate, mediate, and engage with people. I strive for win–wins. Instead of taking a position on something, I tend to look for common goals and common interests that achieve a solution to the issue. So, as a result, I have been able to avoid a great deal of conflict and work with the unionized staff to solve their concerns.

In addition to staff concerns and labor code issues, there are many obligations placed upon the warden, such as ensuring that the rights of the inmates are being met within the parameters of institutional safety. Whether my staff likes it or not, under Canadian law, the only thing the inmates lose when coming to jail is the right of freedom. In fact, in Canada, an inmate is presently entitled to a government pension, voting, and basically anything that a Canadian citizen is entitled to, other than their freedom.

One of the more common issues in the institution is that I have to ensure that their dietary needs are being met. I frequently get grievances from inmates about the food that they are served. For example, there was a formal grievance submitted by an inmate to our federal office when we removed the oranges from his diet. The inmate complained that he wasn't getting his dietary needs of vitamin C.

The commissioner at CSC was fully aware why we removed the oranges from inmates. We learned that the inmates were stealing the oranges and then making home-brewed alcohol. We didn't just take away their oranges; we gave the inmates several warnings last summer. We also met with the Inmate Committee, which represents the inmates and advised them of this situation. Even after all this was done, we still found home brew on several occasions. After three formal warnings, we stopped serving oranges. It became a security and safety concern.

In response to the formal grievance, we brought in a dietician, who verified that we were still providing enough variety in their diet that the needs of vitamin C were still being met. The rights of the inmate were not being violated. Unfortunately, the security needs of the institution sometimes outweigh some of their rights. But, you have to justify this in Canada, as there is somewhat of a reverse onus placed on Correctional Services Canada. We must justify why we are limiting or restricting inmate rights for the sake of institutional safety and security.

RP: There are times when an inmate will die in custody. Can you please comment on your response to inmate violence and deaths within your institution?

MB: One of the things that occurs within the correctional systems of Canada is that we do go through so much change due largely to public pressure. This is a real challenge with offenders, who find the constant change frustrating, and I do sympathize with them. Right now, we are having a lot of public emphasis and scrutiny placed on deaths in custody at correctional facilities and within police holding areas. We just had a death in custody a few months ago within this institution when an individual hung himself.

As a result of this inmate's sudden death, we had a lot of investigative work going on here. The law stipulates that we have to have someone independent come in to investigate these deaths. Typically, the investigators tend to be former police officers who often do not have a lot of sympathy for inmates in general. These investigators work within investigation boards that tend to also look at our day-to-day business and how we manage the inmates in general. This is in addition to the general death investigation.

We also have a "watchdog" system in place for the inmates to ensure that they are being treated professionally and that staff are not abusing them. Members of the Correctional Investigators Office (CIO) visit this institution every 3 months and will sit here for 3 days to listen to the concerns of the inmates. Inmates also have the ability to phone the CIO if they have a concern about their treatment. It is a fair process that is in place, and I appreciate that we need a check-and-balance approach to prisoners when we keep people in custody.

However, the big frustration is with the number of investigations that often come through the institution and the audits that result and the recommendations that are made. The real dynamics are that you are holding these individuals in a prison, you are incarcerating them. Against this backdrop, there are a lot of people advocating out in the Canadian society for them and for their rights. What can be frustrating for an administrator at an institution is balancing what the public expects (half of the public wants you to throw away the key), what the inmate desires, the demands of the advocates, the recommendations of the CIO, the findings of the investigation boards, and finally, the Charter of Rights and Freedoms that are guaranteed in Canada under the Constitution.

The end result is that we constantly have to make changes to our procedures and policies to address all these issues and concerns. This results in an ever-evolving organization, one that is constantly attempting to address gaps that have been identified.

I will give you an example of how this occurs. As a result of the deaths that have occurred in custody, there is a national mandate from our headquarters that each institution will provide an additional "stand to count," allowing us to physically check each inmate. This is to occur sometime between 18:30 and 22:30 h each night. A stand to count is when the inmate has to stand in their cell doorway and be face-to-face with the correctional officer.

As the warden for the institution, I asked the inmates for feedback with regard to what particular time of the evening they wanted the stand to count. I told them of the new national policy and of their options, that the additional count had to occur sometime between 18:30 and 22:30 h. It is your routine, so let me know what works best for you? If we do the count at 19:00 h, that means that all inmate visits have to end, and the inmates must present themselves at their cell block. It's going to impact your routine so tell me what works best for you as an inmate?

The inmates responded by requesting the stand to count at 22:30 h. So, we accommodated their request, and everyone initially seemed happy. We were achieving the new policy requirements from national headquarters, providing better safety for the inmates, and conducting the stand to counts at a time that the inmates thought worked best.

However, after a while, we received complaints from some of the older inmates who stated that they were just too tired or that they were taking medication, and as a result, they could not stay up to 22:30 h for the count. A few of the inmates launched formal legal challenges, stating that the new policy and procedure is violating their rights by forcing them to stay up late at night. This additionally resulted in some of my staff being upset when they see inmates violating the policy.

Some inmates have refused to stand to count, resulting in correctional officers entering their cells to wake them up. When this occurs, the inmate often becomes angry and irritated by being woken up while sleeping. The inmate feels like he is being harassed and may file a separate formal complaint for being woken up.

Eventually, I just have to say that some of these guys aren't following the rules, and then, I start looking at maximum discipline. When an inmate isn't standing to count, he's telling me that he isn't adjusting to the institution. So, although the institution has good intentions and we try hard to work with the inmates in implementing new policies and procedures, it is not always a smooth process.

RP: Could you please discuss some of the other significant policy and procedure reviews that have occurred within the Correctional Service of Canada in recent times? Can you please provide some examples of how these policies have been implemented within an institutional setting?

MB: One of the more noteworthy things occurred a couple of years ago when the Canadian federal minister in charge of corrections ordered a complete overview of the Correctional Service of Canada. A committee was appointed, which resulted in an 18-month review of the entire prison system. The committee visited jails, conducted interviews of staff, and came out with a document entitled "The Roadmap of Public Safety." Out of this roadmap, there were 109 recommendations.

Over the past 2 years, the CSC has been going through what we call a transformation. Based on the findings of this report, the current conservative government agenda for public safety was to implement the 109 recommendation of this report and ultimately change the Canadian federal correctional service. In this regard, one of the more controversial recommendations was to eliminate statutory release and hold the inmate more accountable for their actions by ensuring they serve their full sentence. (Currently, an inmate will serve roughly two-thirds of their sentence in an institution. Then, by way of statutory release, they are released back into the community by way of parole or some sort of conditions, for the remaining portion of their sentence.) I have some concerns with abolishing statutory release and having the inmate serve their entire sentence.

First, this means that we'd have all of these offenders in our jails up to the full expiry of their warrant, serving their full judicially imposed sentence. This would mean a significant increase in our population numbers, which would result in the overcrowding of our current facilities. This equates to increased prison costs, as well as the real possibility of more prison violence. These issues tend to be problems that occur in the U.S. prison system but something that we in Canada typically don't have.

Second, the other issue, as an administrator, as a warden, I also have my own personal values and perspectives of how I look at corrections. As a warden, I think it is a bad thing to abolish statutory release, even though it is the agenda of the current conservative government. To be clear, I will certainly support whatever policy the Canadian government and CSC embarks upon. I will follow it.

However, my concern with the abolishment of statutory release, my personal belief, is that a slow structured release into the community is in the best interest of the community. That way, we can put an individual into the community by way of parole with all kinds of supervision and conditions. That's probably a lot safer than keeping a guy incarcerated until his warrant expiry. Once an individual has done his entire sentence in jail, then you must just kick him out by law. The problem with this approach is that there's no supervision, there are no conditions of release, and he has all of his rights and freedoms. From an ethical point of view, I think it is a lot safer for everyone, and it is also in the public interest to have a structured release into the community.

Typically, federal corrections in Canada have been quite successful with our traditional approach to corrections and statutory release. Our rates of failure are very, very low. Also, I think, overall, the rates of crime in Canada have significantly dropped. This may be in part due to a change in culture, a change in our Canadian community, but nonetheless, we must be on the right path here in Canada and with CSC. We are certainly making a difference in our rehabilitation efforts.

In Canada, we are making much smarter decisions in releasing our inmates back into the community. We are providing much more thorough and enhanced programs to our inmates. We are also preparing them for a safe release into the community. We're much more focused through the transformation of inmate accountability. We are forcing inmates to take accountability for their actions.

That is not to say that we haven't had our challenges with inmates here at Matsqui. We've had guys who have refused to give a urine analysis, which is our way of managing the inmates to know if they're involved with drugs. Many of the inmates in our institution do have drug addiction problems. If they are using drugs, then this will increase their risk factors for violence and for public safety. So, when an individual inmate refuses a drug analysis, they are hindering our responsibility to the inmate, to the inmate population, and to the general public.

When this occurs, we limit the inmate's eligibility for parole and for transfer to minimum security. Our focus is to have the inmate take responsibility for their actions. We try to influence and change inmate culture to achieve positive transformation.

In the past, we were, at times, too focused on getting the inmates out on parole. We were almost giving them a meal ticket to get out. It wasn't always about inmate accountability. Sometimes, it was as if we were almost pushing inmates into programs. Did they actually learn anything from the program? Did they actually get any insight into their entrenched criminal values and how they could change?

Now, we try to place more emphasis on the offender for the inmate to be accountable and responsible. This is one of the concerns with abolishing statutory release. Currently, if an inmate desires to get out early and complete only two-thirds of their sentence, then they are far more likely to make the effort to get into the programs and take accountability. They have to follow the rules and earn parole within an "early parole system" that is ultimately better for the inmate, the institution, and the general public.

RP: You mentioned the issue of drug testing and the challenges that this poses for an institution. Could you please comment on the general issue of drugs in your institution, and how you have addressed this concern?

MB: Well, yes, we have huge issues with drugs coming in to our institution. It is our number one security issue. While it is mostly tobacco, there is a little bit of everything, and all types of drugs do get in. You are likely aware that inmates are not allowed to smoke anymore. We banned tobacco from all federal institutions. Actually, the inmates have a formal complaint in right now, and it is before the federal courts as a challenge. However, the reason for the tobacco ban was with regard to health concerns and labor laws about second-hand smoke.

Initially, the inmates were allowed to smoke outside the correctional buildings but not inside. What we found was that the inmates were not complying with the law. We kept articulate records and caught them smoking inside the institution. After a year, CSC had enough documented violations of inmate's noncompliance that we were able to initiate an entire ban on smoking. We were expecting riots and placed our Emergency Response Teams on standby when the policy took place.

Interestingly, there were no issues or riots. We successfully implemented a ban on tobacco about 2 years ago. For the most part, it has gone very well. But, inmates are still getting tobacco in here. For example, a small bail of tobacco will go for about $13.00 outside on the street, but it will sell here for about $100. There is some currency inside here, but mostly the underground trade and the black market. We've tried to implement really stringent drug strategies. There are consequences for having drugs, but we are going to have to look more at enforcement and adopt the "four pillars" approach.

However, we have done really well with preventing drugs from coming in with visitors. We have drug dogs and scanners, and we even turn away visitors who test positive for drugs. We are of the opinion that we don't want drugs coming inside the institution. We just turn you away as a visitor if we believe that you have drugs.

The most recent challenge that we have encountered are drugs being fired or thrown over the prison fence. What the inmates and their associates have been resorting to is known as "tail guns." Tail gun is the name used for the air guns at sporting events, when they fire t-shirts and prizes into the crowds of spectators. By using the tail gun, they are able to fire drugs and contraband over the walls and fences into the institution.

I will give you an example. About 6 weeks ago, one of our staff heard this big loud noise outside the prison fence, a big loud bang. Then, as he was looking, he turned around and saw two inmates grabbing a package near one of the prison buildings. The staff member called for assistance, and they intercepted the package from the inmates. When they looked inside, they found that the package contained over 600 steroids, as well as cigarette lighters, tobacco, syringes, and a cell phone. The items had been placed in two soup cans that were taped together. Someone fired the cans over the prison fence with a tail gun to the inmates who were waiting for the cans to arrive.

Also, just last week, we recovered 2 oz of heroin that were found in the prison yard. The drugs were wrapped in condoms and balloons and then placed in a coffee cup that was thrown over the fence. There were rocks tied to the coffee cup to weigh it down and get it over the fence.

In another instance, we found a tube full of tobacco that had been fired over the wall/fence. Interestingly, on this particular tube, there were hooks and strings attached outside the tube. It appears that the inmates know that the items are being shot over the wall and are trying to "snag or fish" the tubes by using the hooks and string. As you see, the inmates are getting very innovative and very organized in knowing what is happening outside the prison walls.

This may, in part, be explained by the number of cell phones that we have found lately. Cell phones allow the inmate to circumvent the monitoring systems, to communicate with people outside, and to tell their associates when and how to bring in drugs as well as other contraband. The cell phones allow communication of when the patrol has gone by, when no staff is around, and when the package can be chucked or shot over the wall/fence. We've tried many things to stop this, and this is one area that we continue to work on.

RP: Finally, could you please comment on the Canadian approach to corrections, Correctional Service Canada? What are your thoughts and experiences of the unique approach taken by Canada in dealing with offenders and in ultimately making Canadian society safer?

MB: I think we have a model of corrections that is looked upon across the world. We might even be the leaders of corrections in the world. I teach crisis management at our correctional headquarters in eastern Canada, where we often have delegates from other countries. I have taught correctional staff from other countries such as Saudi Arabia, Hong Kong, China, and other nations. I have also had the opportunity to talk with my partners from other countries in corrections, and I have obviously looked at documentaries and reporting on other prison systems that exist throughout the world, including in the United States of America, where some of the largest prisons are located.

In the United States, there was one report where I noted a sheriff was running a jail in the southwest. I think you could say that the inmates were dehumanized in his facilities. The sheriff was quite proud of himself, as he was saving the taxpayers money, since it was only costing him $4 a day to feed each prisoner.

However, when one looks deeper and into the rates of violence that he has in his jails, there is constant violence. There are constant problems in this system, his staff are being hurt, and the inmates are being hurt. It is a system that is all about punishment and control. It is a process of beating these guys down until they feel like they are nothing, a system that may dehumanize the individual.

Importantly, the stark reality is that these guys have to go back into the community sometime. If you treat inmates like animals in a punishment and control system where they are dehumanized, then the reality is that they will return to the community like animals.

In other correctional systems, like Hong Kong, the prisons are very disciplined, like the military. The inmates are required to salute the officers, and they must be very respectful. There are no guns or gas used in their jails; it is all kept in control by agreement. The inmates all work, and the prisons are clean and spotless. Lots of the men have long sentences, so the prison becomes their home. It's absolutely amazing what they do. They don't have to use force; it seems as if their system is built on mutual respect. It is very militaristic in a lot of ways and seems to function well.

In Canada, we are just the opposite. We are more about communicating and engaging with the inmate. Correctional Services Canada provides inmates with the most appropriate programs to assist them with their transition back to the community. We best prepare the inmate for a safe transition back into the community. And again, it all goes back to CSC policies and administration, our values and ethics about public safety and security, releasing these individuals in the best way possible back into the community.

One of our former commissioners was actually Scandinavian. When he was brought into Canadian Corrections during the 1990s, he was very much about reintegration. In the last few years, it's been more about the safety of our institutions. While some of our policies have changed, the values and ethics have stayed the same. Our mission statement still hasn't changed to this day. The very first line of our mission statement is, "We believe that all offenders have the potential to change."

This mission statement is still very much practiced today. It remains to be a fundamental part of our values. I think that all offenders do have the potential to change and become law-abiding citizens. With the right programs, controls, and supervision, even more offenders can change. However, there are some individuals with psychopathic behavior that will not change, but it is important to remember that the number of these individuals is small.

In summary, I think we have a very good federal correctional service in Canada, and I am very proud of it.

RP: Thank you for providing your candid opinions and your insight into Canadian correctional issues.

MB: You are welcome. I am very pleased to participate in this project and to be part of Correctional Service Canada.

Interview with Robert Jennings on Corrective Services, Western Australia

8

ANN-CLAIRE LARSEN

Contents

Introduction

The Department of Corrective Services in Western Australia (WA) manages 14 prisons statewide, with varying security statuses. As of January 13, 2011, prison beds numbered 5079 for WA's population of 2,300,000 (Department of Corrective Services). WA recorded the largest proportional (23%) and actual (702) increase in sentenced prisoners, between June 30, 2008 and June 30, 2009, among all Australian states and territories (Australian Bureau of Statistics (ABS) 2009, 29). This includes an increase in female imprisonment in WA from 33 to 41 female prisoners per 100,000 adult females between 1999 and 2009 (ABS 2009, 27). In 2009, the Minister for Corrective Services announced an AUD$655 million strategy for additional prison beds (Porter 2009).

Interview with Robert Jennings, May 17, 2011

I drove 206 km from Perth to interview Robert Jennings. I placed an MP3 player on the table between us, introduced the research project, and handed over an information letter. Jennings signed the interview consent form. The interview lasted 1 h and 45 min.

Before retiring in 2010, Robert Jennings was a superintendent at Casuarina, WA's maximum security prison for males. He had worked in corrections for 34 years, including 28 years in WA as a welfare officer, an assistant superintendent, and a superintendent at prisons. He answered each question in a calm, authoritative manner. The views recorded are his own.

Career

Jennings was a pilot in Britain before moving into corrections. He explains,

> I saw in an American flying magazine in the late 1960s that they had programs for disadvantaged kids in trouble to learn to fly and go on camps. I thought it was a good idea to get kids involved. I talked to people like United Biscuits, a biscuit company. We got kids from an approved school in Britain. We'd show them airplanes and teach them various things. Then, I started doing voluntary work for the probation service. Then, I was ill and the chief probation officer said to me, "Why don't you become a probation officer if you don't think you be able to fly anymore?" They paid for me to go to a university, and I got into corrections.
>
> We came to WA, because my wife is Australian. I started off at Bunbury Prison in 1989 as a prison welfare officer. I did an accelerated prison administrators' course. I was chief officer at Fremantle Prison in uniform, and it went on from there. I worked as superintendent at Bandyup (women's maximum security prison), Casuarina (men's maximum security prison), and Hakea Prisons.

Jennings was a superintendent at WA's maximum security prison for women.

> I have been away from Bandyup (women's maximum security prison) for a long while, but they used euphemistic phrases. They talk about the "women's estate." They'd mean the number of cells. Women tend to be overregulated in prison and charged more than they should be internally with petty charges and generally managed as if they are fallen angels.
>
> It is difficult when a woman goes before a magistrate or a judge, given the social background of most judges and magistrates. Instead of being dealt with for what they have done, stolen from their employer, there is a moral imperative. They are a fallen woman, because a good woman wouldn't do that. That's still around.

Although surprised to find himself in corrections, Jennings remarked, "Mind you, aviation was full of crooks as well."

Corrections provided benefits but few rewards.

I have been very fortunate to have independence in my working life. In corrections, you don't always see positives. You can't look back and see a hundred success stories. You will never know your successes, because they don't come back. I enjoyed working with a diverse range of people: prisoners and staff.

Changes

Since the early 1990s, changes abound.

Lots of changes. Corrective services have developed. But, it's like everything. There have been periods when it's gone backward. The role of custodial officers has changed. They are more involved in the total management of prisoners, not just turning keys. In well-run prisons, there's a more integrated approach to managing prisoners. The role of psychiatrists, social workers, the nurse, and the teacher is seen as important. One big team, not just prison officers and others.

The role of prison officers has also changed.

The push by WA to get prison officers involved with managing prisoners rather than just opening doors has worked well. It's gone further than some people would have ever dreamed and is not as good as some people would like.
Prison officers are the best people to manage anger management programs. Getting prison officers involved in change management programs is a good idea. It is still only patchy, but it is accepted. It is not something that you couldn't aspire to because you have seen your mate doing it. Integrating female staff into male prisons is positive.

A wide range of professionals work in WA prisons.

A change has been the integration of nonuniformed staff, for example, psychiatrists, social workers, teachers—everybody into the management of prisoners. When managing at-risk prisoners, it's everyone's responsibility in the prison, from the chaplain to the prison officer. They all sit at the table. That was unheard of 20 years ago. Often, we don't celebrate the successes, because we are too negative.
The superintendent is responsible for everything in prisons. You don't do it all yourself. At Casuarina, for instance, we had a 50-bed hospital, so you've got nurses and an education center and programs people and industries. So, there is a vast range of professionals in the prison system. That is another good thing since the 1980s.

Yes, political changes. WA led Australia in corrective services innovation in the early 1980s, and it doesn't have anything to do with which political party was in power. There was consistency with the same attorney general for a lengthy period and the same head of corrections. There was some genuine change in innovation and reform.

Self-harm has dropped dramatically since the early 1990s. It is interesting at Casuarina Prison or Fremantle Prison, particularly with the disturbed and vulnerable prisoners. It was a daily event with people self-harming. We improved the services, and we stopped them being marginalized. We took them out of the units, gave them work and a structured day. A whole range of excellent ideas came from prison officers and young administrators.

Casuarina, a male maximum security prison, has 572 beds as of 30 June 2011 (Department of Corrective Services 2009/2010). Although Casuarina was innovative on opening in 1991, recent developments seem less encouraging.

Casuarina Prison is an epitome of change. They designed a prison on 100 acres that was expensive, but it couldn't be expanded. Lots of people are now saying, "How awful," but the thought behind it was very intelligent. They thought, the more prisons you have, the more prisons you fill. They are now putting two new units on at Casuarina. I bet the architects were saying, "You have all the space here, and why is it so difficult?" The place was designed that way. That is why Fremantle Prison closed so quickly after Casuarina opened. You don't build prisons that you can add on to, or you suddenly end up with warehousing people, which is what we do at the moment. Warehousing people.

Overcrowding in prisons produces "warehousing," which is detrimental to correctional reform (see the work of Hinds 2006, 211) and prison culture.

Overcrowding changes the mindset of the people who run prisons. Warehousing means not finding meaningful work for the people or education. These take second place to the day-to-day stuff. I have seen the prison system go backward. There are always pockets of excellence.

One political leader was quoted recently saying that double-bunking was a good thing. I'd like to see what piece of research supports that. It must be new stuff. Double-bunking is fine sometimes if you have people for their first night put in with buddy or people who are going through crisis, but people need their own social space. I find it (double-bunking) beyond reasonable debate.

"Warehousing" is exacerbated when too many indigenous people and people with a mental illness are incarcerated.

Casuarina opened in 1991, and the total number of prisoner population was 1650 in WA. Shortly after, the Frankland unit at Graylands Hospital opened for forensic patients. Now, the prison population is about 4500. The number of beds at Graylands hasn't expanded. So, our management of mental health and people with disabilities hasn't improved. Prison is a warehouse for a lot of people who shouldn't be there.

Twenty years after the Royal Commission into Aboriginal Deaths in Custody, Mick Gooda, the Aboriginal and Torres Strait Islander Social Justice Commissioner, claims that most of the commission's 339 recommendations have been disregarded (Standing Committee on Aboriginal and Torres Strait Islander Affairs 2011, 1). Aboriginal and Torres Strait Islander people comprised 3.8% of WA's population (ABS 2006, 16); yet, prisoner census data show that the number of indigenous men and women in custody has increased markedly: 55% for indigenous men and 47% for indigenous women between 2000 and 2010 (Standing Committee on Aboriginal and Torres Strait Islander Affairs 2011, 8). Approximately 40% of the prisoners in WA are aboriginal (see Loh et al. 2007, ix).

Jennings attributes indigenous imprisonment rates to drug-related crimes.

> For anybody who manages corrections, we'd say a pivotal change in corrections was injecting drugs. The way management ran the prison, the culture of the prison, it had a massive impact on prisons.
>
> I suppose when aboriginal people developed a needle habit, when they first started using speed in the early 1990s, not many aboriginals were using heroin in WA. That had an impact on aboriginal people.
>
> I get bored silly hearing people quote the imprisonment rate and what they are going to do, but the reality is, what major changes have we enacted to deal with that issue? We have played around at the margins.

Throughout Australia, "indigenous juveniles are 28 times more likely than nonindigenous juveniles to be incarcerated" (Standing Committee on Aboriginal and Torres Strait Islander Affairs 2011, vix). As of June 30, 2007, indigenous young people were 43 times more likely to be detained per population in WA (Taylor 2009, 30). Their overrepresentation in WA "has been consistently higher than the national average" (Richards 2011, 3).

WA prisons are consequently overcrowded. Jennings attributes overcrowding to law and order politics, "which has dominated the crime control debate as well as policy making since the 1960s and 1970s" (Hinds 2006, 204). WA has had the "highest proportional increases in prisoner numbers" (17%; ABS 2009, 26).

> We had a significant population of remote aboriginals in Casuarina. It was never designed for that. We started a special program, and we redesigned a whole unit just for that. A change in policy came when Sue Gordon (Aboriginal magistrate) did the stuff of domestic violence and then child abuse in the aboriginal communities, which generated a bigger custodial population, as did a greater police presence in Warbarton and places. We haven't built a prison up there. They are down here. So, when people wander around and yell about prisons being overcrowded, if they were doing the job they were set out to do, there would be no more need for more maximum security prisoners than the original design of Casuarina if everybody was housed how they should be.

Changes in custodial culture occur inadvertently.

By default, Casuarina was a great place for indigenous people from remote areas. They were locked in the walls at Fremantle Prison. At Casuarina, they had trees to sit under and open space and could wander around. More importantly, there was no bureaucracy about them seeing management. You didn't have to put in a form or go to a parade. You could see the boss just walking around, and for aboriginal people, that is really important.

Relatives phone the superintendent in most WA prisons. You are walking around talking to prisoners all day, every day. It would be unheard of in other prisons. You don't run prisons from offices. If you want to reform prisons, you have to walk around. Years ago, someone asked me, "What is it like trying to change prisons?" It's a bit like stirring custard with your eyebrow. Painful and slow. There is an unholy alliance between prisoners and prison officers to stop change.

Technologies affect WA prison practices.

Prisoners didn't have access to phones in the 1980s. They could write letters if they could write. Now, quite appropriately, they can go and pick up the phone. A lot of the girlfriends are on home detention. You see these young men on Saturday morning saying, "Where were you? What time did you get home?" There is very controlling behavior. Yes, there can be problems. The prison system is very good at controlling this, but it's another issue that prison staff have to manage. Restraining orders mean a letter can't be sent to this person, and trying to keep track of all that is horrendous. Prisons do an excellent job of dealing with all that.

As of June 30, 2009, females comprised 7% (2125) of the total Australian prisoner population (ABS 2009, 8).

Women's imprisonment has changed dramatically. When I first ran Bandyup, if there were two women in the cell, they had to have their feet on the floor when they watched the TV. They couldn't have a blanket over them.

Jennings' approach to corrections was grounded in practice.

You can get change, but leaders have to be visible and have a presence. That is a lot of rhetoric about leadership, but it's a bit like horses and carts. The horse is at the front. You don't push a cart. That sounds a bit arrogant, but it's true. For most superintendents in WA, there is not an area in the prison where they won't walk alone.

It's all meaningless if a prison officer can't go up to you and say, "What is going on in that unit is not right, the way the female staff are being treated," or a prisoner says, "This is happening, Mr. J. Just check it out." Once you get away from that and into the compliance model, where it's all tick and flick, there may be a veneer of ethical management, but is it actually happening on the floor? I don't know.

The aging prison population needs attention.

One issue about offending late in life that is often scoffed over is how much offending is linked to gambling habits, both male and female. Men kill loved ones or their lover's boyfriend or the grandfather for a crime he committed 30 years ago. That wasn't around much in the 1980s. The police got better at protecting kids to give evidence.

How prisoners are managed reflects societal attitudes that influence prison values. WA's Department of Correctional Services will offer to test new prison entrants for sexually transmitted infections and blood-borne viruses (Watkins et al. 2009).

Before Fremantle Prison closed, the big issue was how many people with HIV would be managed in the prison system. At its height, there were only three or four known HIV carriers. Originally, we isolated them completely. Now, we mainstream them. You tell the staff to use universal precautions. Has the world fallen apart? Not at all.

The other thing was transvestites. We thought we would have a huge problem. We made a revolutionary decision in WA that, if we assess them and they were genuinely living a female lifestyle, we would manage them in a female prison, which we did, pre–sex change. It was a better environment, and it worked. That is progressive.

High-profile people can be difficult to manage. It's important they receive the services they are entitled to; no more, no less. One of my colleagues once said that Fremantle Prison is the most egalitarian society in the world. "I don't care what religion you are or where you come from. I am going to treat you all the same." He meant that, and he was right.

As sentencing changes and the length of sentencing, it is a huge issue caring for dementia people who are not mobile. At the moment, we tend to default to the hospital area of prison. It isn't a good place. It was never an issue for us in the early 1990s. Hopelessness is all a part of the aging population. We will end up with a geriatric unit in a prison. At the moment, Casuarina manages those people. They need medical attention; they don't need maximum security.

Jennings' personal correctional philosophy:

First, have a long-term philosophy: strategic thinking, not a 4-year political cycle. Genuine changes take about 10–15 years. When law and order suddenly became sexy for politicians, you got this cycle of mediocrity in decision making. Correctional change doesn't fit into a 4-year cycle. Corrections need to be taken outside politics to get real change. It's fairly naïve of me to say that, but that's what I believe. In WA corrections, we are bombarded with law and order.

We have a dumbing down of strategic thinking on corrections. "We are going to get tougher than this one, and we are going to stay in longer." You end up with more people in prison. You build more prison beds. You have overcrowding. We went from a system that had single beds everywhere to when I left; every bed was double-bunked. I was 130% over the design capacity in 2008/2009.

Prisons are businesses.

Prisons are expensive places to run. In maximum security, it's AUD$100,000 each prisoner. It's a complex business that costs taxpayers a lot of money. They deserve to have their money spent wisely. Prison superintendents must have a business approach.

Serco manages WA's private medium security prison holding 1000 male prisoners. In 2011, the WA Department of Corrective Services was fined AUD$285,000 for an aboriginal elder's death from heat stroke (ABC News 2011). Mr. Ward died in the back of a prison van operated by a private security company GSL (now G4S; Baldino et al. 2010, 418). Consequently, the issue of appropriate oversight frameworks essential for quality control has emerged. Jennings' view on WA's privately run prison:

> I have philosophical difficulties about WA's private prison. If we say the top end of our scale of measures we take against our citizens is to deprive them of their liberties, we don't execute them anymore. Do we feel it appropriate to put it in the hands of a private operator? The private prison was introduced almost as if you don't have one private prison; we are going to privatize others. So, officers had a fear about that.
>
> They do run the private prison 30% cheaper. They pay people less and have less people on the ground. Do they do it better? I don't know. There are tremendous hidden costs about private prisons. The compliance costs are high to have an army of people to supervise how the prison is running. When you factor their wages into it, that puts up costs.

Politics and economics are primary concerns, but the damaging effects of incarceration on prisoners need attention.

> It all needs to come back to two simple things. One, if someone comes to prison, you make sure they don't come out worse than when they come in. You need programs in prison to deal with the debilitating effects of institutionalization. Two, as a society, there is a reasonable and right expectation that you should try to help people in prison.
>
> Prisons are closed institutions, like mental hospitals. A prison is doing an excellent job if it stops people from being institutionalized, one factor in stopping them coming back. But, many people put too much expectations on prisons.
>
> When you make a mistake, just say, "We have made a mistake. We got it wrong." Don't tie it up in bullshit.

Problems with WA Corrections

Providing quality prison services means knowing prisoners' fears.

The minute someone comes to prison, it's a stressor. It upsets people's sensibilities. If you ask any kid when he comes in what his biggest fear is, it is sexual assault. That's not saying it's a real fear, because fortunately, it is far less than people advocate. So, you have got to balance that with who they are in with and what the reasons are. So, you end up with a long bureaucracy of assessment and prison officers filling those tick-and-flick checklists, which are really about compliance, not quality. They are to say, "We checked, and he is alright to go into that cell with that person." No. In the long run, they are better off having their own space.

Despite the Royal Commission, 20 years on, little has changed.

Suicide, either indigenous or nonindigenous, was not a prevalent thought in correction managers' minds or architects' minds. Casuarina was designed so that prisoners could open windows that give them access to a horizontal bar. It's designed like an airplane to see the space outside. When looking through, you don't see it as a hanging point. I had my head torn off by the coroner. "How could we have places like that?" But, those issues were not around then. We have gone through terrible rates of suicide in WA, far too many, unfortunately. I have been the superintendent or the assistant superintendent with between 17 and 20 deaths. The rate of suicide has gone through peaks and troughs. Back in 2001/2002, we went through a bad time, but that has to be seen in the context of suicide in young males in WA anywhere, and that is pretty high. It's a low point when you deal with suicide.

Drugs in WA prisons are problematic.

Alcohol was the thing of the 1970s and 1980s. Mentioning drugs in prisons is not politically correct in some circles. Any superintendent or administer who stood in front of camera or went to an inquiry and said, "There are no drugs in my prison," should be sacked immediately. He is a fool, a liar, or both. We had contact visits in the WA prison system, not conjugal visits like in other states. People sit with loved ones. It is inevitable that drugs will be passed. Some staff bring drugs in, very rarely in the last 15 years in WA, not so many hard drugs as cannabis. The bush lawyers in prison would argue that, when we introduced urine testing, we encouraged the use of opiates. Cannabis can be detected 74–76 days after you've taken it. If you take heroin, 36 h later, it's not present in a urine test.

We have entered a dangerous philosophy: sentencing to be helped. From a judge's point of view, it is far more palatable to say to someone, "I am going to sentence you to x number of years in prison, and during that time, I want you to address your anger management, your sex offender management," and then we have these hurdles. If they don't do it, they stay in prison longer. So, if I were a kid, I'd say, "Just lock me up, because I am going to get out quicker." In our society, if you are a child and taken into care, you are being looked after by the state for a very long time. I'd rather get 4 months and come out.

Prisoners are like that. They are getting longer sentences, because they are getting sentences to be helped. It is more palatable to keep them in, because we are going to treat them. We went through a period where we were deferring people's parole for 8 months, another 8 months in prison, while they do an 8 h course. Absolutely crazy. It's a bit like the emperor's got no clothes and nobody is allowed to say.

It's very fashionable to treat prisoners. It is totally inappropriate, because treatment is a medical model, and if you are being treated, you are not responsible. So, I would not tolerate things like treatment.

Prisons serve as a societal yardstick, but serious management problems exist.

We need prisons. A yardstick for me to know I am good is that I am not in prison. We need to put bad ones in prison. A lot of money is wasted on people who don't need secure custody. Probably 35% or up to 45% of the people in maximum security prisons don't need to be there. It is an expensive way of running prisons.

The remand situation is problematic legally. Look at the number of people in custody on remand who get a disposal with a noncustodial sentence, and we have kept them there for 12–14 months.

The issue of the sex offender is a never-ending debate in WA. Without legislation, an indefinite sentence is a worry; we do it more than anyone. A sex offender was released today with 38 conditions by a judge. A woman said, "Why should one more child be put at risk with this man?" So, the judge said, "We will put him out on these conditions," and the people in the community will say, "If he needs 38 conditions, why is he out, and look how expensive it is."

Considering the issue of inappropriately housed prisoners:

If we had facilities with less of a custodial flavor and more a nurturing flavor, more caring, where those people went and didn't come out of, the ethical issue/debate would not be there for the judge. He'd be happier to leave them in there. Having dealt with people who are institutionalized for a long time, many would be happier to stay in that sort of environment, the sort of place that nuns run. I am not advocating we go back to the sin bins for people or put them in psychiatric hospitals and they never got out. We need a place for intellectually handicapped people who can't survive in the community, because what happens is, as you close psychiatric institutions, patients went into prisons. If I had my way, we would be doing a lot to deal with that as it's very expensive.

Keeping people out of prisons will reduce recidivism.

People become institutionalized when they spend time in an ordered structure where there is little autonomy for them to say how their life will run or how the organization is run as an institution. Many people in custody have gone through the juvenile system. They were trained long before, so they don't consciously reoffend to come back to prison. The biggest deterrent is when it is unknown. The longer you keep kids out of going to the juvenile court, the bigger deterrent it is. When they go to prison, it's no big deal, because they have learned to cope.

Successes Achieved by WA Corrections

Few prisoners escape from WA prisons.

Lots of things work well. The safety of the WA public is maintained. The first responsibility of a prison system is to keep people in. Justice has sent them. We do it very well in WA. There has been one escape from Casuarina in 20 years. WA should be proud of that. The number of escapes in minimum security has dropped.

In general, we treat prisoners with dignity, more so than other jurisdictions. Staff care about their job, which is excellent. If you speak to some wizened old prison officer, he will tell you the negative and walk away. But, watch him do his job and ask the prisoners, "Why do you go to him, grumpy old sod?" "Well Mr. J., he always does it." What that means is, "If you are entitled to it, he goes and fixes it up for me." When you are in prison, you are powerless, so you rely on prison officers for everything. If it's a genuine no, not a capricious no, that's fine. Prison officers mostly care about their jobs more so than people in the community.

Theory and Practice

Jennings believes theory informs good management. His practice was informed by prison management theory, promoting security, control (order), and justice for prisoners and staff, as well as Andrew Coyle's work. Much research is already done on prison management. However, for the government to allow research, timing has to be right. Research has shown that, for example, "it's a furphy (rumor) that long sentences reflect community safety." *Throughcare* is a management strategy requiring prisoners to be cared for from presentence through to release and is practiced in WA. Jennings explains WA's theoretical position on punishment.

> We had a basic philosophy of WA prisons, but I haven't heard it expressed for a long while. Prison is a place where you serve your punishment; you don't come to be punished. That doesn't go down well with a lot of people. Prisoners were to be treated in a humane and just manner, provided with opportunities to "better themselves" in the broadest context, education and work. At Casuarina, we used to make people get ready to go to work, and it was their choice whether they had breakfast or not. "I am not your lover or your mother." A lot of people did not have structure in their lives. Bettering themselves has been a part of corrective service philosophy when it is not a warehouse.

Prisoners are regulated and given opportunities to work (mostly).

> When you are an unsentenced prisoner in WA, you can only be made to clean your cell and areas you use. When you are a sentenced prisoner, you are obliged to work. If you don't, you are sanctioned. You can't buy anything, or you may be secured in your cell during the working day. That is rarely done. People have obligations as well. Very few people refuse to work in prisons. When a prison is overcrowded, there is not enough work. We offered the whole spectrum of work: mental work, wood work, leather work, print work, cooking, baking, everything.

Jennings' views on student placements are telling.

> Community corrections moved to a compliance model with people reporting. They have adopted a British model. I've got friends that work in community corrections. They are terribly disillusioned. They are overworked, and there has been a dumbing down of the training.
> When I came from the U.K., there was a real elitism about WA probation services. They were all tertiary trained in sociology, but I was thinking that this is not exactly probation training. You haven't been trained in counseling and supervision. If you want to talk about ethics and reaching high standards, it really depends on the supervision of social workers and probation officers and whatever; on the academic training, they are doing their placements out of university. What is the quality of supervision on the floor? How much is the university supervising when they are out? You have supervision to get rid of the bad ones on placements. There is a poor level of student placement in WA compared with the U.K.
> In the U.K., you had status if you were to supervise a probation officer or a social worker student on their final placement. You were a qualified probation officer or social worker who had good academic skills, were good people with analytic skills, and had done training in student supervision. I have never seen that in WA. The 4-year social work degree, it is very Mickey Mouse.

Prison officers have a difficult job.

You have to switch off from what prisoners have done. When prisoners received a sentence, my job is to do this, this, and this. I am not there to judge him. That is same with prison officers, or they don't often stay long as prison officers. It is difficult to deal with people who have committed offenses against young children; however, when you look at those who are managing those people, you often find the best interaction of any service. Despite changes, stereotypical views of prison officers remain in the community.

A prison is a negative environment. People are surprised at the level of report writing expected of prison officers. But, if they go to a party and most people have a vicarious interest in corrections, everybody says straight away, "You are a do-gooder," if you talk about what you try to do for a prisoner, or they ask, "Do you thump them?" That's what they want to hear. Or, they want to tell you what to do. Everyone has a view on corrections or law and order. They want you to lock them up and leave them, or you are too tough. That is difficult for everyone in corrective services.

Long-term planning for corrections is essential.

Money for prisons is becoming tougher. So, those charged with running prisons will find it more difficult, because the dollar will not be there. Costs won't go down. In the short term, we rush to build more beds in prisons. But, what is the purpose of that? You got to have infrastructure around it. We have got to have a long-term plan.

In the last 6 years, I worked in corrections; I never saw a long-term plan. We're building new prisons as a knee-jerk response. I don't blame the individuals at the top. It's the nature of the business. So, the future is not particularly rosy for corrections. In 5 years' time, the same debate will still be there.

Institutionalization must be balanced against prison routines that may be advantageous for some prisoners.

Everyone is different. When people have serious substance abuse issues, they dry out in prison. Parents say, "I've got my son back. He would have been dead on the street." A mum says, "at least we know where he is." Some people improve their health. They didn't eat on the outside. Some psychiatric people get on the right medication. They are stable and a different person.

Cognitive skills programs work well. Having a team approach to programs involving prison officers who speak the same language as prisoners and provide feedback is essential.

Preventing recidivism has remained elusive. In WA, "70% of indigenous male prisoners reoffended following release from prison compared to approximately 40% of nonindigenous offenders" (Senate Select Committee 2010, 21).

It's interesting what changes people. You get someone who says, "I have had enough of this life. I don't want to spend prison time with these kids." They don't come back. The penny drops. So, it's nothing we have done. They mature in their thirties. It's mostly males between 16 and 28 years. We also know once they reach 28 years, they don't come back. But, research does not tell us who to target; who is going to be serious recidivists. We are no further there.

Evidence-Based Corrections

If you think prison deters people from committing crime, evidence-based philosophy doesn't support that much. If you think being punitive in prison stops people committing crime, the evidence-based philosophy doesn't support that either. The recidivism rate from Fremantle in the 1970s was no higher than it is now, and that was pretty punitive. Everybody wants a quick answer, and there isn't one. Corrections need a more holistic approach.

International Developments in Corrections Have Influenced WA Corrections

In the late 1980s, the influence was Scandinavian. Now, whether that was a good model or not, given the social fabric of Scandinavia and the conservativeness of WA, but we were influenced by Scandinavia, and that's when unit management came in. Then, we looked to Canada; they seemed to impress government; they seemed to connect with particularly the indigenous population of Canada. Then, in the last 5 years, there's been a strong English influence in prisons. I am not quite sure now what corrective philosophies are worthwhile, taking on from the U.K. There may be good ones.

The British run a very rigid prison system. A more subtle influence that affects the way prisons are run has been about the prison officers as a uniformed corp. WA's superintendents never wore a uniform. Now, we are requiring prison administrators to wear uniforms. While you want people to be proud of their uniform, you want them to think outside the box of just being a uniform officer; you want them to do lots of things.

There has been a huge change in accountability and human rights for prisoners such as the ombudsman. A lot of foreign prisoners in WA jails would prefer to stay in WA than go back to other countries. Huge changes in those conventions on human rights have affected WA. The management of Muslims, providing them with food, all little issues, and the tensions between non-Muslim, and how do you make sure that a person's ethnicity or religious rights are being met without giving them more than the rest? Those issues are a part of it.

The openness of WA prisons. You get human rights commissioners wandering around. There is much more accountability that is positive. There are more open prisons than in the 1980s. In the 1980s, the *Prison Act* said, "Supreme Court judges could wander around unfettered." But, I never met one. Now, we have the ombudsman, the inspector of custodial services, the Human Rights Commission. Prisoners can go to the Equal Opportunities Commission about issues or to a whole range of outside agencies. It causes management problems and tensions, but they are necessary.

Events overtake people. Because Casuarina was designed based on a Danish philosophy, unit management was introduced, where you get small groups of officers managing a group of prisoners. It never got developed quite as the original plan.

General Assessment

Despite some progress, Jennings calls for theoretically informed decision making.

I have dealt with superb people for both the Liberal party and the Labor party. But, we have been caught up with a whirlpool of quick TV grabs of who can be tougher. You do not lead corrections administration by being popular. The first thing to learn as a corrections administrator is you are not popular. You do not make meaningful change on the back of the editor of *The West Australian* newspaper. You do it by having a philosophical base. All you need to do is sit back and ask, "Is this right? What is the right thing to do?" It's never about it suiting shock jocks or do-gooders.

Ask, "In the twenty-first century, is this the way we should be dealing with people?" Some procedures may be tough. Is it right that we have a prisoner who cannot read and write? We keep them in prison for 7 years, then we let them out, and they still can't read and write? The government needs to have tough love. To say to a young man, "You are going to read and write. If you don't, or if you don't try, there may be some more sanctions in the prison." Don't you think that's right? That we teach people? We get too complicated.

What we do is compliance. In Victoria, when some awful prisoner gets out of prison, there is no big deal. In WA, there is heat on the minister. This is the politics of WA corrections. I haven't heard a minister talk about what his philosophy is for WA. Without Liberal bashing, at the last election, they came up with the argument they wanted a young person's prison for 18- to 25-year-olds, and no child should live in poverty either. But why? What is your thinking behind it?

If you go into a juvenile detention center, look around. It's full of aboriginal kids. If you are a superintendent in the adult custodial system, you talk about when they come to you (in the adult prison). I am happy to be tough, but there has to be evidence to the toughness. If you want that, there has to be a purpose. Not because it makes you look good. I hope someone calls me a do-gooder when I am dead, because I am sure the people who got rid of slavery were do-gooders and people were do-gooders who stopped children 8 years old in the eighteenth century from working in factories in Britain.

There is not much statesmanship in politics. I don't see much change coming.

The English-speaking world had seen increasingly punitive policies (Roberts and Indermaur 2007, 56).

The public has a perception that sentences are far too lenient, and that's got worse not better, despite efforts of the chief justice. It's got worse by the constant shock jocks on the radio producing great discord. Public perceptions change dramatically when it's their friend or relative. It's (sentence) far too harsh.

I don't miss it. I miss the people. It was a 24-h job. I enjoyed going to work.

It's changed a bit. A riot had a dramatic effect, and it took time for the staff to get their confidence back. You are managing dangerous people in a university campus environment. It takes staff a while to adjust.

WA has made favorable changes, but much could be improved.

I have always had rapport with remote aboriginals and those with mental illness. I have always spent a lot of time trying to improve mental health services in prisons.

Despite their prison experiences, prisoners need support following release to affect recidivism.

When someone leaves prisons, if they don't have social support, a roof over their head or don't have money or don't have work or skills or opportunity, the chances of them succeeding are very low. That has not changed in 50 years. A book written in the 1950s or early 1960s by a probation officer in London was called *I Give Them Money*. He said, if they haven't got any money for a roof over their head, no amount of making them feel good on the inside is going to change them. It's a balance. A lot more emphasis is needed on what happens to them on release, not tokenism, if we genuinely want to stop people coming back to custody.

Release procedures have improved dramatically. But, coming from an appalling low base, it is caring tokenism. I read yesterday about people coming out of prison and getting state houses. If we don't want people coming back to prison, we got to have a whole government approach to managing it. NGOs don't have resources. If I had to decide between how much money I'd spend on prison treatment programs, I would spend the bulk of the money on transition to community, how you manage them the first few months.

We all hope to change young people by nurturing them when they come into custody. They show a work ethic. Some of the aboriginal kids are exceptional at sport. But, when they leave, they will not have the status they had in prison from staff or peers and no support mechanisms. The chances of them going back into a law-abiding lifestyle are pretty slim. That is sad. Stressful.

My biggest regret is we have not moved forward in dealing with aboriginal imprisonment. I wish I could say something more positive. We learned how to manage them better, and most junior staff have a better understanding of aboriginal culture and treat them in a more appropriate way in programs in prisons, etc. But, reducing aboriginal incarceration, nothing has changed in 40 years. No. The same rhetoric.

Jennings preferred not to comment further on developments. He said, "There's been an influx of people from the U.K. with a different philosophy, and that's up to them to explain that."

Despite the changes and working with offenders, Jennings enjoyed his work.

Stressful? I never found it too stressful. My staff used to say I am a carrier, not a sufferer. No. But, that is not true. The mere fact that anybody is working in prison, you become institutionalized, unless you're careful. People don't like to admit that.

The only real change you will get with the community on penal change is when they realize how every time you want us to build more prisons, that means one less school. Our rate of imprisonment has gone up dramatically. Is this place any safer?

Conclusion

Years of practice informed Jennings' views on corrections. For him, practices in prisons must be researched, evidence based, and have a sound philosophical base. A long-term strategy rather than vote-catching politics is essential for corrections. New thinking is required to address overcrowded prisons, as building more prisons is not the answer, and double-bunking leads to "warehousing" prisoners. How indigenous offenders and those with mental health problems and dementia are dealt with currently is inappropriate, ineffective, and financially wasteful. In turn, prison culture is adversely affected. Thus, alternative facilities are required for some prisoners. Furthermore, institutionalization must be guarded against as prison processes tend to contribute to recidivism, particularly juvenile recidivism. A team approach to managing prisoners, which involves prison officers, advances WA corrections. For him, prisons are a closed microcosm of society heavily influenced by politics.

However, there is no place in prisons for treatment programs. Jennings' message is to ask: Is this the right thing to do? Although frustrated by the imprisonment rates for indigenous and other vulnerable offenders, Jennings is proud of his achievements in corrections.

References

ABC News. 2011. http://www.abc.net.au/news/stories/2011/07/07/3263929.htm?section =justin. Accessed July 7, 2011.

Australian Bureau of Statistics. 2006. *Population Characteristics, Aboriginal and Torres Strait Islander Australians.* No. 4713.0. Canberra: Government of Australia. http://www.ausstats.abs.gov.au/ausstats/subscriber.nsf/0/526FE126443EBCC6 CA257718001D547F/$File/47130_2006_reissue.pdf. Accessed July 7, 2011.

Australian Bureau of Statistics. 2009. *Prisoners in Australia.* No. 4517.0. Canberra: Government of Australia. http://cdn.justice.act.gov.au/resources/uploads/Neo/ abs/45170_2009.pdf. Accessed June 24, 2011.

Baldino, D., M. Drum, and B. Wyatt. 2010. The privatization of prisoner transfer services in Western Australia: What can we learn from the Ward case? *The Australian Journal of Public Administration* 69(4): 418–430.

Department of Corrective Services home page. http://www.correctiveservices.wa.gov .au/prisons/default.aspx. Accessed July 12, 2011.

Department of Corrective Services' Annual Report. 2010/2011. Government of Western Australia. http://www.correctiveservices.wa.gov.au/_files/about-us/statis tics-publications/dcs-annual-report-2010-2011.pdf. Accessed May 30, 2012.

Hinds, L. 2006. Challenging current conceptions of law and order. *Theoretical Criminology* 10: 203–221.

Loh, N. S. N., M. G. Maller, J. A. Fernandez, A. M. Ferrante, and M. R. J. Walsh. 2007. *Crime and Justice Statistics for Western Australia Statistical Report (2005): 1 January 2005–31 December 2005.* Crime Research Centre. The University of Western Australia. http://www.crc.law.uwa.edu.au/_data/page/38151/stats_ report_2005_without_maps.pdf. Accessed July 11, 2011.

Porter, C. 2009. Eastern Goldfields Regional Prison. Questions Without Notice No. 433 Asked in the Legislative Assembly on May 19, 2009. Parliament of Western Australia, Perth. http://www.parliament.wa.gov.au/parliament/pquest.nsf/ 969994fcf861850d4825718d002fe7fb/9c986014517e1e0ec82575be000ef2e6? OpenDocument. Accessed July 11, 2011.

Richards, K. 2011. Trends in juvenile detention in Australia. *Trends & Issues in Crime and Criminal Justice.* No. 416. Australian Institute of Criminology, Australian Government. http://www.aic.gov.au/documents/D/6/D/%7BD6D891BB-1D5B-45E2-A5BA-A80322537752%7Dtandi416.pdf. Accessed July 12, 2011.

Roberts, L. D., and D. Indermaur. 2007. Predicting Punitive Attitudes in Australia. *Psychiatry, Psychology and Law* 14(1): 56–65.

Senate Select Committee on Regional and Remote Indigenous Communities. 2010. *Indigenous Australians, Incarceration and the Criminal Justice System.* Discussion paper prepared by the committee secretariat. http://www.aph.gov.au/senate/ committee/indig_ctte/Final_RRIC.pdf. Accessed July 7, 2011.

Standing Committee on Aboriginal and Torres Strait Islander Affairs. 2011. *Doing Time—Time for Doing: Indigenous Youth in the Criminal Justice System.* Canberra: Parliament of Australia.

Taylor, N. 2009. Juveniles in detention 1981–2007. *AIC Reports Monitoring Reports 05.* Canberra: Australian Institute of Criminology, Australian Government. Accessed July 7, 2011.

Watkins, R. E., D. B. Mak, and C. Connelly. 2009. Testing for sexually transmitted infections and blood borne viruses on admission to Western Australian prison. *BMC Public Health* 9: 385.

Interview with Timothy Leo, Chief Psychologist of the Singapore Prison Service

9

ANDREW DAY
SHARON CASEY

Contents

Introduction

Singapore is a small but densely populated country, with a resident population of just over 5 million people. It is near the equator, located south of Malaysia in Southeast Asia, and although made up of more than 60 different islands, has a total land mass of only 272 mi² (704 km²). Singapore is a relatively new country, which became independent only in 1965, when it separated from the Federation of Malaysia after a long period of British rule. Lee Kuan Yew, Singapore's senior minister and prime minister for more than 40 years following independence, developed a strong vision of how Singapore should be governed which has profoundly shaped not only the economic development of the country but also the current criminal justice system. According to Hor (2000) the major thrust of this policy was, for many years, "the progressive removal of 'obstacles' to conviction, severe punishment of the convicted, and where conviction is not possible, executive detention as a fallback" (p. 1). Nonetheless, the Singaporean criminal justice system has a strong British colonial legacy, and Singapore courts interpret the legal codes in much the same way as occurs in any system of common law.

In this interview, Timothy Leo, chief psychologist with the Singapore Prison Service (SPS), describes how the Singapore Prison Service has undergone transformational organizational changes in its efforts to develop a correctional system that optimizes opportunities for offender rehabilitation and reintegration. A broad suite of rehabilitative initiatives are now routinely offered to prisoners which rivals those offered in any other jurisdiction [for example, see the work of Heseltine et al. (2011)], and the number of specialist rehabilitation providers now includes more than 80 full-time psychologists and correctional counselors.

Leo is a Singapore national who completed his postgraduate education in Auckland, New Zealand, before working as a clinical psychologist in forensic mental health and with the family court. He joined the Singapore Prison Service more than 10 years ago, at the time when interest in offender rehabilitation was reemerging after a period in which it had not been considered core business. As in other jurisdictions, the rehabilitation of offenders was relatively undeveloped at the time.

Over the course of his career in Singapore, Leo has been responsible for the development of psychological services and psychology-based programs throughout the prison system, and he has been a key driver behind the rehabilitation policies that now characterize the service. This interview with Leo, conducted in his office in Singapore, utilized the semistructured format used for all of the interviews that are described in this book. It is, however, reported here in relation to four key questions. These relate to his personal philosophy and motivation for working in corrections, the main changes that have been implemented in Singapore over the last 10 years, and his views about some of the directions for the future. Finally, Leo reflects on how the Singapore Prison Service has been able to achieve so much in what is a relatively short period of time. These responses are then discussed in relation to a commentary from the authors on modern correctional policy and what other jurisdictions can learn from the Singapore experience in implementing organizational change.

What is your personal correctional philosophy and motivation for working in correctional services in Singapore?

Leo began the interview by offering a brief description of the context in which correctional services are offered in Singapore. This was presented as an important factor in both his decision to join the prison service and, more broadly, in the subsequent development of rehabilitation services:

> Singapore is an Asian country that is also multiracial. Being a small densely populated nation, the need for racial harmony and a mutual respect for each other's culture is paramount to the nation's survival and competitive edge. Yet, we are also a pragmatic nation, benefitting from knowledge and approaches from the outside, while holding on to our core values that are intrinsic to our cultures and heritage. We inherited much from the British legal and parliamentary systems. The East–West mix also applies to how we run our prison

system, applying what fits in our system and filtering out what is not useful or conflicting with our values and coherence as a people.

In Singapore, the general sentiment among the public here is that the criminal justice system is tough but fair, and within this, there is support for rehabilitation; the Government takes a tough stance toward crime through legislation, enforcement, the inculcation of civic mindedness from the young, and through engaging the community and grassroots leaders in crime prevention programs. This provides the backdrop and foundation on which correctional work is done. Public confidence in the government being able to keep Singapore safe and relatively corruption-free allows prisons to take on rehabilitative efforts without public outcry and antagonism by victims of crime or pressure groups in society. In my view, and this is shared by many in the community, rehabilitation work contributes to making Singapore safe.

At the time he joined the prison service in the early 1990s, Leo had become interested in research that was being conducted in Western countries suggesting that offender rehabilitation programs could have socially significant effects on recidivism if they were designed and delivered in particular ways. In particular, he was interested in how accurately future behavior could be predicted and in the development of assessment methods such as the Level of Service Inventory–Revised (LSI-R), an assessment tool which has been designed to classify those who were most likely to reoffend based on a relatively small number of demographic, personal, and offense variables.

What excited me in the 1990s was the development of structured and actuarial risk assessment instruments and, later, better risk management systems— the debate about purely actuarial instruments versus clinical judgment and the development of clinically structured decision-making models in assessing and managing offender risk.

Leo's interests were, however, more than just academic. It was the opportunity to apply this new technology in ways that could form the basis of a modern prison system that was structured around the need to rehabilitate that he found most exciting:

What got me into Singapore was the organizational change that was underway. When we decided to launch the LSI-R, Singapore was right where the action was to be. I was excited by that—I was coming to work in a system that was really changing for the better. There was a lot of scope for psychology here.

Importantly, there was broader interest within the service in the development of evidence-based programming on the basis of the structured assessment, and a number of new rehabilitative initiatives framed within a focus on secure and humane containment enjoyed strong support from both within and outside of the organization.

No one (in Singapore) has ever challenged rehabilitation. Because we have an evidence base to say that rehabilitation can lower reoffending, thus making Singapore safer, we have greater grounds to say why we should use public funds—this strengthens support.

Rehabilitation in prisons has to be predicated upon a safe and secure prison. With this as a basis, prisons have the foremost duty of executing justice in a humane manner. Apart from this, which involves incarceration as punishment and incapacitation, the prison regime is also meant to deter both the individual offender and the public from committing crime. With these functions, prisons also provide rehabilitation using evidence-informed practices.

What are the main changes that you have seen since joining the prison service?

The last 10 years have witnessed a whole series of changes in Singapore's prisons, which can probably be best described in terms of a paradigm shift. These include the development of a mission statement that privileges rehabilitation, the restructuring of prison housing units, changes in the role and function of custodial staff, and engagement with the community. In Leo's words, there has "been an evolution in correctional thinking from the idea that nothing works through to evidence-based programming on the principles of risk, needs, and responsivity." He was able to readily describe a wide range of different initiatives that had been implemented:

The prison system in the 1990s was distinctly different from today. Major developments in the last 10 years include a risk/needs-based classification system to guide the allocation of rehab resources, a rehabilitation system that is founded on evidence-based practice, a cadre of specialists in psychology and correctional counseling, criminogenic programs for higher risk offenders, increased community involvement within prisons to augment rehabilitation efforts, prison officers who have both custodial and rehabilitative functions, a move from single non-purpose-built prisons to purpose-built clusters of prisons, technologically supported prisons, correctional research and program evaluation capabilities, strategic planning systems, a compelling vision and mission statement crafted by staff, risk-guided release decisions, different early release schemes, diversionary schemes, staff who are proud to be prison officers, the formation and development of the Community Action for the Rehabilitation of Offenders (CARE) network, and public support for rehabilitation and reintegration through the Yellow Ribbon Project (YRP).*

A number of new diversionary programs and alternative sentencing options are also available in Singapore.

---

* The CARE and YRP programs are described in more detail later in this chapter.

Currently, there is a scheme for people with no previous criminal antecedents and where the offense is less serious. These people are diverted from prison but report to a center and are placed on electronic tagging. We also have inmates who are released into Work Release Centers, halfway houses, and home detention. The supervision imposed on them maintains a measure of control over their behavior. These are for people who are at a lower risk of recidivism.

What are some of the future directions for corrections?

Leo described a strong commitment to the ongoing development of the service, particularly in relation to collecting the type of evidence that can directly inform practice.

One of the greatest challenges in the corrections systems today in trying to be faithful to evidence-based practice is to integrate the different components of rehabilitation for a diverse group of offenders who come under different regimes and sentences. The complexity is trying to ensure that the right inmate gets the right service or intervention, especially when we have to balance the provision of rehabilitation with operational demands and challenges.

Our challenge now is not to say we are doing a "good job" and, hence, rest on what we have achieved so far but to push ahead to see what we can do differently and better.

I believe that Singapore is at the threshold of moving to another level of correctional practice. The experience and learnings of the last 10 years have given us a good head start.

Three more specific areas were identified as avenues for further service development. The first of these concerned the environment in which rehabilitation programs are offered.

There is a growing recognition by correctional practitioners that the correctional operating environment and milieu provides a vital context for learning, skill practice, and generalization of learning. This needs to be balanced with the idea of keeping prisons spartan, which gives people the idea that prison is no-nonsense and discipline is paramount.

Within program delivery, a particular challenge for many rehabilitation providers is how to sustain offender motivation to change. It is in this respect that current criminological thought and other models of rehabilitation such as the Good Lives Model [GLM; see the work of Ward and Maruna (2008)] are being considered.

I think the "what works" risk-needs-responsivity (RNR) literature will, in the future, include more Desistance- and GLM-related findings. Both perspectives involve seeing the world through the eyes of the offender. I am also heartened by the recent developments by Andrews, Bonta, and Wormwith on expanding the understanding of the RNR model to include some of the key concepts found in the GLM and Desistance literature.

Finally, the need to develop the whole area of throughcare services and the transition from prison to the community was identified as an emerging area of current activity.

More correctional systems are moving from mainly incarceration to include rehabilitation and then becoming a partner with the community in offender reintegration and prevention of reoffending. In essence, we are talking about the concept and practice of throughcare, where the inmate's rehabilitation can continue even as they reenter society.

I see three movements from incarceration, rehabilitation, and then working on community postrelease initiatives. We are dealing now with more complex systems—the boundaries have expanded.

The expansion of more community-based sentencing options as community rehabilitation capability develops and increases to support such options. I see the community as playing a larger role in offender rehabilitation, both in helping us within the prison but more so in helping to scaffold offenders as they reenter society. Both the scope of their involvement and the extent of their involvement will increase in the next few years. Prisons have begun to work toward developing strategic plans to work toward such a realization.

What do you think have been the drivers of change in Singapore?

We were particularly interested in understanding more about how these changes had been possible in a relatively short period of time. Leo identified a series of internal and external drivers for change. The internal factors included the identification of the following:

I think the marriage of correctional technology, leadership, political will, commitment, and partnership with stakeholders and the community are the vital ingredients for successful correctional practice.

Multimodal organizational transformation using strategic planning, employee engagement in organizational change processes, strategic use of media, introduction of what works practices into prisons, and expanding rehabilitative capabilities while maintaining the safety and security of prisons.

Visionary leadership at the top.

A compelling vision and mission statement.

Development of internal systems of inmate management that allowed for dual roles of prisoner management and rehabilitation.

Openness to learning and a desire to develop and progress further in terms of correctional management and rehabilitation.

Those external factors that were identified included

Support of government.

Public confidence in the legal, penal, and enforcement systems.

Encouraging the public through the YRP and targeting general public and specific segments, e.g., potential employers.

Developing community partner capabilities through the development of the CARE network comprising community partners and various government bodies.

Public awards for SPS in organizational excellence and choice employer in Singapore.

Discussion

Leo was invited to participate in this interview because of his deep understanding and knowledge of the Singapore correctional system and how it has developed over the last decade. In this interview he portrays the Singapore Prison Service as a vibrant, forward-looking organization that has established a system of rehabilitation that possibly rivals that found anywhere else in the Western world. In many ways, Singapore is offered as an example of what is possible when there is the will to implement organizational change in corrections. It thus becomes important to consider aspects of this interview that can help us understand more about how this transformation has occurred. What follows are some comments and reactions to the interview from the authors of this chapter (who are not Singaporean nationals but have worked with the Singapore Prison Service over the last 5 years) that we hope will be of interest to those who work in other jurisdictions and who are interested in developing rehabilitative services.

What Leo is really describing is a deep personal commitment and an organizational embracing of the notion of evidence-based practice in correctional service delivery. Guided by the research evidence that rehabilitation works beyond just incarcerating offenders [for example, see the work of Andrews and Bonta (2010)], the Singapore government broke new ground in its deliberate and concerted effort to develop offender rehabilitation initiatives in corrections. The organization was keen to learn about research conducted in other countries and apply the learnings to the local context. Most obviously, this applied to the identification of a series of offender rehabilitation practice principles that have been derived from meta-analytic reviews of the outcomes of a series of program evaluations that involved thousands of offenders around the world [see Day and Howells (2002)] and have subsequently been widely endorsed by prison and probation services around the Western world [for example, see Ogloff and Davis (2004) and Wormwith et al. (2007)]. These principles currently form the basis for most program accreditation, inspection, and review processes and have been adapted for use in Singaporean prisons. In brief, these suggest that therapeutic efforts should be focused on those who are most likely to reoffend (the higher risk offenders), target those factors that are directly associated with offending, and deliver interventions in ways that have been shown to be most likely to bring about change. Although these three core principles (of risk, needs, and responsivity) are the most well known, Bonta and Andrews (2007) have now identified a total of 17 different principles that are thought to be associated with improved service outcomes.

The first, and possibly most significant, stage in the change process in Singapore was to review the system of case management and sentence planning such that offenders were able to be classified according to the level of risk of reoffense that they presented. The development and local validation of risk assessment tools provided the impetus for this. However, what is apparent from talking to Leo is the level of acceptance for this approach and the commitment to rehabilitation generally, which exists both within the prison system and in the broader community. This is, in our view, a defining feature of the Singaporean system that differentiates it from other Western correctional systems.

Our observation from visiting and working in Singapore's prisons is the level of acceptance that staff at all levels of the organization have for the mission statement of the prison. It seems, then, that a critical first step in organizational change is the development of a shared vision for the service as a whole. Chua Chin Kiat, an ex-director of the Singapore Prison Service, paved the way for change, resulting in the creation of the Prison Vision.

"We aspire to be captains in the lives of offenders committed to our custody. We will be instrumental in steering them toward being responsible citizens with the help of their families and the community. We will thus build a secure and exemplary prison system."

The phrase "Captains of Lives—Rehab, Renew, Restart" is displayed throughout Singapore's prisons, along with messages that align with this mission statement such as "Our mission is to get criminals out of prison," or "We're trained to look for the sparkle, not just the flaw." These reaffirm the values of a service in a manner that is both visible and persuasive.

Perhaps the most impressive thing about the way in which changes have been implemented in Singapore, however, is the strategic approach that has been developed to introduce rehabilitative ideals. Neo (2010) has identified six discrete strategies that have helped the Singapore Prison Service achieve its goals. Each of these strategies is evident in Leo's description of how the organization has changed. For example, the first strategy, the employment of established risk/needs tools, saw the introduction of a case management system that determined rehabilitation pathways based on the assessed risk of reoffense and criminogenic need. The second involved the development of a suite of offending behavior programs and a commitment to program evaluation. The next steps were to develop a throughcare and reintegration framework, to mobilize the community, and to set up a network of community providers and agencies to support prisoners following their release. The final strategy has been to develop the capabilities of correctional workers. These strategies offer those jurisdictions that have yet to fully embrace rehabilitative ideals the basis of a template for service development or for reflection on their current status. For example, although many Western jurisdictions offer a range of offending behavior programs to high-risk offenders, there are few places in the world that have focused their attention on how to mobilize the support of the community for rehabilitative efforts with serious offenders.

In any interview of this nature there may be a tendency for those in leadership positions to portray the achievements of the organization in which they work in an overly positive light. As such, it becomes important to consider the extent to which each of the strategies identified above has been successfully implemented. Certainly, and as Leo describes, the Singapore Prison Service has been able to implement a system of offender case management based on the principles of risk and need. There is also a wide range of offending behavior programs that are offered to moderate- and high-risk offenders, although the effect of these programs on reoffending has yet to be fully established. It would also seem that the needs of correctional workers are being addressed— the prison service has recently achieved one of the highest awards for organizational excellence in Singapore after being rated as a "top 10" employer.

The area in which, in our view at least, the Singapore model has achieved most success has been the ability of the prison service to mobilize community support for rehabilitation. Leo makes references to two important initiatives that, in many ways, illustrate the differences between Singapore and other countries in relation to community support. First, the CARE network is a formal structure within which key government and nongovernment agencies work together toward offender reentry back into the community. Through the Singapore Corporation of Rehabilitative Enterprises (SCORE), offenders are offered vocational training and work programs in market-relevant industries. Second, the YRP, launched in 2004, is an annual campaign aimed at promoting community support for giving offenders a "second chance." The Yellow Ribbon initiative has three objectives: 1) to create *awareness* of giving second chances to ex-offenders; 2) to generate *acceptance* of ex-offenders and their families in the community; and 3) to inspire community *action* to support rehabilitation and reintegration of ex-offenders. It attracts extensive media coverage in Singapore, which is used as a strategic tool for campaign messaging, and was launched with a series of televised and printed advertisements. The program of activities includes a series of activities, such as art exhibitions and concerts, designed specifically to engage the public.

Inmates and ex-offenders participate widely in activities, and this is seen as an integral part of the campaign. It is generally accepted that the message of "help unlock the second prison" has now permeated all levels of society; for example, between 2004 and 2009, nearly 2 million yellow ribbons were distributed, more than 300,000 Singaporeans participated in events, and more than 800 new employers registered to provide employment opportunities to ex-offenders (Soh 2010).

In conclusion, then, Singapore can be considered an Asian country that has embraced the notion of evidence-based practice in its approach to criminal justice. It has embraced some of the ideas from other correctional systems while developing a system of rehabilitation that is uniquely Singaporean. Although there are many areas in which service delivery can still be improved, it represents an example from which other correctional leaders who are interested in rehabilitating offenders and reintegrating them back into society can learn.

References

Andrews, D. A., and J. Bonta. 2010. Rehabilitating criminal justice policy and practice. *Psychology, Public Policy, and Law* 16, 39–55.

Andrews, D. A., and C. Dowden. 2007. The risk–need–responsivity model of assessment and human service in prevention and corrections: crime-prevention jurisprudence. *Canadian Journal of Criminology and Criminal Justice* 49, 439–464.

Day, A., and K. Howells. 2002. Psychological treatments for rehabilitating offenders: Evidence-based practice comes of age. *Australian Psychologist* 37, 39–47.

Heseltine, K., R. Sarre, and A. Day. 2011. Prison-based correctional rehabilitation: An overview of intensive interventions for moderate to high-risk offenders. *Trends and Issues in Crime and Criminal Justice* 442, 1–8.

Hor, M. 2000. Singapore's innovations to due process. *Proceedings of the International Society for the Reform of Criminal Law at the Conference on Human Rights and the Administration of Criminal Justice*, Johannesburg, South Africa.

Neo, L. 2009. Offender rehabilitation and reintegration: A Singaporean model. *Proceedings of the Reintegration Puzzle Conference*, Perth, Australia. Accessed 4/5/2011, http://www.acea.org.au/Content/2009%20Papers/Neo%20lee%20hong.pdf.

Ogloff, J. R. P., and N. R. Davis. 2004. Advances in offender assessment and rehabilitation: Contributions of the risk–needs–responsivity approach. *Psychology, Crime & Law* 10, 229–242.

Soh, W. W. 2010. The Yellow Ribbon Project Story (Singapore)—Reaching Out and Touching a Nation. Accessed 1/05/2011, http://www.unafei.or.jp/english/pdf/Congress_2010/30Soh_Wai_Wah.pdf.

Ward, T., and S. Maruna. 2007. *Rehabilitation: Beyond the Risk Paradigm*. London, UK: Routledge.

Wormwith, J. S., R. Althouse, M. Simpson, L. R. Reitzel, T. J. Fagan, and R. D. Morgan. 2007. The rehabilitation and reintegration of offenders: The current landscape and some future directions for correctional psychology. *Criminal Justice and Behavior* 34, 879–892.

Interview with Sue Hall, Chief Officer of West Yorkshire Probation

10

CLARE BECKETT

Contents

The probation service is sometimes described as the "third arm" of the British criminal justice system. It allows courts to sentence offenders to serve time under supervision in the community either instead of or after a period of imprisonment. Probation officers supervise "community orders" where offending does not require a custodial order. In addition, the probation service offers supervision for adult offenders "on license" after release from prison. Established more than 100 years ago, the service has roots in religion and was always intended to be a force for reformation and change. The first person who could be called a "probation officer" was employed as a result of a gift of 5 shillings to the Church of England Temperance Society, to be used to "rescue people who fell into drunkenness" and to prevent individuals committing a series of small crimes and, therefore, entering the prison system.

The modern service can be traced back to the Probation of Offenders Act 1907, when the requirement to "advise, assist, befriend" offenders became a statutory duty. This act created probation officers and probation orders and gave the courts the ability to sentence offenders to a mandatory period of supervision in the community. Courts could now recall and imprison people who breached probation orders. By the Golden Jubilee, in 1957, there were approximately 30,000 people serving probation orders. Probation officers were trained with social workers. They challenged offending behavior but also provided more general help and support. The values of the organization, in which every person is capable of change, given adequate support and motivation, echoed the postwar welfare consensus in Britain, where the economy was growing, and unemployment was low.

Local probation services had a large degree of autonomy within national organization and aims. Chief officers of different area services had a degree of self-rule, approaching the recruitment of officers differently and allocating their budget on a local level. This allowed the service to reflect local geographical differences, which also meant that it was hard to assess national advantages or disadvantages. There were national trends that also reflected government priorities: juvenile offenders moved out of probation interest in the 1960s as other services began to provide for them, and since the 1980s, drug treatment and drug-using offenders have been a core probation constituency. Today's probation officers still supervise drug users in the community, providing behavioral intervention to prevent a spiral of drug use, crime, and imprisonment.

However, the winds of change moved against "advise, assist, befriend" and against localized delivery. In 1979, the election of Margaret Thatcher and a conservative government signaled the end of the British postwar welfare consensus, already damaged by increasingly poor industrial relations and increasing unemployment. Successive Conservative Home Secretaries and their Labour shadows promised a strong and concerted approach to crime and punishment. In 1984, the government published the first statement of national objectives and priorities for probation. This was followed by moves to focus the service on enforcement and control of offending and on protecting the public. A new probation officer qualification was introduced, distinct from social work training. Arguably, this period marks a distinct break between the early probation service values and the modern National Probation Service.

Over the last decade, the probation service has been in the process of further transition. The Offender Management Act 2007 initiated the abolition of the 42 Probation Boards to create 35 Probation Trusts. There is a growing emphasis on competition, innovation, and efficiency. This move has come as part of a drive to modernize, which has fallen under the banner of the National Offender Management Service (NOMS) since 2004. On May 9, 2007, NOMS, along with the entire correctional services element of the Home Office, joined the former Lord Chancellor's Department in the newly created Ministry of Justice.

These moves have been accompanied by growing stress on the role of probation in protecting the public and on probation officers in taking responsibility for assessing the risk an offender poses. Protecting the public and reducing reoffending are the two main aims of the modern probation service. Training frameworks for probation officers emphasize the value of evidence-based practice, building on a "what works" agenda. The modern probation service is dominated by public protection, risk assessment, and effective management of offenders. At the same time, increasing prison populations and drastic prison overcrowding make community penalties an increasingly important option. Where probation "missionaries" would once have been the friend of petty criminals and drunks, the twenty-first century officer will have a caseload of dangerous and prolific offenders, including sex offenders and life sentence prisoners on release from jail.

Sue Hall, chief executive of the West Yorkshire Probation Trust and chair of the Probation Chiefs Association, has seen many of these changes in her time as a working probation officer. She gave this interview in the boardroom of the probation service, in an area that was, at that time, in the process of applying for trust status. She was a warm and friendly officer who knows her field staff by name, even though West Yorkshire is a large area, including two major cities: 1) Leeds and 2) Bradford. The account of her work was clear and strong, rarely faltering. As an interviewee, she was unlikely to have strayed into areas she was unwilling to talk about, but on the other hand, she was sufficiently confident to contribute, sometimes critically, to wider debate. The whole interview took about 2 h and was conducted without a break. The transcription shows very little need for interviewer prompts.

The Interview

Hall had previously received a list of the topics to be covered and had no reservations about being taped. The following excerpts from the transcript may be reported out of order for clarity but are verbatim (interviewer's comments are set in italics).

Career

Q: What brought you into probation in the beginning?
A: It was complete chance. After leaving university, I started doing some voluntary work and found I enjoyed it. I hadn't really heard of probation, to be honest, and saw an advert in the paper and thought, "Oh that looks interesting," applied and amazingly got in. In those days, it was much easier to get in than it is nowadays. I'd not have a chance nowadays, because the selection criteria are really quite tough, and perhaps, the public is more aware of probation than it was back in the 1970s.

Q: (This is a reference back to the early probation service, where different areas recruited independently. Modern probation officers go through a national selection process and training.)

A: My entire career has been in probation; I trained in Cardiff University and did what was then the Home Office–sponsored course. The arrangements have changed two or three times since then. But, going back to 1977, which was when I trained, the Home Office sponsored probation students. I qualified in 1979 and joined the Humberside Probation Service as a probation officer, working in places such as Grimsby and Scunthorpe. I became a senior probation officer based in the student training unit, where I spent 4 years working very closely with Hull University, and then went on to be an ordinary team senior. Then, I became an assistant chief officer in Humberside, moved into West Yorkshire as a deputy in 2000, went to South Wales as a chief officer in 2004, and then came back here (West Yorkshire) as a chief officer in 2005. A few weeks ago, I became the chief executive of the West Yorkshire Probation Trust, because we've become trusts this year. In a nutshell, it's 30, 31, nearly 32 years now in the probation service.

Q: Hall has kept a spotlight on probation training throughout her career.

A: When I was a basic grade probation officer, I was a practice teacher, and I did my social work practice teaching award, and then, of course, I was involved in the student training unit in Hull, which was designed for people doing the probation element at the Hull social work course. I did that for about 4 years and was very involved in the development of the "Dips,"* the diploma in social work. When we moved from the diploma in social work to a specific probation qualification, I was very much involved with that, and I've been a great supporter of the importance of training ever since and remain so to this day.

Major Changes

Q: Hall's career started in the 1980s, very soon after the election of Margaret Thatcher and at the beginning of movement away from probation as a form of social work. At this time, there was no national qualification: officer training was linked to social work.

A: When I started, the training wasn't very good if I'm absolutely honest; we were trained as social workers with very little input into working with offenders, and we sort of picked it up on the job essentially. I

---

* This is a common abbreviation of diploma qualifications.

think there really wasn't a strong theoretical base to what we did. We "advised, assisted, and befriended," and I think in those days, we would have seen the police as on the other side of the line. It was a very different culture, and I don't really know how effective we were. We worked with a whole range of people that we simply don't work with now, particularly first-time offenders and "lower level"* offenders.

Q: The next decade in probation reflected political interest in centralizing probation service and establishing the evidence-based "what works" agenda.

A: In the 1980s, national standards were developed, and the managerial approach to probation began to emerge toward the late 1980s. I remember something coming out called the "Statement of National Objectives and Priorities" in the mid-1980s, which was the first inkling really of what's become the dominant culture throughout the 1990s and, indeed, into the current decade. Alongside that, the understanding of public protection and risk began to emerge, as well as the "what works" agenda in the 1980s; so, from not having a very strong notion of how probation was different from social work, by the end of the 1980s into the 1990s, we were very clear that we were about reducing reoffending and protecting the public. We had a clear set of national standards and began to work to objectives and targets. So, the way the probation officers do their job now is… there are definite benefits, and there are definite downsides. The huge benefits that I see are that there's much more professional weight to what we do, there's academic basis around particularly working with risk, working with public protection, there's a basis around how you influence people to stop offending, a very interesting academic debate around that and, you know, that's very good. I think the work we do, for example, with sex offenders, with violent people, the cognitive behavioral approach that we've adopted is helping people look at their behavior, change their behavior. I think those are huge advantages. Where it's gone too far is the managerial approach, which, in the early days, was very good to make us focus on the right things: When you have limited resources, you need to deploy them to best effect for the community, but it's gone too far. Everyone I think agrees with the knowledge that there are too many targets, and as a result, operational officers spend too long in front of the computer inputting records. In some ways, that

---

* This is a reference to risk level. Offenders are categorized according to the level of risk that they pose to the general public. A level-1 offender poses the least risk.

allows the work to be measured. I think the pendulum has to begin to swing backwards on that one.

Q: A marker of current probation practice is the use of "targets" to assess the usefulness of intervention. These targets are set nationally and attract considerable controversy. Debate polarizes between those who see targets as limiting professional judgment by imposing a "tick box" approach and those who see targets as an effective way of measuring and making accountable supervisory performance [for a complete discussion, see the work of Beckett (2009)].

A: I'm in favor (of targets). I'm not in favor of doing away with targets. I believe in the adage that "what gets measured gets managed," and it's about being clear about what it is that you want to measure and manage. Unfortunately, the current system tends to measure what you can as opposed to what you should, because some things are just too hard, so we have too many targets that are about process and timeliness as opposed to outcomes. I do believe in having clear goals that are measured, that people are accountable for, but they shouldn't be so all consuming and so restrictive that they stifle creativity or they mean that too much time is taken from face-to-face work with offenders, and that's why I think the pendulum will start to go back. I'm not advocating that we just dismantle what has happened over the last 10 years.

Q: Debate has centered on the role of the probation officer. Should it be one that reflects the original "advise, assist, befriend" principles, or should the officer play a pivotal role in enforcing compliance to a community order?

A: Well it's (the probation role) not just enforcement; for example, if you believe community sentences' can make a difference, then you have to believe that people should comply with them, because otherwise, why have them if people... if there's no consequences to not complying? You have to have a justice system that's seen to be fair but is also seen to be executed robustly, so if you get the confidence of the sentencers, they have to believe that, when they are passing a community sentence, it will be managed properly, that there will be consequences. However, many magistrates could say they are not in favor of some of the technical breaches that we are obliged to take back to court. They would rather we had more discretion around the breaches so that we breach where it is appropriate to do so, but we don't breach because somebody's 5 min late for their appointment. Many magistrates might be in favor of not being so technically tough and managing the spirit of the order, but they would not favor people just not turning up with no consequences. They do see that the purpose is not just punishment but rehabilitation and change.

With the rise in the prison population to the level that it was year before last (2008), we were strongly encouraged to use discretion, and I think that we did that. Certainly, in West Yorkshire, we spent a lot of time looking at judgments and when it's appropriate to send somebody or request that somebody's returned to prison and when you can continue to manage that risk in the community.

When I was a probation officer, basically, you did a bit of everything, you did a bit of counseling, (for instance) you did alcohol counseling—you did your alcohol diary with people. Now, the introduction of offender management means that we're much more likely to have offender managers managing, if you like, the core of the order, but we will be using other bodies, for example, to do the work on alcohol or to do, I don't know, work on employment or whatever. There's less of that done directly by offender managers, and obviously, we have a specialist manager's program team that run the programs.

Q: Currently, the probation service is part of the same organizational structure as prisons. This is a new initiative, and the effects are only beginning to show. There is also an unsettled political climate. It is not clear as to what extent the 2010 coalition government will support the state provision of services or require privatization. Since its inception, NOMS has also changed direction, as different political ideologies are foregrounded.

A: I think that what we haven't really talked about is NOMS, and I suppose if you wanted a sort of "this is how it is in England and Wales," it would be remiss of me not to mention the fact that NOMS is responsible for managing work with offenders and for custodial and the community sentences (National Offender Management Services 2008). While NOMS has a line management relationship with the public sector prisons, it's more complicated with probation. We have a director of offender management based regionally, who has a contract with us as a probation trust, and that's a contract that will be renewed every 3 years, if everything continues as it is. In theory, we could lose that contract if we don't come up to scratch. In theory, there could be other providers. That's not how it feels at the moment, where probation is still provided by a public sector probation service across England and Wales, but the legislation that went through in 2008 essentially ring-fenced some aspects to the public sector, and that ring fence ends in 2011. If a government was so minded, they could—they really could—make us jump through market testing hoops later down the road.

Q: Is the difference ideological and managerial?

A: What it says is, "Yes, it is the state's responsibility to make sure probation services are provided," but it doesn't believe that only the public sector can provide services. You see that, with the prisons, you know we have some private prisons. NOMS values things that probation does; it would be wrong to suggest that it doesn't. It hasn't tried to make us do or be very different; reducing reoffending is still the priority, not just punishment. We can't be complacent about the role of the public sector in the future. It could change. The difference I would like to see is a probation service becoming commissioner of local services.

I think that one of the things this country has done not terribly well is tried to bring the market into the public sector. Having said this, you can't just leave the public sector on its own to get on with it—you do need to have challenges and to be kept on your toes. Look across, for example, at some European probation services, which aren't really held to account, and they're possibly more wasteful in how they spend their time and their money. I think we're highly efficient in England and Wales. I really do think the public gets extremely good value out of us, but this endless redesigning to somehow artificially bring competition in... I don't know that there's evidence to suggest that, at the end of the day, the savings you get justify the amount of money and resource you've put in. I think this endless bidding and competing is just... I don't know that it produces the goods.

Q: However, NOMS was introduced partly to facilitate "end-to-end" offender management.

A: The thing that I think NOMS has brought in, which I think has been good, has been the idea of end-to-end offender management through prison and probation. We certainly work very closely with our prison colleagues now. We see a lot of them; we talk to them a lot. End-to-end offender management holds a lot of currency, still, within the criminal justice system, because everybody accepts that it's not helpful for those prisoners who are most highly recidivist and dangerous people in the system to get a service in prison that isn't then sustained when they come out. If they're getting drug treatment when they're in prison and that stops when they get out or if they can't get somewhere to live, it means that work done in prison is completely negated. It doesn't make sense not to work with prisoners when they're in prison, particularly if they're in a long time, so everybody would accept that you need end-to-end offender management. Making it work is quite difficult in a pressurized, pressure cooker prison system where people are moved around a lot.

The one bit we've never been able to resource, which is probably the most important gap in our system, is work with prisoners serving 12 months or less. The "revolving door" prisoners, who go in, spend a short time in prison, go out—their ties are fractured, and they have a hugely high reoffending rate, the highest in the whole system. Not to have found resources for that is one of the failures of the Labour government, and possibly of NOMS.

Q: In some areas, three short prison sentences like that lead to life sentences—three strikes, and you're out.

A: Just indiscriminately to impose a life sentence on somebody for offenses that might not be very serious makes no sense at all other than in a highly punitive system, and it imposes an impossible strain on a prison system. I would say a position where you can't have hope—where life means life, and you have no hope of parole—is an inhumane system. For the vast majority of prisoners, giving them something to work toward is important, is a motivating force in prisons, and if you don't have that, you move to a position where you're into tougher and tougher enforcement.

Personal Philosophy

There are frequent pointers in answer to the other questions: Almost every section includes a statement of belief. In particular, in discussing theory, Hall says, "But it all adds to the ethos of 'you don't just do you have to do, and reflect and evaluate.'" *This comment, coupled with a stress on the belief that people can change and that evidence informs practice, would seem to be the "drivers" of Hall's personal philosophy.*

Q: In other places, links are made between personal philosophy and national philosophy.

A: In the last decade, I suppose risk and public protection became the number one priority. What I see at the moment is that reducing reoffending is gaining greater ascendancy. I personally would say that you protect the public by reducing reoffending. Clearly, with higher risk offenders, you are more focused on managing the harm they might do, but at the end of the day, reducing reoffending is what makes communities safe, not just concentrating on managing higher risk offenders.

Q: Because behind that, there is also a belief that people can change.

A: Yes, and that's one of West Yorkshire Probation Trust's values—this came out of a consultation exercise with staff earlier this year. It came back loud and clear: "People can change" is a value that staff see as one of our core values.

Q: And so, do you?

A: Yes, oh yes, absolutely. Yes, I believe staff can change as well. "People can change" isn't just about offenders; it is about staff also being prepared to develop their practice and change to meet the needs of the moment.

Links between Practice and Theory

Q: Hall's personal commitment to and knowledge of the training given to probation officers is unusual. She takes active interest in staff career development and in staff training, personally attending award ceremonies and giving individual congratulations.

A: If I just look back, historically, there's no doubt that the "what works" initiatives in the late 1980s and the 1990s absolutely changed probation. Previously, we used our creativity and experience in the work we did with offenders, but no one had looked at the theoretical underpinnings and evidence of effectiveness.

Q: The first theoretical study of probation intervention programs came from Canada in the 1980s and was taken up by the service quite quickly.

A: Accredited programs were developed based on some of the work that Canada had been doing and were implemented within England and Wales—more than anywhere else outside North America. Staff welcomed the quality of a lot of the programs, and programs staff often became passionate as proponents of their programs. Even the huge cultural change of working to a manual and being videoed and all that sort of treatment integrity aspect was accepted. I think what we saw was, if we targeted people on the correct programs, if we supported them through the program and if they completed it, then they had an impact. This is supported by research.*

Q: Assessing and forecasting the risk an offender poses have been a key training point.

A: Of course, you can't manage all risk; you can't guarantee no one will ever reoffend again. All you can do is to do your best to reduce the risk. Unless you lock everybody up forever, there will always be a risk when people remain in the community.

For probation officers, risk assessment is absolutely imbued in how you operate. What we're seeing now is, I think, a really interesting emergence of desistance research. This has had a huge impact in Scotland. Links between academic research and probation have not been strong over recent years, but very interestingly, NOMS has

---

* The National Association of Probation Officers offers evidence that the successful completion of programs reduces average reoffending rates from 50% to 35%.

become interested this year in offender engagement—that's about the relationship between the offender manager and the offender. NOMS has initiated research looking at the value of that relationship and has also commissioned a study about the implications of desistance research for offender management. I would anticipate over the next couple of years as we begin to think through what this means for what we do—that there will be some changes in the way we do offender management. I don't think we're going to throw the baby out with the bath water. I don't think that we are going to be saying we're not going to be doing accredited programs now, but what we will be saying is, in order to support somebody through their journey to desistance, you need the right interventions at the right time, but you also need the relationship with the offender manager to support them and to engage with the circles of support that will help an offender on the journey to desistance.

Q: Over the last 10 years, the training for probation officers has been reviewed. The current qualification is delivered by partner universities working on NOMS guidelines and retains an academic qualification at the BA level. The interviewer has been involved in these negotiations.

A: The new qualifying training is both an academic and a practice qualification. We held on to that being at the degree level. One of the, I suppose, issues for us that we haven't talked about yet is having gone into NOMS, which is predominantly a prison-run organization. There was danger when the new qualification was developed, that a very narrow cost-cutting approach would have been taken to it, which said "Prison officers only take 3 weeks to train. Why do probation officers need 2 years and a degree?" If that argument hadn't been won, it would have devalued probation as a profession. I believe that you can't just pluck somebody off the street and stick them in front of a serious offender and expect them to be effective. They need to have some tools in their toolbox. They have to be able to work with some of the most difficult and dangerous people in our society.

The expertise, I think, we bring is that we are experts at managing relationships with offenders. We do understand about engaging, motivating, and supporting people. We are tuned into assessing—awful term—criminogenic needs and working to resolve some of the issues. That's where the link with theory has come. The "what works" agenda was around what aggravates and what mitigates offending, what makes it more likely that someone will offend, what makes it less likely. We're all very clear on that. Probation officers, I think, have a holistic view of an offender and bring that understanding of how you work with offenders.

Q: What do you like about your job?
A: I like the fact that I think probation can make a difference. If you meet
   an offender who has become an ex-offender, there is nothing more
   inspiring for probation staff—when it goes right. Somebody regains
   their life, and that has an impact for their families and their communities. It's those things that inspire probation staff to keep going.
   We know we don't do it with everybody; we're not naive, we're not
   stupid. There are a lot of people who don't make that change, but
   we know it's possible.

Problems and Successes

I think where we are now is that probation staff are very committed and driven
to probation by a sense of vocation. That hasn't changed, despite changes in
the job itself. None of that has dampened people's commitment to doing the
job, and that's really important. We're a value-driven profession, and people
hold on to the belief that offenders can change, and that's really, I think, very
precious. Probation officers are realistic but believe that it's worth persisting
with somebody, because at the end of the day, there may be a change.

I would like to see more effort given to research in probation. West
Yorkshire has a research team. I hold on to that through thick and thin—we're
possibly almost the last locally based probation research team in the country.
It's really important to me that we have on-site access to researchers who can
look at the work that we're doing and help evaluate it, but are also in touch with
research agendas outside. What's lovely is that they run the practice research
network internally and put out research bulletins. For those practitioners who
are very keen, it gives them an opportunity to be involved in bits of research or
manage bits of their own research, on a very small scale, but it all adds to the
ethos of "you don't just do, you have to do and reflect and evaluate."

*Much of the conversation here concerned the immediate future of the West
Yorkshire Service. This reflects the timing of the interview at a period of uncer-
tainty in the British political climate.*

Q: What does probation do at the moment?
A: Probation is involved with offenders. We become involved at the court
   stage when somebody is appearing before the court. If the courts
   wish for assistance in sentencing, they'll ask us to write a report,
   a presentence report, which will look at somebody's offending
   behavior and look at the sort of risk that they pose and will make
   proposals for community sentences or indeed comments around
   custodial sentences, to help the sentencers in magistrates and

crown courts reach a verdict. Once the sentence is passed, we are responsible for supervising community orders and offenders on license who get more than 12 months in custody. We run probation hostels or approved premises. We're based in courts; we're based in prisons. Our focus is the offender. We know that you can't reduce reoffending and reduce risk on your own as a criminal justice organization; you need to work with partners, because we know offenders have to access health resources, they need to have access to accommodation, employment, and treatment facilities for their substance misuse. Our knowledge of working with offenders is also really important for communities to feel safer, so we bring our knowledge to the table. We work with partners to try and get access to resources for offenders to enable them to, hopefully, become better citizens.

Q: What do you hope for in the immediate future?

A: I think there needs to be a clear policy steer, a clear mandate around what the purpose of probation is and what we should provide. I think we should be given outcomes to work toward, and I think we should be given a clear budget to achieve those outcomes. I think we should not necessarily seek to provide everything ourselves, but we should be involved in working locally to commission services. I think that I'd like to see probation continue on the West Yorkshire–wide basis, because I think there are economies of scale. If you go very local and have very small services, you struggle to provide things. I wouldn't like to see regional or national bodies. I do think you need to have local flexibility to work with your local authorities and community partnerships to develop the services that each locality needs, and I'm very in favor of a sort of "total place" approach, which says that public services and, indeed, private and voluntary services should look at what their complimentary aims are and where it makes sense to pool money to develop processes across agencies. You should be able to do so, because there are huge efficiencies and savings to be made.

Q: Changes in Bradford and Leeds have become possible, because West Yorkshire has become a probation trust. This changes the management structure, giving the local service heads in the two cities more direct management responsibility under Sue Hall's overview. As chief officer of the Trust, Hall negotiates with "the center," or NOMS.

A: We've put a local delivery unit (LDU) in each of the five local authorities in West Yorkshire, each led by a head of probation, so you've now got a head of Bradford probation, a head of Leeds probation, etc. We've been devolving responsibility from head office down to the

LDUs, giving them real control over their budgets, setting up business units to support them in their local delivery units, and with what's left at the head office, becoming much more geared to supporting what's happening out there rather than micromanaging it.

Q: These changes have not yet been reflected in the change between the Trust and NOMS.

A: I'm trying to model with them (NOMS) what I'd like the center to do with us. At the end of the day, I'm still responsible for the use of public money in West Yorkshire. Therefore, I have to make sure there's accountable and responsible use of it. I'm responsible for our overall performance, and I have to make sure that each of the five LDUs is working to standards that we'd expect of them, but the trick is, within that, to give people the opportunity to be creative. I think that the new duty that community safety partnerships have is to reduce reoffending, alongside an understanding of place; all of that has the potential, even at the time of dire finances, to be exciting. It could deliver savings. If, centrally, the view was, "We can't maintain this huge central structure, we'll have less targets, because we can't afford to monitor them anymore, we'll give you more freedoms locally, but you'll get less money," I could live with that.

Transnational Links

Q: Hall is an active member of the European Association of Probation.

A: We're one of the older probation services, and we have a huge reputation. By many European standards, we're well resourced in terms of the number of staff and the number of offenders that we work with, and we have resources on hand that aren't available in Europe. For example, the resource that we have in accredited programs, approved premises, all of those things. Strapped though we are for resources, one of the reasons for that is that a lot is demanded of us—how often we see people, the intensity of the work that we do with them, the provisions we make, the services we provide really stretch us, but the fact is, we are expected to do that. What you have in Europe is a real hotchpotch of arrangements. In many countries, you don't have a probation service run by the state but by not-for-profit organizations. A lot of countries have social workers based in prisons who don't connect with probation on the outside, so you don't have an idea of a probation service running through prison into the community. This is a major issue for some European countries. Many of them don't have the idea of supervision on license after release from prison; many don't provide reports for the court. Some countries are much more into the restorative justice approaches, victim–offender mediation. There is little research being done in the many European organizations about the quality of work. I think the U.K. and North America are far in advance of much of Europe in terms of research that's available. Then, you have the emergent* European countries where probation services are all brand new. Certainly, we've been involved in the U.K. with a lot of twinning projects in, for example, Bulgaria and Romania, Czech Republic, and Turkey to help develop probation services. So, it is interesting to consider the new developing practice in Europe and the more established practice in England and Wales, which is seen as very state dominated.

General Assessments

I went to a European probation conference, and someone was talking about England and Wales being a correctional system and about how other European systems aren't correctional. I was really struck by that. I thought, "Are we a correctional system?" I don't know that we are in the way that North America is much more correctional. I probably don't understand the term *correctional* enough, but if it means that what we do is only about punishment enforcement, then that's certainly not true. Even our prison system here would say they don't do that. Our prison system also has reducing reoffenders as a goal, and reducing reoffending has been the priority for governments really since Charles Clark was Home Secretary (1997–2006). Very interestingly, this is now reflected in community safety partnerships. Reducing reoffending became a cross-government priority after the last comprehensive spending review, so it wasn't just for criminal justice systems to reduce reoffending—it was a cross-government aim. That became reflected in the agreements that each local authority had to negotiate with their partners, and that's now, as of the 1st of April (2010), become enshrined as a priority for community safety partnerships. Probation has become a statutory partner in community safety partnerships. Our job within that is to work with community safety partnerships to develop strategies for reducing reoffending within localities. So, there's social support now for reducing reoffending. Even the new government† is talking about the "rehabilitation revolution"—they're using those terms. Where you might have thought they

---

* This term is used for countries that used to be part of the Communist bloc in Europe.
† This interview took place just after the 2010 general election, which returned a coalition government.

would have come in on a punishment ticket, they're saying prisons are too full and we believe in rehabilitation.

Conclusion

The interview lasted nearly 2 h. Perhaps, the most striking thing about this account is the ability of this chief officer to locate her probation area in the context of social and political change. Demands on probation personnel are high at any time, but currently, successive policy changes and financial cutbacks have challenged the ability of the service to provide coherent core provision. This can only be done through the clear iteration of values. It is clear that the core commitment to individual change and protection of the public run side by side here.

It is also easy for highly stretched public services to be overly critical of the management structures above them. In this context, Hall's concerns about NOMS and her hopes for the future are constructive and relevant. The movement to the management of public services through centrally targeted performance indicators is controversial, and Hall's support for that system, in general, with concern for particular application is interesting in this context.

References

Beckett, C. 2009. Organisational experiences of performance targetting: Police, prisons and probation. *British Journal of Community Justice* 7 (3).

McGuire, J., and P. Priestly. 1995. Reviewing what works: Past present and future. In J. McGuire (Ed.), *What Works: Reducing Reoffending. Guidelines from Research and Practice.* Chichester: Wiley.

National Offender Management Service. 2008. *A Century of Cutting Crime 1907–2007*, London, UK: Home Office.

Trotter, C. 1999. *Working with Involuntary Clients: A Guide to Practice.* Sage, London: Publications Limited.

Glossary

Accredited program: A program consisting of a series of planned sessions with offenders based on cognitive behavioral interventions. A specific program will be "accredited" for use with groups of offenders by probation (or prison) authorities based on the evidence of behavior change on completion. West Yorkshire provides such interventions around, for example, enhanced thinking skills or sexual offending.

Approved premises: Controlled accommodation for offenders under the supervision of the probation service. Residents follow a structured regime, which includes an overnight curfew. There is 24-h supervision by trained staff.

Breaches: An offender will have received an order of sentence. This order will include such stipulations as the number of times they should attend probation, where they are to live, or areas of the community or individuals they must avoid. Breaking any of these terms or conditions by, for example, missing probation appointment without good reason results in a "breach" of the order. An offender who has breached a community order can be sent back to court and given a custodial sentence instead.

Charles Clarke: A Labour politician who served as Home Secretary from December 2004 to May 2006.

Community orders: Introduced in April 2005 under the Criminal Justice Act 2003. It will eventually come to replace all current community sentences.

It allows magistrates and judges to make a different sentence tailor-made for each offender based on their crimes by choosing from a range of 12 different requirements rather than having to match an offender with a preexisting order.

It is hoped that this added flexibility will further increase the success of community sentences by allowing them to target an offender's needs more specifically. In addition, technological advances such as electronic tagging are now easily added to the conditions of a sentence, providing innovative ways of denying liberty, reducing reoffending, and ensuring that community sentences are not a soft option.

The 12 requirements that sentencers can choose from are listed as follows:

- Unpaid work (between 40 and 300 h)
- Participation in any specified activities
- Accredited programs aimed at changing offending behavior
- Prohibition from certain activities
- Curfew
- Exclusion from certain areas
- Residence requirement (e.g., in a probation hostel)
- Mental health treatment
- Drug rehabilitation requirement (provided by the drug treatment and testing teams)
- Alcohol treatment
- Supervision treatment
- Attendance center requirements (for younger than 25 years)

Community safety partnerships: Responsible for coordinating a joint agency response to community safety issues across cities. The partnerships were formalized as the Crime and Disorder Reduction Partnership

(CDRP) to comply with the Crime and Disorder Act 1998. In 2010, the term CDRP was dropped in favor of the more encompassing "Community Safety Partnership." The overarching goal has been to reduce crime, disorder, and the fear of crime and to build a safer place for those who live, work, and spend leisure time in the area.

Criminogenic need: Criminogenic needs are attributes of offenders that are directly linked to criminal behavior. Effective correctional treatment should target criminogenic needs in the development of a comprehensive case plan. Any treatment not targeting criminogenic needs is counterproductive to efficiency and effectiveness.

Desistence: Desistance from crime—the process through which people cease and refrain from offending—is a research topic that is of significant import for criminal justice policy and practice.

End-to-end offender management: The term was introduced by the 2003 Report of the Correctional Services Review (known as the *Carter Report*). The Carter Report was the last in a series of reports into the correctional services, which all concluded that handling offenders was fragmented, good work was not being followed through, and better coordination was needed to reduce reoffending. The report recommended that a single named officer should become responsible for managing a complete sentence from start to finish, including periods in custody and periods of sentence in the community. The offender manager should be responsible for assessing risks and needs, for sentence planning, for choosing and ensuring compliance with interventions, for reviewing offender progress against the plan, and for adjustments in light of any changes. Other officers and agencies would be involved in the delivery of parts of the sentence, but there would be consistent overview.

License: A period of "licensed liberty" in the community after a prison service. Offenders are subject to probation supervision and can be returned to prison at any time.

National Offender Management Service (NOMS): An executive agency of the Ministry of Justice responsible for the correctional services in England and Wales (separate arrangements exist in Scotland and Northern Ireland). It was created by combining parts of both of the headquarters of the National Probation Service and Her Majesty's Prison Service with some existing Home Office functions. It was initially created in 2004 after a review by Patrick Carter (now Lord Carter of Coles), a Labour-supporting businessman. Carter had been asked by the government to propose a way of achieving a better balance between the prison population in England and Wales and the resources available for the correctional services. He proposed three radical changes. First, there should be an end-to-end management of each offender from first contact with the correctional services to full completion of the sentence. Second, there should be a clear division between the commissioners of services and their providers. Third, there should be "contestability" among these providers. By these means, he argued, efficiency would be increased, unit costs would be reduced, and innovation is encouraged. Growth in the prison population, which had increased by two-thirds over the last 10 years, would be constrained by giving the courts greater confidence in the effectiveness of community sentences as opposed to prison sentences through the better management of offenders, leading to reduced levels of reoffending. The government accepted these uncosted proposals in full, without consultation and in the face of concerted pressure from Probation Unions and Criminal Justice practitioners.

After a period characterized by changes of political leadership, crises about foreign national prisoners, and a burgeoning prison population, on May 9, 2007, the correctional services element of the Home Office was moved to join the former Lord Chancellor's Department in the newly created Ministry of Justice. In January 2008, the Secretary of State for Justice announced a major organizational reform, which resulted in the Director-General of Her Majesty's Prison Service, Phil Wheatley, becoming the chief executive of NOMS and assuming responsibility for the National Probation Service and Her Majesty's Prison Service and management of contracts for the private sector operation of prisons and prisoner escorting.

Offenders: The term used to describe people found guilty of an offense and sentenced through the court. Many offenders' organizations argue that the term is stigmatizing and campaign for different terminology. However, all government interventions use the term offender.

'What works' agenda: In 1974, authors D. Lipton, Robert Martinson, and J. Wilks, using "meta-analyses" and assessed all the evaluations of criminal rehabilitation programs between 1945 and 1967. They reached the following conclusion: "With few and isolated exceptions, the rehabilitative efforts that have been reported so far have had no appreciable effect on recidivism." Later, in a 1978 publication, they admitted that they had left out of their study some pieces of research that may have shown rehabilitation to be more effective than they had publicly stated. The phrase "nothing works," however, became the mantra of those opposed to rehabilitation and had some influence in moving the public away from the Liberal programs of rehabilitation. McGuire and Priestley (1995) considered a number of interventions underpinned by the cognitive behavioral theory (CBT), and Chris Trotter (1999), "working with involuntary clients," looked at research evidence in Canada and the United States and concluded that CBT interventions did work, sparking a new "what works" agenda.

Interview with Robert Ambroselli, Director of Parole, California Department of Corrections and Rehabilitation

11

MARY MAGUIRE

Contents

The social and political landscape of California has seen much change since its original statehood in 1850. California, the 31st of the 50 states, is currently the largest state in the union with a population of approximately 37 million people (11.95% of the United States population; U.S. Census Bureau 2010). The path of corrections in California has mirrored the state's robust expansion and has experienced some of the challenges that come with the largess associated with California.

Soon after statehood, in 1851, California opened its first prison on a ship docked in San Francisco Bay. The 30 inmates housed on the prison ship were responsible for building California's first brick and mortar facility, San Quentin State Prison (California DOJ).

One hundred years later, in 1951, a time of prison reform in the United States in general (Rotman 1995), the then California State Detentions Bureau changed its name to the California Department of Corrections. Finally, in another attempt to promote reform, the state again changed the name, adding "and Rehabilitation" to the end. With an 11 billion dollar budget and 35,000 sworn officers (65,000 employees in total) the California Department of Corrections and Rehabilitation (CDCR) is now the largest law enforcement agency in the United States. Since the opening of San Quentin in 1852, California has built 32 additional prisons and acquired a prison population of 171,000, more than twice the number of inmates those institutions are meant to house.

The rapid growth of the CDCR through the 1970s and 1980s left the system with extremely high costs, poor inmate–staff relations, and the highest recidivism rates in the nation. The Civil Rights Act of 1871, although it did not initially grant inmates civil rights protections, now allows inmates to file suit against state officials. Under Section 1983, inmates may contest the conditions of their confinement, including improvements in conditions, medical care, return of property, or compensation for abuse by staff (Civil Rights Act of 1871). With prison overcrowding, California has experienced a myriad of lawsuits related to treatment by staff, medical and mental health care, and general conditions. Severe overcrowding and a system that appeared to be careening out of control have prompted several independent reviews of the mammoth system with recommendations for reform.

In 1990, the Blue Ribbon Commission on Inmate Population Management predicted that, without serious reform in California correctional policy and practice, severe overcrowding would become a major risk to state and local government in the future. Their 38 recommendations targeted sentencing guidelines, parole, drug offenders, prison construction, and community corrections (Blue Ribbon Commission 1990).

In 1962, California developed an independent state oversight board modeled after the United States' Hoover Commission of 1947, the Little Hoover Commission on California State Government Organization and Economy. Similar to its predecessor, the Little Hoover Commission is charged with investigating government operations and affecting change through reports and legislative proposals. In 1994, the Little Hoover Commission published its first major report on California Corrections, *Putting Violence Behind Bars: Redefining the Role of California Prisons*. The report made 30 recommendations largely related to sentencing and parole reform as well as returning to an earlier model of rehabilitation. Later in 1994, the Commission issued another report focused on the prevention of youth crime, which recommended that the California Youth Authority (the entity then responsible for juvenile detention) be given the ability to provide the treatment and education delinquent youth needed (Little Hoover Commission 1994). In 1998, the Commission issued their report on overcrowding, *Beyond Bars: Correctional Reforms to Lower Prison Costs and Reduce Crime* (Little Hoover Commission 1998). By this time, the system was described as being in a state of "crisis that worsens each day." Again, multiple recommendations were made, now specifically targeting reducing crimes made by those on parole. Little Hoover has gone on to publish eight additional reports with investigative findings and recommendations for improvement.

Despite a myriad of warnings, in 2002, California was the site of the nation's largest class action lawsuit, *Plata v. Davis/Schwarzenegger*. The inmates in the *Plata* case alleged that correctional staff were inflicting cruel and unusual punishment by being indifferent to the serious medical issues of inmates. A settlement required that the CDCR overhaul their medical facilities, policies, and procedures. An independent medical panel was instructed to audit the state's progress, and in 2005, a Federal Judge charged with overseeing the *Plata* case found the prison's medical conditions to continue to be extremely neglectful and to constitute medical malpractice. Stating that the system was "broken beyond repair," the judge placed the CDCR medical care under the control of a court-appointed receiver. Additional lawsuits ended with court-appointed special masters to monitor the progress of the CDCR in meeting court-mandated improvement guidelines in areas of mental health, dental care, and use of force (*Perez v. Tilton, Budd v. Cambria, Coleman v. Wilson, Madrid v. Gomez*, and *Gates v. Deukmejian*). Yet, additional lawsuits have brought changes in the area of parole: for the availability of parole options for lifers, for the due process rights of those experiencing a parole revocation, and for the rights of parolees on disability (*Rosenkrantz, Valdivia v. Davis* and *Armstrong v. Davis*, respectively).

After a series of lawsuits, some that would later result in the state's loss of control of services, in 2004, then Governor Schwarzenegger appointed former Governor Deukmajian to direct the Independent Review Panel (IRP) in a thorough investigation of the California Department of Corrections and make recommendations for reform. In their findings, the IRP stated:

> From the 1940s through the 1970s, the California correctional system was looked upon as the national leader. Innovative and daring, California pioneered the way for standards that were adopted by other jurisdictions as a model of efficiency. What, then, has happened to this jewel of a corrections system? How did it fall from the pinnacle of success? The answers are complex, yet simple: there has been too much political interference, too much union control, and too little management courage, accountability, and transparency.

The IRP made 239 specific recommendations, which targeted every aspect of the correctional system. The scope of the recommendations was daunting. Governor Schwarzenegger did appoint appropriate task forces and continued to facilitate attempts at reform; unfortunately, the legislative and political forces that were part of creating the problem had not changed.

In one of its latest accounts to the State, the Little Hoover Commission (2007) reported:

> The problem does not need further study. The State knows what the answers are, thanks to nearly two decades of work by such groups as the Blue Ribbon Commission on Population Management, the Corrections Independent Review Panel, and a series of reports by this Commission. Despite ample evidence and recommendations, policy-makers have been unwilling to take on the problem in a purposeful, constructive way.

The consequences of failing to act aggressively now leave the State open to losing control of the State correctional system and, with it, control of the state budget. The debacle developed over decades. Solutions, likewise, will be years in the making. But making a start now is essential.

The bare facts have earned California's Department of Corrections and Rehabilitation an ignoble distinction for systemic failure. Inmates have swelled prisons far past capacity. With cells already full, new inmates camp out in hallways, gyms, and classrooms. The goals of punishment and confinement have left little room, or budget, for rehabilitation. The bulk of the State's prisoners are not succeeding once released. California's recidivism rate, at 70%, is near the highest in the nation. The ranks of correctional officers have not kept pace with the rising prison population. The department has thousands of openings, resulting in huge overtime bills and mounting stress for correctional officers.

The Commission's 2007 report provides many recommendations, one of which is to implement earlier recommendations. One notable recommendation, however, is to reinvent parole. The nearly 70% recidivism rate is making a significant contribution to overcrowding, and many on return are recidivating due to parole violations, not for committing new crimes.

The United States currently imprisons well over two million Americans, more individuals than ever before in its history. This represents a penal system that was 10 times larger in 2000 than it was in 1980 (Dyer 2000). Ninety-eight percent of inmates will be released, taking the prison culture back to their communities (Clear 1995). The person most responsible for making a successful bridge from incarceration to reentry to the community in California is Robert Ambroselli, the Director of the Division of Adult Parole Operations for the CDCR.

Ambroselli made himself available to discuss the California Correctional system in general and reform in California Parole in particular. What follows is our interview, which took place on October 12, 2010 in his office at the CDCR Headquarters in Sacramento, CA.

M: We are interested in your career trajectory and how you came to your position as the Director of Parole.

R: I started out as a correctional officer in the department in 1990. I opened up Pelican Bay State Prison. We activated that institution, and I worked there for a number of years, about three and a half years. I went on to activate another prison. I worked in the prison system for about 6 years as a correctional officer (CO), and then, in 1996, I became a parole agent. I transitioned from the prison side of the house to the parole side.

M: What precipitated that change?

R: I was always interested in parole. It always seemed fascinating. There was always a lot going on there. More than just incarcerating, at least in my mind, it seemed like parole had more innovative things going on with trying to rehab people and the process of doing all of that.

Parole was going through a downsize rather than an increase in its workload in the mid-1990s. About 1992 or 1993, parole took a really big hit. They actually decreased their workforce quite a bit. The budget situation was a little bit like what we are looking at today, but today is much worse than what we were looking at back then.

In 1996, the parole division started ramping back up again and filling positions that it had downsized. So, that was my first opportunity to come to parole, and I took advantage of it and became a parole agent (PA) in Bakersfield. I lived and worked down there for about 4 years. Here in Sacramento, I was promoted to a PA II and started climbing the ladder of the parole agent series. I became a supervisor, then an administrator, then associate director, then deputy director, and then the director. It was a slow progression from one to the next.

M: Is there something you can identify about yourself that helped you make that progression?

R: In my mind, what drives me has always been pushing to the next thing: the desire and the need, at least from my perspective, to improve my environment. It is less about what the department is doing for me and more about how I can improve my environment, my work, my surroundings and do things better, more efficiently, and with more logic. Always progressing and looking over the fence.

M: So, it's a professional drive.

R: Yes, never stopping. I never looked at what I did. It is always where we are going until you make the touchdown, and then, you go up the field the other way. Always driving the ball. Never mind what you did yesterday, that is done.

M: Things really have changed in California since you started in 1990.

R: Absolutely.

M: This is one of the largest states in the union, and we have a correctional system to match. I am wondering how much of an effect one administrator such as yourself or even a small group of administrators can have on such a large and complex system with so many external stakeholders.

R: As leaders, we always have the primary responsibility of public safety, be it the prison system or in parole; that is our primary responsibility. If you can't provide for the safety of your employees, the inmates, or the parolees, then everything else falls apart at that point. There are several things that impact our environment.

First are external stakeholders. In the mid-1980s to early 1990s, California was driving a number of laws related to heavy responses to criminality. Regardless of whether it was serious or not, this state was pushing hard to drive a point that it was not going to tolerate any criminality at all from its population, and so, we went through a prison boom. We were not just building one or two prisons; we increased by 25% and almost doubled again. So, over the course of a very short period, we went from a dozen or so, to 15, 20, 25, 30, and now we are up to 33 prisons. Three strikes legislation and other strict sentencing guidelines impacted how quickly and how many people would be sentenced to state prison.

At some point, like anything else, you get to the realization that you can only do that for so long before the population rises beyond building prisons, and unless you are just going to continue building prisons indefinitely, you realize that something else has to happen with this population. And so, I think, other states that had similar laws got to that point much earlier and started making changes to their sentencing laws or how they supervised their offender populations sooner. Those experts also help craft how we respond, because they have experienced similar results. As such, we can learn from those practices and make changes internally. Our ability to impact change is to work with those external stakeholders and learn, in some cases, from their practices to improve our situation.

M: To what extent is the difficulty in making change contributed to by the legislative process in California itself?

R: It is a number of parties, so to speak, that are involved. For starters, our own department has its culture that is steeped in whatever the norms are at the time. Changing a large paramilitary organization takes time and great effort.

The second piece is the media, which also drives public perception in some cases and/or reacts to those perceptions. Our responsibility is to work to provide them information so they can report the changes and communicate with the public. Finally, the legislators and our law enforcement partners. As budget situations change, so do the requirements to respond to our offender population related to program placement and rehabilitative services. While many people agree that they need those services, when there are funds, there are great expectations to use those programs. In California, a panel of experts consisting of academicians, correctional trends, and other program-related staff were assembled to make recommendations for program placement. Oftentimes, there is a great expectation that we place everyone in programs.

When the fiscal situations change and there is a decline in revenue, the ability to place the offenders in those programs becomes greatly reduced, and we begin to find that we can't put offenders at the same rate in programs anymore. While the expectation is still there, the reality is that the money isn't. So, the department started to look at making decisions based upon either a matrix or decision-making instruments, essentially saying, we cannot pick all of you, we have to just pick some of you and this is how we get there. And, that does not happen easily. There are competing interests. There are a lot of people that are experts, and those experts don't necessarily all agree. They provide a foundation. They agree on certain basic things but not always the approach. So, that requires sometimes even more work than taking the instrument and getting past it. That can be an uphill battle. It took us every bit of a couple of years to get through the number of possibilities and the avenues that we could have taken before we finally picked the path we were going to take.

M: That's a cumbersome process.

R: That's a very cumbersome process, because a lot of times, it's not the journey; it is the preparing and planning and negotiating before that takes all the time. Once you got it, you know where you are going.

M: And it was prior to dealing with the expert panels and working with the complexities and politics that they bring that we had the prison growth boom, right?

R: Yes.

M: And then, perhaps, because of the growth boom and due to the nature of corrections in the 1990s, it looks like California also had a series of lawsuits in which one followed the other. Can you respond to some of those lawsuits, perhaps Plata, Coleman, or some others that you think have really made changes in this state in terms of how we do business?

R: From my perspective, a number of the lawsuits have come from the sheer size of this department and its ability. I don't want to sound like the apologist, but it is just like trying to stop a freight train that has already picked up speed. It just takes time. All of the well-intentioned processes that are in place still require some progression to slow the train down. What you have got is a very, very large population at the time of those suits—and it is dropping now but at the time—of more than 160,000 incarcerated plus 125,000 on parole, so you just have a population of some pretty large cities if you think of 350,000 people being in prison and on parole and then trying to deliver services to that number of people.

You have prisons that were trying to deliver mission-oriented services while people are going in and paroling at a very quick pace. Some offenders have serious mental or physical disabilities, while others just accept their inevitable return to prison. All of that churning of inmates while still providing basic delivery of medical services to our inmate population, providing dental, providing mental health, and overcrowding in and of itself can cause an inability to move people to the right place.

The lawsuit that originally dealt with getting people to their parole revocation hearings and getting those hearings to occur on a timely basis started with the timeliness of hearings and progressed into the delivery of programs and placement of offenders into those programs. Coupled with the mental health and physical disabilities and constant movement of returns and releases from prison, the ability to get the right offenders in the programs or to deliver services becomes very difficult. The sheer size of the population, the geographical location of certain prisons, and the need to deal with the offenders' needs can restrict progress that other smaller correctional environments don't experience.

M: It's a very complex process.

R: It requires the department to move quickly. So, in some cases, the department reacted as quickly as it could while other court cases had special masters appointed.

M: Were you in Pelican Bay when the court case arose that originated in Pelican Bay?

R: It was in 1990 when I was there. I was an officer at the time. So, my perception of what was going on versus the much bigger picture of what the department was going through was a little different, because I was looking at it from the ground level. I was there during that time, but I don't know if I can speak about what the department was doing at that time, because there were other administrators in place dealing with those circumstances. But, I can go back to my thinking as an officer and how policies and/or the culture was dictated at the time and how I changed into the parole series and how it was then and today, how we are trying to change that culture and how important it is. And, I can certainly tell you where I learned or what I learned from back then to try to change how we are communicating with staff today. As far as I am concerned, we are doing it much differently.

We didn't have the technology to communicate with people then. I want to spend a little bit of time explaining how we are trying to change the culture, because, fundamentally, if you don't have the buy-in and begin a culture change at the very bottom of your organization, then you are going nowhere. I could spend all day talking to folks, printing documents, but if the people at the ground level who make things work don't buy it, then you are just not going to get anywhere and in this business more than anything else, it is very, "show me what you are talking about, because I like what I am doing." They are not resistant to change, but I think they are steeped in tradition and you have to really sit down and say, "this was good at the time but we have to move in this other direction" and get them to understand why it is that we are moving.

M: The "why" seems crucial. If you are going to ask me to change how I do my job, why should I?

R: Yeah, and for how long will I be doing it this new way and for how long are you going to be around, because I can wait you out.

M: Because they know they will be asked to do it differently by the next person who comes along.

R: Exactly. And, the next guy is going to come along and do it differently. So, I think that is the biggest piece of how we deliver our message. Why it's important and then also to try to get some buy-in at their level.

M: You mentioned the matrix programs and who goes where and how those choices are made. Do you have the specifics, Robert, what percentage of inmates are able to have access to programs through your evolving system?

R: There are two or three things we have to do that are changing in corrections that we did not have in the past. One of them is truly understanding our business and looking to see what other people have done. The second piece is understanding your data. Get data and understand your data so you can put yourself in a position to do things more effectively than in the past. Because if not, then all you really have is anecdotal information and you're not able to really put that into practice.

We never really have enough program slots or beds to put the people that need them into those beds. Our offender need to program availability is somewhere between 30% and 40%. In other words, close to two-thirds of our population have a need that we don't have programs for.

Parole also uses community-based programs like Alcoholics Anonymous and Narcotics Anonymous, to balance between the need to get an offender in a program and availability in the community.

The second responsibility right after programs is reintegrating the offenders into the community and to be able to do that you have to have people who are oriented to that mission who understand the difference between reincarcerating an offender for public safety reasons and being willing to put them into the program in the community because their risk is not great.

The shift in our cultural change from where we were to where we are going now is: how do you decide who goes into that program, and how is it that you know best versus somebody else? How do I get 2500 parole agents from one end of a large state to the other end of the state to react similarly?

M: How do you?

R: That's when you start to change a department's reaction to how it does business. In the past, we used a number of documents that looked at the incarceration history, the substance abuse history, and the criminal background. Staff used varying levels of experience in which, given the same sets of circumstances, they all reacted differently. Some staff felt that one or two uses of narcotics warranted program placement and higher levels of supervision while others felt criminal history and offender violation history was what should dictate supervision and program placement.

About 5 or 6 years ago, we started moving away from that process. It came at the suggestion of the expert panel we assembled as well as other external stakeholders that suggested or recommended looking at what other states did related to making decisions differently.

Other states had begun using risk assessments to help them make decisions like the delivery of services and revocation decisions. It not only standardized the decision making, it also used program space more efficiently given the limited resources.

At first, it was a difficult transition and many internal administrators in our organization felt there was no need for change. As we looked to other states like New York, Ohio, or Illinois, we noticed their need to deal with change and their progression to the use of assessments or decision-making instruments. Their population was really no different than ours, so if it worked for them, it could work for us as well.

Organizational change is not easy and in a division as large as ours, we felt that we needed to bring external experts that had helped other states make that transition much more smoothly than going at it alone. They have worked with other states in similar circumstances and could guide us in lessons learned from those changes and could also provide research and suggestions on how to implement the changes over the course of time. Their responsibility was to work with our internal experts in reorganizing our priorities so that they could be implemented successfully.

Although we needed to change what we were doing in offender responsivity, we also needed a risk and a needs assessment to be able to supervise our population more effectively. In collaboration with the University of California, Irvine, Corrections developed the California Static Risk Assessment also known as the CSRA.

This instrument is predictive in its ability to say how it is that offenders recidivate: it is either low or moderate, or high drug, high property, or high violence.

The use of the CSRA and training on the instrument required much effort on our part as staff felt in some cases that it supplanted their decisions about what risk was. Trying to change perceptions and train 2500 staff required communication, patience, and constant training. Additionally, members of the legislature and the media also had to be informed.

Although the CSRA was an evidence-based risk assessment, the division needed a violation decision-making instrument to respond to violations more consistently. Our department worked to establish an instrument that used the CSRA as a basis for the risk while looking at violations of parole and options available to staff when offenders committed violations to establish a matrix of responses. In short, if an offender had a low risk assessment and had committed a violation that was considered to be low, the matrix would suggest a program referral. On the other hand, if the CSRA was high and the offender committed a more serious violation, the matrix offered more restrictive responses to include incarceration. The difficulty in getting standardization without a matrix is where the risk is moderate and the offense is moderate as well. Using this new decision-making instrument, we had an opportunity to get that consistency. Ultimately, staff always had the right to override the instrument based on their personal experience. That was a critical piece in the process. Staff felt they could use the instrument but could always adjust accordingly.

M: So, the agent maintained his/her discretion?

R: Always should, if you take away the discretion, what the agents will say is that you don't really need me, and they see it as adversarial instead of something that is supposed to help. We also tried to market it as an instrument that will help with consistent decision making. It is not there to agree or disagree with you, but it is there to give you a set of options that, regardless of where you are in the state, you should consider these things before you return somebody back to custody. What we told folks is that when you have these various levels of experience, people going in and out, and nobody is there to help you make decisions as an agent, at least this instrument is something you can reach to for assistance. Most people, when they start a job, want to know what the rules are and what the expectations are in case they need to make decisions they have something to go on. And so people were more likely to move toward something that helps them make the decision but it is not the end-all.

M: And then, there is a risk/needs assessment?

R: There is a RNA, because the needs piece is important. We needed to be able to assign risk, but we also needed to assign needs. So, you could have very low risk but high need or high risk and low needs. Agents would say they are all confused. "I don't know what you want me to do with this guy." So, you have to have these very clear lines that say this is the direction I want you to go. I want you to deal with people (the individual as a whole) and also deal with risk. I want you to put the right person in those programs.

M: I am interested to see the instruments, but recently, we had some changes in parole caseload. Can you speak about that?

R: Sure. So, along with these things moving along, you've almost got to go on a bit of a media blitz with your folks. At one point, we decide that it is not just that this change is afoot, but there is also a fundamental change that has to occur in parole to shift away from how we have been doing things in the past, not because it was not right but because we need to move in this new direction. To get there, we had to ask, what is it we want to do that is different from how we were doing things in the past?

That's where we established our Five-Year Road Map, which outlines 12 major changes that we plan on enacting over the course of 5 years.

The first component was the California Parole Supervision Reintegration Model, and that is what you were talking about, which is restructuring our caseloads. We found that our agents were supervising too many offenders to be effective. Seventy parolees to one parole agent is the current caseload for parole agents, and unless you had a specialized caseload, you basically had 70–85 parolees at any given time. We found that our agents did not have the time to effectively supervise that high of a case count. Our agents were responding from fire to fire, never taking the time to personally deal with all of the things that impact an offender's success in the community. Oftentimes, due to high caseloads, the common response was to meet the basic specifications of supervision and when the parolee violated their condition, return them to custody.

Our division brought in representatives from the field as well as external experts to reassess every aspect of parole work. They reviewed the policies, the studies that were available, and looked at what other states were doing to establish not just lower caseloads but also to tie the supervision specifications to practices that had been proven to be more effective. In this new process, agents have lower caseloads, specifications that are proven to be effective, a true risk assessment, and a decision making instrument that compliments best practices.

M: Are you at the beginning of the 5-year road map?

R: Yes, we started in January of 2010. We are piloting this approach. It is in four parole units in California. One of the things that was recommended was not to shotgun this process out with 110,000 of your offenders and 195 parole units. It is just too big, too massive of a change and you won't get the converts you need. The recommendation was to start small and find out where your mistakes are and gradually refine the process until you are ready to roll it out statewide.

M: In piloting, you are looking at the interface between the parole agent and how they are working with the instruments?

R: Yes, how they work with everything. How they work with the risk assessment. How they work with this radical change from dealing with offenders differently, incentivizing parole, talking about case plans, and talking to the offender. We use something called motivational interviewing now, so those techniques are being assessed. It is all part of that and so it sounds good in the academic circles and it makes sense because it's been done before. But trying to convince 2500 peace officers that—I really need you to spend more time talking to people and you need to listen to the parolee—is not just a simple thing to get to them.

So, we started in the pilot sites and those pilot sites were broken down into three phases. Those four parole units were brought to one training session, and we started phase one, which really dealt with motivational interviewing and case planning prior to the offender coming out on parole, and then it works on the basics of doing things differently when the person comes out: motivating them to understanding the parole plan. Phase two just started 2 weeks ago and is much more intensive. It gets into discharge planning and decisions about the offenders themselves—their needs assessment, the risk assessment, how agents are expected to work with their parolees. Each one of these phases lasts 60 days. These folks go out after the initial training. They test the 60-day process and we make changes that are necessary to make sure that it is

effective and practical for the case carrying agent. We communicate via an Internet portal so staff can see the changes immediately
and can post requests.

M: This is seemingly a major change, albeit a great example of the use of
technology, but a major change to get frontline people to talk to
one another in front of administration.

R: Absolutely. At first, the training sessions did not yield any major suggestions for change or even criticism because staff felt that making
comments would be seen as being critical. We had to convince staff
that they had the right to make comments but more importantly
suggest changes so we could be successful. Our trainers needed to
be patient and listen rather than offer a defense to all the suggestions and the positing on the portal had to be taken seriously with
changes to the suggestions to make staff feel that they had a voice
in the process. It took time, but staff understood that we needed
their suggestions and criticisms to improve on the process.

M: Are they doing it?

R: They are. Some are much more into it and do it with a lot of ease. Others
not so much, but when we go to our meetings, we all get together
as a group, we take notes and post the minutes on the site. The
name is not as important as the issue that is being posted. It helps
to post the training notes as a way of holding ourselves accountable to the change that staff want to see and also to be transparent
in the process.

Phase three is the last 60 days, and that is the closing end. There
is some documentation, paperwork, and discussion of how we discharge people. When we are done with phase three, and this group
gets done testing it, we will fall back and make the final policies
and lock down the forms. Then we can all agree, pretty much, that
this is how the process will work. We will then start to roll out the
process statewide.

M: What is the role now of the outside groups?

R: Our own department collects the data but University of California, Irvine
(UCI) works with us very closely. They are there at our training sessions. They take notes. They're about documenting and also following
through with whether or not our parolees are being impacted later.

The researchers have a software program that measures how the
questions are asked and then the responses by the parolees. There
is a matrix they follow that indicates whether it is effective or not
effective. Their role is to review from their position how our staff
are interacting, make suggestions, and finally, test the effectiveness of what we are doing against groups that have not gone to

the training yet. It is a critical component of understanding our effectiveness in this process.

M: Your relationships with these outside stakeholders seem really critical.

R: Very important. Yes. It is critical. We've had a relationship for a long time. They are very supportive and they have to be critical and present the information in a manner that says—this is how we think it's best. Without them, then all you are really doing is looking at yourself in the mirror and you don't tend to be as critical as you have to be to get out there.

M: It's hard to see what's happening when you are in the middle of it.

R: Yes, and you don't want to believe it some of the time. To some extent, you want to migrate to what you think works.

M: It's difficult to simultaneously be watching the ball and watching what everyone else is doing.

R: Yes, you cannot be the coach, the offensive, and the defensive person at the same time. So, our first big change was getting info out to our agents about what it is that is going on. Our Five-Year Road Map clearly defines where our division is going and it explains what the expectations are. By defining the steps and laying out a timeline, our staff know how long it will take and can follow the progress.

We also asked our managers and administrators to use the road map and the documentation for interviews as a way to get staff motivated to read it. We felt that staff would be willing to learn in some cases by practicing for promotional processes.

M: We've discussed that one of the challenges with this reform is getting frontline staff to buy-in, and even leadership to buy-in, but what are the other challenges in making this new plan come to fruition?

R: Two things. One is execution, because this is an organization that says we are going to do something, we really need to make the time to explain it to staff and give them an opportunity to understand why it is important to them. The second is follow-through—using data collection to see where you are in that process.

For execution, we detailed every single one of the 12 points in something called Microsoft Project. We explained the 12 points and the subtasks within those points. By carefully mapping out the requirements, we were able to detail the steps, how long it would take, and who was responsible for ensuring the tasks were completed. We also made the leadership responsible. We said, "You are responsible in your region or area to implement this piece of it." We all sat down over the course of 3 or 4 days, and we painstakingly detailed every single one of the things that had to happen. So, as a group, we voted on and established timelines and said YOU are responsible for it, YOU are responsible. Everyone has a certain number of tasks and days or months to complete those tasks.

M: They have ownership.

R: Yes, that was part of it, but each person is now prominently displayed online. We are going to track how effective you are percentage-wise on whether or not you've gotten there. Of course, no one wants to be left behind—most people are all in the 50% or the 75% range. A benchmark has been established and they know what it is. When we have meetings, weekly or monthly, whichever one it is, we will pull this out. Just like my parolees, we pull out their benchmark and say, where are you in this organizational change? How is it that you are behind by 20% compared with somebody else? I don't want to hear about such and such.

So, the ability to clearly display this and make it public information—nothing is hidden. When you stand out there with everyone else in comparison to this process, you get conformity. Not with everybody.

M: Informal social control.

R: Yes, but not with everybody.

So, the ones that aren't doing it have moved on or found other places in the organization while others come in and say, I understand what my expectations are, and I know how far I am on this timeline, and I am willing to lay the plan out for you.

They are starting to understand when they are either behind or ahead of the curve.

M: This represents a shift in strategic thinking.

R: Yeah, the steps have to be very well laid out, because if not, there is mass confusion. There are more than 1000 components to this thing, and there is no way I can manage, at the Director's level, the thousands of components. With so much going on and so many moving parts, I have to lay out the big picture, identify the tasks and subtasks within that project, and then manage at the highest level.

The second piece is using our data—looking at literally how far along we are and if everyone is complying with expectations. So, we use our reports server that we recently launched. It tracks unit by unit, district by district, or person by person.

One of the components of our model was to put 1000 people on GPS and the rest on Electronic In-home Detention. The report server automatically populates data in a statewide process to show any variable we need. For example, we can look at the entire parole population or just a region or just an individual. We can see who is employed or unemployed by population type or by region or however else we would want to organize the data.

Every report looks the same but you can drill down in various levels and it will pull out how you compare to someone else. We can compare units to units, and say, how is it that one parole unit versus another parole unit in this district spends a lot more money or a lot less money and with a recidivism rate of a certain amount than these other units?

How are you different than these other units?

What are you doing that is wrong or right? What is different?

We call this the agent report card. It is YOUR report card. It is how you are doing or how your district or unit is working.

This is new. Of course it is going to cause, at first, a lot of questions. People will say, we shouldn't be putting this out there, because people will question it. But there is nothing to hide. This information should be out there so you can manage things differently.

We have to understand our data. Now that we've got this up, don't just tell me you made these changes or that you had a radical change in your area, when I see that you are spending or not spending enough money, or your return to custody rate in certain areas for technical violations of parole is dropping or not dropping. I can take points in time and say, you were going to make some changes, but I don't see a change in revocation rates. Or I do see a change, and they are trending down, and it was right after we had training.

M: With such a large population, will you expect differences in one region versus another?

R: Sure, they are all different. Each one is based upon this road map. The first part focuses on reintegration. The second part of the road map was the reduction of caseloads. Then, next was placing 1000 GPS units on the most severe gang members, and that is up and running. Placing 1200 electronic in-home detention (EID) units as an alternate sanction was included. Then, we will reduce our span of control for supervisors, and then we start to get into our Parolee-at-Large rates for our regions. We scheduled apprehension rates for our regions. Their mission was clearly outlined toward dealing with returning people who have been absconding back under parole supervision.

We did find differences in regions. Sometimes in larger cities, the agents are more impacted. San Francisco has one kind of a problem; San Diego has another. The populations are different. In San Diego, people are released who are much closer to the border. Those people tend to be different than the people in other metropolitan cities. All of those things go into how populations look.

But, for once now, we can look at a unit and say, "You know, I noticed that your employment rate is higher, your people abscond more often, you agree or disagree with an instrument maybe a third of the time, and you are not referring the number of people you need to, and you are returning people back to custody more than anyone else. And when I look at your type of returns, it actually looks like the types of returns are technical." We can start to set a trend line that shows, "You know, I don't know yet, but you are not spending any money, your people were unemployed, they tend to abscond, and your responses to those kind of violations is to return parolees back to custody. How will that change if you don't change your responsivity or agree more with an instrument or less?"

M: You now have a statewide comprehensive picture. Do you think it is easier or harder to be a Corrections Officer today than it was when you were an officer in the early 1990s?

R: It may have been easier as a CO then, because we were still able to... It was kind of like being a police officer in the 1950s when you did not have half of the laws or half of the problems. There was and continues to be a progression toward doing things such as effective communication with our population, etc., where in the past, it was said, "You have a disability, deal with it." And now, obviously, you cannot do that anymore.

With the parole agents, I think the same things have changed. We have evolved from doing whatever we did with some anonymity. There were some things that we did then that we had to get away from. For example, one of the biggest changes that we are employing here is a field office trainer program. We look at outside law enforcement agents who graduated from a police academy but you don't go out with a gun until you go through a field officer training program. It says, OK, you have the basics, but now you have to pass a battery of tests that tells us you are capable of making good, sound decisions out there. Los Angeles, California is nothing like small towns. So we are going to teach you these processes.

We found that our parole agents graduated from their academy. They've got an education and have some minimum requirements. They've got some experience. They are a little older than your average 22-year-old. They are a little more mature. But they still did not have the basics of Parole Agent work engrained in them. They would have a caseload that was stacked high and all of a sudden it is YOUR problem to figure out. You moved from a small town in Northern California to a large metropolitan city. You have 80 cases. Good luck! Your partner is right there, but he is too busy trying to figure what he is doing to help you out. This was not working well.

We established a Field Training Officer (FTO) program that is 10 weeks and starts in January. Every single one of the agents who will go through the program will go to a classroom program put on by California's Peace Officers Standards and Training that teaches them how to be good instructors and good mentors. At first, they will show the new agent how to interact with people— the first 3 weeks are just that: here is how you book someone into the county jail; here is how you get through the file or what freeways to travel—the basics.

The second 3 weeks, the new agent takes over the supervision of the FTO's caseload and starts to get involved with the parolees and gets acclimated to how that works. The last 3 weeks, the FTO is watching the agent work by him or herself and is just going through a process of evaluating that person. Those evaluations go to the supervisor who now has, at least, a tangible process in place and can say—based on your FTO report, here is what you can or cannot do. If you failed the FTO program, you have to remediate or you are not going to become a parole agent. This is a big change from the way we used to do things in the past. Radical difference.

That took a lot of convincing and there were some financial requirements that we had to work hard to get in this fiscal environment. We had to show them that we are paying through the nose because people are making mistakes or getting fired or making decisions that are not consistent with good practices.

We also have a Supervisors Academy now. It used to be one day you were told what to do and the next you are telling people what to do. Now you go through basic supervision which includes standardized supervisor training like sexual harassment, then there is a specialized parole supervisor academy that gets into specific parole unit operation. I remember being promoted to a supervisory position and saying to myself, "I don't know what I'd do if we had a bomb threat." I thought that was ridiculous, so we initiated a 3-week academy and it goes through the ABC's of supervisory issues. What do you do if someone is stuck with a needle? How do you go through the basic processes of a bomb threat or riots—just basic supervision.

We have a mix of new supervisors and experienced ones. It's the experienced ones with their arms crossed, saying, "I've been doing this for 10 years and you are going to have to explain to me why I have to go." So, when we ask them to respond to critical situations and they can't answer them correctly, we remind them that time in grade doesn't necessarily mean you have all the answers. And, if you do, we need you to help teach.

M: What would you consider to be the greatest problem facing the correctional system at this time?

R: Tradition and probably just culture.

M: Internal challenges?

R: Absolutely.

M: It sounds like you are leaning heavily on external agencies/institutions that are providing you with guidance and empirically based literature. What should the relationship between theory and practice be in corrections?

R: I don't know how anybody can get through something as complex as corrections without the assistance of people that have either been there before and studied it or who understand trends. It is not that they know more than you, but they have been through some of these situations with other states or they understand that A and B comes before C, and they will help you avoid doing some of those things.

M: We have a narcotics war on the border of this state, I am sure you must have to deal with that to some extent. We also have two wars abroad that you have had officers called away to fight. To what degree has the California Corrections system been impacted by international relations or transnational relations?

R: Just like anything else, our agents serve in a number of wars or military exercises. They go out and come back. The biggest impact they have had with us is less about the understanding their correctional practices work to ours. We cannot get to their countries to see how it is that they are doing things.

I think laws have impacted or at least other countries' responsivity to things like drugs and how they deal with those things. Our federal system, the U.S. Immigration and Customs Enforcement (ICE) system, and whether or not they deport people or push them off on to us has been what has impacted us more so than what is going on in another country.

For example, there has been a policy shift related to deportation. It used to be that people who complete their time in a state prison would come out to parole and we would keep that person on active parole even though they have been deported back to their country of origin, mostly Mexico. When they enter the United States illegally, the first thing we would do is snatch them up for violation of parole and turn them back to custody. There was a change in policy that now says when that person completes their time and they come out and are deported, we actually discharge that person from parole.

Of course, locally, that push from a number of people was that you pushed it off on to that other country or to someone else to deal with it. It is not really about pushing it off but the responsibility really falls on other federal agencies to deal with that person. They entered the United States illegally, so they should be prosecuted if they entered illegally. There are federal laws to return them. It is not because parole doesn't want to do it, but at some point, we have a finite number of resources, and there is only so much we can do. We are clogging up state prisons with parole violations for 5 months before returning them back to where, in fact, they should be getting prosecuted. So, I am not saying, and the administration is not saying, that we don't want to deal with it, because they do. People need to be prosecuted, and the spirit of the law needs to be applied to these people. We are saying that 4 months for a return to custody for violation of parole for illegally reentering the United States is not really the true response. It should be 3 years back to state prison.

It gives the parole division an opportunity to deal more specifically with our parole population as opposed to this other group of people who should be dealing with someone else. And that is sometimes hard to communicate with other agencies.

Externally, that is related to narcotics and the movement our parolees are involved in it, but it is a much bigger problem than just the parole division. The trafficking of narcotics up the United States corridor and the guns that come back down and the southern Latin American or Mexican borders that are a problem are just bigger than the parole division can tackle.

M: The border has a strong interface with Corrections.

R: Oh yeah, our parolees are involved in that kind of activity, and to the extent that we can limit their movement and their criminality when it comes to those kinds of endeavors, we do, but it is a very big problem.

M: Would you say that you are basically satisfied or dissatisfied with the developments in the field of corrections as a whole?

R: I'm never satisfied, but it is not unsatisfied in the sense that we have not done a good job, but I just think that the minute you are satisfied, somebody is passing you up.

I said that earlier as the leadership of this organization, and not just me but my bosses, we always have to be looking to the next step. We completed this, but our eye always has to be down the road as to where we want to go. So you say, where do you want to go? I don't know because 5 years from now when we have reached the goals, there may be some changes in corrections or law enforcement of things that haven't been tested or new things out there.

We still have lots of work to do, not because we are slow, but again, I liken it to a large aircraft carrier. You can't just turn on a dime, but you always have to be ready. The day you sit down and say you are going to bask in your success is the day that somebody passes you up and says you've missed the ball. Fundamentally, you have to be intellectually inquisitive about what it is that is going on out there and you have to search the Internet, you have to attend conferences. I sit in on a number of law enforcement meetings with my partners, and I have conversations about what they are unhappy about and sometimes about what they are happy about. But it is important to hear about their perception of what services you are delivering to them, because those are the people who are talking about you when you are not there. Again, you are constantly looking at information and assessing yourself. You are not changing from what you have done because this is our road map, but you make changes about the way you communicate with your constituents, about how you get this information out there. I make these presentations to them constantly about what it is that is going on and what is happening, constantly informing them, pushing out these sites, saying this is what it is.

I'm satisfied that we're making the changes, but I'll never be satisfied about where it is we have to go because I'll never retire.

M: Is that day going to come?

R: I don't think so. I'm not the kind of guy who takes a lot of vacations. My deputy director is extremely faithful to the mission of our division, as are all the managers.

We spend time after hours talking about what is going on. We e-mail each other. We're always in communication. You want to hire people who keep it moving and live and breathe that. When you have everyone chained up together—WE are one front. We travel together. We spend time together outside of work. Last weekend, we went on a 5 K fun run. What is important is that when people see you together as an organization outside of work as well as inside of work, they don't use systems to divide you from other people.

The people who aren't interested move on or find something else in the organization and those who are interested want to join it because they see it moving in the right direction or want to help it get along.

M: What you describe sounds like a tightly woven cohesive management style. Can you see other management teams that function like you do or make an organizational comparison to another sort of model?

R: It does a couple of things. For starters, in any organization, you are at the top worried that somebody is not carrying the water of the mission and not moving things together. When you get enough of that kind of thing, things start to fall apart. So, in this organization, it took time. From my perspective, I was promoted through the ranks. I came in through the floor.

I made a number of relationships, personal and professional. They became my friends. We worked hard.

My standard is that you can be my friend, but if you are not effective, I am not going to put you in a place of leadership. We are still friends, and we can have a beer together, but you are not going to be the person who carries that process.

It was important to me that the people that surrounded me were tied to the mission and I could trust them to get that done. You have to have organizational trust and measures (or managers) of that trust, and you are responsible for doing X, can you? And those people, over the course of time, are the people I can send out, and they are going to do my work for me and report back. Always though, the core group of people talk about what is going on and recalibrate. We are very honest with each other. There are times when we have very heated debates and laughs and there is name-calling.

It is good, though, because I get to say that was a stupid thing that you did. Let's change that and you have to be willing to roll with that.

We have public discussions and then get in the car together, and you have to be brutally honest. What did I say or do? You ran your mouth off too long about this, and you did not get to that, and next time I change based on that. We improve that.

Other organizations that do that out there, I've noticed, to some extent, are our law enforcement organizations. It's the same type of thing, you know, coming through the ranks, and their chief or deputy chief and maybe they have a core group of people. The people who work for me, I trust with my life. I trust them with the mission of the division.

The mission is bigger than the person behind it. Do not let me step outside of what it is that we are supposed to be doing. If I am out there, it is your responsibility to say this piece was not right and bring me back to the center and stay true to the mission.

As long as they do, then they own the mission with us.

Glossary

Armstrong v. Davis: This case resulted in a federal injunction mandating the Board of Prison Terms to remedy its failure to comply with the Americans with Disabilities Act during parole hearings.

Budd v. Cambria: This case resulted in a federal mandate for the CDC to have all in-patient healthcare facilities licensed.

Coleman v. Wilson: This case found that the mental health care services delivered by the CDCR were inadequate. The Court appointed a Special Master to evaluate the CDCR's level of compliance with the Court orders of improvement.

Gates v. Deukmejian: This case found that the California Medical Facility was overcrowded and medical care, psychiatric care, and the treatment of HIV-positive inmates needed improvement. The CDCR agreed to improve conditions, and the compliance with this order is now managed as part of the *Coleman* lawsuit.

Plata v. Davis/Schwarzenegger: This case is the largest class-action prison lawsuit to date. It resulted in a complete overhaul of medical care delivered by the CDCR and a federal receivership to manage the process.

Rosenkrantz v. Davis: This case upheld the Board of Prison Terms parole decisions related to lifers' lack of suitability for parole.

Valdivia v. Davis: This case found that that delays in the parole revocation process violated due process protections.

References

Armstrong v. Davis, 275 F.3d 849 (2001).

Blue Ribbon Commission on Inmate Population Management. 1990. *Blue Ribbon Commission on Inmate Population Management: Final Report.* Sacramento, CA: Blue Ribbon Commission on Inmate Population Management.

Budd v. Cambria, San Francisco Superior Court Case No. 319578 (2002).

California Department of Justice. 2010.

Civil Rights Act of 1871, 42 U.S.C. (1983).

Clear, T. 1995. *Harm in American Penology: Offenders, Victims and their Communities.* New York: State University of New York Press.

Coleman v. Wilson, 912 F.Supp. 1282 E.D. Cal. (1995).

Dyer, J. 2000. *The Perpetual Prison Machine: How Americans Profit from Crime.* Boulder, CO: Westview Press.

Gates v. Deukmejian, 987 F.2d 1392 9th Cir. (1993).

Little Hoover Commission. 1994. *The Prevention of Youth Crime—California Youth Authority.* Sacramento, CA: The State of California Little Hoover Commission.

Little Hoover Commission. 1998. *Beyond Bars: Correctional Reforms to Lower Prison Costs and Reduce Crime.* Sacramento, CA: The State of California Little Hoover Commission.

Little Hoover Commission. 2007. *Solving California's Corrections Crisis: Time is Running Out.* Sacramento, CA: The State of California Little Hoover Commission.

Madrid v. Gomez, C90-3094 U.S. District Court of California (1995).

Plata v. Davis/Schwarzenegger, 329 F.3d 1101 9th Cir. (2003).

Rotman, E. 1995. The Failure of Reform: United States, 1865–1965. In *The Oxford History of the Prison: The Practice of Punishment in Western Society*, edited by N. Morris and D. Rothman. New York: Oxford University Press.

Rosenkrantz v. Davis, 80 Cal. App. 4th 409 (2000).

Travis, J. and S. Lawrence. 2002. California's parole experiment. *California Journal.* Urban Institute: Justice Policy Center.

United States Census Bureau. 2010. Retrieved from http://www.census.gov/popest/estimates.html.

Valdivia v. Davis, 206 F.Supp.2d 1068 (E.D. 2002).

Interview with "CM"

JOANNA SPINK

12

On June 30, 2010, Ken Clarke, the British Justice Secretary, announced a £4 billion cut in the prisons budget, raising the prospect of a sharply reduced prison-building* program after years of expansion in inmate numbers and the probable slashing of the previous government's plans to support another five, 1500-capacity jails managed by private contractors.*

Financial cuts across all areas of public spending had been anticipated because of the global economic crisis, and the prison budget reduction of up to 25% was in line with other government departments. What was surprising was the apparent ideological change of the dominant Conservative section of the Conservative/Liberal Democrat coalition government's beliefs about the efficacy of prison as a deterrent or suitable punishment. The last Conservative government of 1990–1997 is remembered in part for its hard-line approach to offenders:

> "Let us be clear. Prison works. It ensures that we are protected from murderers, muggers, and rapists, and it makes many who are tempted to commit crime think twice" (extract from a speech by the then Home Secretary, Michael Howard, to the Conservative party conference 1993).
>
> "We have built 22 new prisons since 1980… we will provide another 8500 prison places by the year 2000" (Conservative Party Manifesto 1997).

Hence, it was surprising that this Conservative orthodoxy was challenged by Ken Clarke in his first major speech as Justice Secretary. Although certainly appeasing to many of his Liberal Democrat colleagues, his views would have been much less welcomed by hard-line right-wing Conservative Members of the Parliament, and the change in direction was certainly absent from the Conservatives election manifesto. Clarke said he was "amazed" that the number of people in prison had grown to 85,000 and maintained that keeping a prisoner in jail was "a costly and ineffectual approach that fails to turn criminals into law-abiding citizens."

Cynics might suggest that these strongly argued but directly oppositional views from ministers who were and are vocal in 1990–1997 and present administrations correlate more to available funding rather than to any ideological debate based on empirical data. Nevertheless, the outcome of the budget cut, whatever its rationale, will be fewer prison places and more community-based sentences.

---

* In Britain, the words "prison" and "jail" are synonymous terms and used interchangeably.

Two weeks before the announcement of these budget cuts but anticipatory of them, an interview was conducted with a person who has a history of working in resettlement both inside and outside various prisons in the north of England but has never been directly employed by HM Prison Service, referred to as CM throughout this chapter. For several years, CM had worked for and managed a charitable organization with a mandate in resettlement with bases in many prisons. Their services were not compulsory for inmates, so all the prisoners who asked for assistance were presumably already motivated to change their lives in some manner on release. The following extracts from the interview outline his background, the rationale of his work, and his personal recommendations about the future of the resettlement and rehabilitation of offenders. These views are not intended to represent any organization but are based solely on CM's personal thoughts and experiences.

CM: I had just less than 20 years working in BT* in various management roles. Toward the end of that career, I spent time managing a help desk in a redeployment unit, which was about helping people who'd been displaced out of their job within BT. They didn't make people redundant, but they actually helped redeploy them within the company, so my role in there was to help find people roles within that company. That's where I kind of got the views that I did about enjoying helping people—having them move forward with their lives. A friend of mine was working for a charity that was working in the prisons and asked, would I be interested in doing some work with them. So that's how I got into prisons, and I started at a young offenders institution,† which is basically adults under 21, male. I

---

* British Telecommunications.

† In England and Wales, prisoners are assigned security classes when they are sentenced. Thus, prisons are given security classifications depending on the prisoners they are designed to hold. Prisons classified as "A" would typically house prisoners assigned the "A" category during sentencing and would be designed with the level of security necessary for that class. The categories of prisoners in descending order are as follows: Category A prisoners are those whose escape would be highly dangerous to the public or national security; Category B prisoners are those who do not require maximum security but for whom escape needs to be made very difficult; Category C prisoners are those who cannot be trusted in open conditions but are unlikely to try to escape; and Category D prisoners are those who can be reasonably trusted not to try to escape and are given the privilege of an open prison. Subject to approval, prisoners at "D Cat" (as it is commonly known) prisons are allowed to work in the community or to go on "home leave" after a period of their imprisonment is concluded.

The British prison system is also divided into "open" and "closed" prisons. Categories A through C are considered "closed" prisons as prisoners cannot be trusted to interact with society, whereas Category D prisons are generally "open," which means that prisoners who have a good record and are approved can be allowed limited function in society.

A Young Offenders Institution (YOI) is for persons aged 18–20 years, occasionally also housing offenders as young as 15 years.

was working as a coordinator, which was helping them look to see what they wanted to do when they got released. To either get into some sort of work or some sort of training or education, I learned various things as to how to find training opportunities, education opportunities, things along those lines.

Q: So the philosophy was always how important work is really, even in a corporate setting, for anybody?

CM: One of the prisons' key aims was to help reduce reoffending and people coming back into the prisons was that they needed to have some kind of focus once they got out. So, ideally, jobs to go to, and then, they were less likely to reoffend but if not a job, then some sort of formal training or education that would move them forward toward a job or at least even a focus while they were outside. So, the project was very much aimed at looking at the first month of them being released. I would work with them up until the release date, and then, they moved on to someone else.

Alongside this work, I was actually monitoring what was going on *(resettlement work)* throughout all the prisons in the area. Monitoring what their results were, monitoring the quality of their work. It gave me a chance to go round all the other prisons, which included male and female prisons, high and low category prisons, plus open prisons where people can actually go out to work while still serving their prison sentence.

That project ran for just 3 years; then, the contract got taken over by a different firm, and I got moved as part of my job to actually go back to working directly with offenders again but working in a female prison, an open prison, which was, I found, very enjoyable. The ladies there were very much focused on going out to work while they were still in prison, getting jobs, and what they wanted to do when they got released. Now, I am managing this project, which again is going to work in the prisons, but it is also working with probation and people on orders to actually do some sort of corrective behavior work while with probation. So, it might be people who are doing unpaid work community orders, it might be people who are actually released from prison and living in hostels. The whole ethos of it is that, if people are employed or more likely to be employed, then they are less likely to reoffend, so the whole aim of the project is to reduce reoffending but it's doing it through making people more employable and having employability skills.

Q: When you started your work in prisons, was that a major focus?

CM: The ethos wasn't so much focused on employment; it was very much on what was called ETE, employment training education. We still know that we are not going to get every person we work with into employment, and it could well be that the right move for somebody is to actually get them onto some sort of formal accredited training or education course. The whole ethos is that, if they're occupied and doing stuff when they get out, they have not got spare time on their hands, and if they're actually working and they are getting some proper money coming in through the correct channels, then that means that they're less likely to get themselves in with the wrong crowd doing the wrong things but also looking to have money that they've already earned.

Q: Looking at this politically, we had the Thatcher* years and probably less emphasis on training and education in prison service, and then "Tough on crime, tough on the causes of crime."†

CM: I think the whole resettlement concept has come in more recently. It has really moved forward with a pace during this last decade or so. It's very much saying that the aim of a prison is not just to keep people off the streets, but while they're in here, let's do resettlement work, so they can lead what we would consider to be a proper life back in society and not be a burden on the justice system and society.

Q: Theoretically, there are lots of arguments about what prison's for: punishment, to act as a deterrent to others, to try to change somebody's life, or to help somebody stop making wrong choices. You do hear in the popular press more talk about let's throw the key away…

CM: I think that is borne out of a little bit of ignorance of what actually goes on and actually meeting some of the people that you do meet when you're in prisons. There are some people about whom you think "you're never going to change"—that is their lives, that they will permanently be criminals, some to a higher degree than others, but you have the ones, possible with mental illness, that just don't understand that what they're doing is wrong. And obviously, right down the line, you get to the serial killers. But, I think the key thing that you do notice once you start working in prisons is that you do come across a high number of people that, for various reasons, have just got themselves on the wrong track. It could be that they've actually met with the wrong people. Some people have just been in the wrong place at the wrong time, you know, generally not bad people as such, and I think they're the ones that you really do feel that you can help and support them.

Q: Some are just immature?

CM: Yes, you get some. I started working with the under 21s, and some of those, it hasn't clicked at all what they've been doing. When you say

---

* Margaret Thatcher, British Prime Minister, 1979–1990.
† New Labour "sound bite" first used by British Prime Minister Tony Blair in 1992.

how many times have you been in prison, and this is their seventh or eighth time, and you look at them, and they don't know any difference, then you get someone who asks for your help, because it's suddenly clicked with them, this isn't the place I want to be. Yes, I do accept that you do get people out there who say they should just be in prison, breaking stones and serving their time. But, my own view now is, what's the point of sending them back out, without any help when they are just going to make the same mistakes and end up back inside again. Ultimately, it's going to cost me money as a taxpayer. It's going to cause me grief when these people are out in society.

My work is very interesting and rewarding on a personal level. No two days are ever the same, but the key reason that I like doing this job is how good you feel when you realize you've changed somebody's life. When you actually do something and because of what I've done, that is going to make a difference to that person for the rest of their life. That is an incredible buzz, and that is the rewarding part. It doesn't happen all the time; it doesn't happen often enough. I've been to people and told them here's what I've got set up for them, and it was basically thrown back in my face and said, I don't need that, I'm going back out to rob some people when I get out.

There's a lot of genuine people who come into prison, who just need a bit of, I was going to say reassurance, but its more confidence within themselves and showing that there are people who actually care what they want to do and giving them that bit of a push. There is an incredible amount of help that's available out in the community once people get released from prisons. I think, on the whole, there has been a change in the whole community aspect of what's available to help people—funding or free courses and things specifically to help offenders. It's quite ironic that you can get more funding if you have actually been taking drugs. When I ask offenders if they've been taking drugs, they're a bit reluctant to tell you. I say, ironically, you know, if you've taken drugs, I can get you this course for free. I couldn't get it for myself for free, because I've never taken drugs. Is that really fair that some people can get these things for free when you get a law-abiding citizen who's just out of work that they can't get that training?

It all comes back to this; ultimately, is this going to benefit society as a whole?

Q: Is it government money that's funding projects in resettlement or...?

CM: It's very much government funding, but there are also other funding streams coming on board. European funding comes into things. It comes under the term social funds, so it's actually to help society as a whole, but it's aimed at combating antisocial behavior to a certain degree and trying to make everybody's life better by reducing the elements of crime that are out there, but the main source is through government and LSC funding and things on those lines.

Q: LSC?

CM: Learning and Skills Council.*

Q: Oh right.

CM: So, they produce funding to help people, improve their basic skills and knowledge, and things on those lines. It might primarily have been a knock-on effect, because prisons were getting so overloaded. I think what they're looking at is getting more community orders in place so people, when they're actually sentenced at court, they're actually given orders that send them back into the community to do work for the benefit of the community. They might have to start wearing orange fluorescent jackets with community payback on them so that the public can actually see that here is somebody who's done something wrong, been to court, and has been ordered to go out and do some work to help the community. Be it by painting the local halls or sweeping the roads or things along those lines.

Q: And these are people who may have had a short prison sentence before?

CM: Yes, in the past, they might well have been sent to prison. Also, they have set up the National Offender Management System† so that you have your district and national offender managers. So, the offender manager structure in charge of all of Yorkshire is responsible for a pot of money. So, what they're now trying to achieve is having prisons in Yorkshire having prisoners who are going to be released back to Yorkshire. It also helps us to... why are we penalizing the families more by saying go and see your son, daughter, husband, father whatever, we're making you travel 150 miles when okay, you can

---

* The Learning and Skills Council was a nondepartmental public body jointly sponsored by the Department for Business, Innovation and Skills and Department of Children, Schools and Families in England, until March 31, 2009. It was established in April 2001, but after severe criticism and claims of financial mismanagement in March 2008, the abolition of the LSC was announced; funding responsibilities for training young people were transferred to other organizations.

† The National Offender Management Service is an executive agency of the Ministry of Justice. It brings together HM Prison Service and the Probation Service to enable a more effective delivery of their services. It is responsible for commissioning and delivering offender management services in custody and in the community, helping to deliver punishments and reparation and coordinate rehabilitative, health, educational, employment, and housing opportunities for offenders to reduce reoffending as well as overseeing the contracts of privately run prisons, managing probation performance and creating probation trusts. There are nine regional offices in England and one office in Wales (http://www.hmprisonservice.gov.uk/abouttheservice/noms/).

just travel 30 miles down the road. It helps keep families together. We do have prisons where they have mother and baby units. So, you can have a mother who's coming into a prison who can bring her child with her up to the age of 18 months. Again, that's very much to foster family relationships. The women's prison I worked in previously had a facility where families can come and stay for 1 or 2 nights or a weekend or during the midweek. A mother who was in there could then have her children up to the age of 18 years coming and living in this house, which was on the prison grounds but not part of the prison. And again, that's all to keep maintaining those family links. Those visits are just for children and not conjugal or anything on those lines. It was a category D prison, but when I was there, I think there were 12–15 prisoners who had life sentences but they were coming to the time where they were eligible for parole. They had served life sentences for murder, so very much high-profile people in there and high-profile crimes as well.

Q: I know that you use voluntary help from members of the community to work for your projects. That's an interesting change. Opening up what has always been viewed as behind closed doors—literally—prison life. You are asking individuals to befriend or work with or help with this sort of work on a voluntary capacity. I don't think that's been common practice before, has it?

CM: It's not been common in the prison environment, and it's something that my organization is very keen on promoting. There are a high number of people out there who, for whatever reason, do want to volunteer and actually help people. They might not be able to commit themselves to a vast amount of time, so from our point of view, we are looking at people volunteering for 1 or 2 hours a week. It might be that prisoners just need somebody who's got a bit more life experience to talk them through things, or it might well be that you actually have somebody who has some specific skills that they can help people with. But, it's certainly something that the prison managers are keen on, and they see it as a huge benefit. The prisoners accept the help more openly as the person helping is not an authority figure. That's one of the key reasons why our work is successful. Prisoners don't see us as people who are going to start telling them that you can or can't do this, and certainly, what we want is for the volunteer to continue that relationship with the prisoner on release, so they can help them get reintegrated back into the community, potentially meet them when they leave prison to actually help them go to the job center to get things set up, if they need to apply for any loans, things like that, if they need to go to a doctor, dentist, anything like that and then potentially giving them help to look for work. Quite often, all a person needs is just somebody to be there to give them a bit of support when they go for a job interview, when they come back and say, this happened, that happened, and so on.

I was very pleasantly surprised when I realized how many people actually put themselves to be volunteers. I think it's very commendable, and it shows up very well on the British public.

Q: Do all inmates have access to some program or some other sort of training or other if they want it?

CM: I can't talk for the very high security prisons, because I really don't know. I would guess that, when you get to high-profile, very dangerous people, no. They won't have any provisions to actually do things, but certainly, the prisons that we work in, when you get down to a less of a risk category, then certainly our programs are open to everybody, and the range of resources is very much tailored to what their needs are. Recently, it has become clear that rather than offering a provision that everyone can go through, the prisons think more about what the specific benefits for individuals are. So, rather than somebody going through a carpentry course, then doing a hairdressing course the next week, and then doing a chef's course the week after, well you know, where's all this leading? Now, it's very much focused—well, here's where you want to go and let's channel you down a very specific route. You do get some in there that want to do everything on offer, because they just see it as an opportunity to get out of their cell.

Q: If you were to be given as much money as ever you wanted and to redesign a prison in any way, shape, or form you thought was the best way, in the ideal Utopian world, what would you like to do?

CM: For a prison to be really effective and work, it works in the first few weeks. So, my view... when you get an individual who has broken the law and is deemed to go to prison, I think that it should be a very short sharp shock to the system. To say, right, you're in here for 4 or 5 weeks, we will give you as much help as we can, but this is prison, your liberties are taken away from you. Some of the prisoners that I've seen who come to prison for the first time, after 2 or 3 weeks, they're at their most vulnerable. This is the opportunity to educate them about what they should or should not be doing. When you then see them again in 6 or 7 months' time, what you find is someone who's almost become hardened to being a prisoner and saying you know, no problem, I can do this, and it's not a big deal to me anymore. So, I think my first thing would be that you need to hit them hard in the first few weeks. Make it so they don't want to be here. What I would also do is concentrate resources on the first time somebody comes in. I think you need to give them the message that we are going to help you, improve your life. If they come back in for a second time, I think you still do that, but as time goes on, those opportunities become less and less. If somebody had all this help and is still going out and committing more crime and coming back to prison again, then, perhaps on a sliding scale, the harder prison life should be for them. Right now, it is, well, now you are back in for the 12th time and you still get all the benefits and you still do this, that, and the other.

Q: So, they are progressing to more of a punishment?

CM: Yes. So, resettlement, to begin with, but a limit on the chances they are given. It's a sad thing, but you do get people who actually feel safer in prisons. They feel more secure in their life in prisons, so they'll go out, and straight away, they'll do something to get arrested to come back into prison, because that's where they see themselves as being in a safe environment. I think they need to be looked at slightly differently, because obviously, there's some kind of mental issues there.

Q: Have you found an increasing number of people with mental health problems and similarly obvious drug issues? This is very current, isn't it, the debate about more and more people becoming involved in drugs and people being in prison purely because of drug addiction, trying to fund that drug addiction? Perhaps, they are not a "bad" person intrinsically, but they have been stealing purely to feed an addiction.

CM: I haven't personally seen the numbers rising. Referring to people who might have mental issues, they really don't grasp the concept that their lives are not the norm. Maybe it's through experiences in their childhood or whatever, and I think that to them the norm is that you do this crime and potentially you might get caught and sent to prison. Then, you have to look at prisoners with mental issues who really don't have any concept of right and wrong anyway.

The people admitting to substance addiction of one kind or another is quite a high proportion. One of the questions we ask them is: Have you got any drug use? It's very rare for them to say no, they've never taken drugs; you do get some, but not many. And, I think that's another key thing. A lot of people do go to jail because they are stealing to fund that habit. There is a debate as to whether you make some of the drugs legal and make it available. Would that reduce crime in a big way because you have then taken away all the drug barons and your taking away the need to go out and steal if you can get drugs quite openly?

Q: Would get drugs on prescription or...?

CM: I think something on those lines. I really don't have a strong particular view on that one way or the other, but I think it's an interesting debate to discuss to what extent would society be better if drugs were legalized to a certain degree and be readily available. On prescription or even just to go out and buy at a quite sensible price, as opposed to what they have to be normally.

Q: Philosophically, we accept alcohol as a legal substance and the damage alcohol does, which is huge... but politically, that is a dangerous debate to start. Nobody dare raises that sort of question, or they are immediately unelectable. Talking of politicians, when politicians make decisions about how they are planning to fund the prison service, how they are going to tackle recidivism, how they're going to fund resettlement projects like yours (or not), do you find it frustrating? Do you think that they understand the issues and make policy decisions based on evidence rather than political bias?

CM: I don't think that they don't know what they're talking about, but at times, you just wonder if they actually spent any time talking at the grass roots, when they're talking about these things and can be sitting there thinking. Well, that isn't my experience and how I see things happening. Potentially cutting money from the resettlement budget, for example, I think it seems a very shortsighted way to actually save money. Ultimately, the type of work I do is to reduce the numbers of criminals. Well, you should be pumping more money into that area. Some politicians have to be very careful, because they need to favor public support anyway, and if the public view is lock people up and we don't want to see them, then that's what they're going to have to do to make sure they are going to get reelected.

There has been a lot of research done looking at the number of people who reoffend if they are or are not employed, housed, and things like that. Employment is the key criteria to reduce offending, and the other key statistic was that people are more likely to reoffend within 3 months of leaving prisons, so again, if you get them past that initial period.

Q: Do you think too many people are sentenced to prison? People are sent to prison that could be dealt with better in the community?

CM: I think there's a mixture. From my experiences, there are people you just think, why on earth were you sent to prison? Before I say anything else, I'll put a slight rider on it, as this is from what I've gained from them. You've always got the caveat that you might not have the whole truth (*about their crimes*) from what they've said. From the perception you get, from the background they come from, their home, social life, and for the crime that they've committed, you just wonder why this person is in prison. I think it all depends on which magistrate, judge,* or whatever you get as to how they actually view you. I don't particularly think that there are too many people sent to prison. What I think you need to be quite careful at looking at in the future is, how do you get the balance, as we said before, of keeping the public safe and ensuring the public believe justice has been done and providing the best situation for the individual. Is it to actually send them to prison? The last time I looked, I think it was something like 80,000 people in prisons, and 5,000 are women. Now, I do not believe that the proportion of male offenders to female is 75:5. I think that's somewhere; there's a particular imbalance.

Q: Definitely. So finally then, none of us knows where the financial cutbacks are going to come from. What are your expectations or fears?

CM: I think looking at it from what we're doing, I really do have a passion now that what we do is actually going to help people, it's going to benefit them, and it's going to benefit society. I think there are a lot of individuals out there that just need a little bit of support, a little bit of a hand on the shoulder, and come on, you can make something out of your life. A lot of the people I work with just need that little bit of help and guidance, and they could actually make real progress themselves and turn their lives around, because you know, there are a number of people in prison who really have just made a silly mistake or just have been very unfortunate. For example, when I was in the female prison, there was a lady there who would have been in her sixties, absolutely model citizen, been driving home one night on the motorway doing 80 mph, lost control, crashed, killed somebody, straight away in prison. Now, she's not a criminal. I understand the family of the person she killed. She was speeding, she wasn't drunk, she wasn't on drugs, and she was just driving too fast. When she eventually got out of prison, she had got her family to go back to. She had a successful business you know. Should she have been in prison? From the point of view of was she a danger to the public, no. Was she at risk of reoffending? Well,

---

* In Britain, there are two types of court. A magistrates' court does not have a jury but rather three magistrates or laypeople who are not legally trained but are assisted by a professional legal advisor and are responsible for declaring the guilt or innocence of the accused and then sentencing. They have prison-sentencing powers of up to 6 months, and if the expected prison sentence for the crime is higher than this, the case will be referred up to the higher, Crown court. Magistrates' courts date from circa 1327 and are considered to be the workhorses of the criminal justice system in England and Wales because they handle more than 95% of the criminal cases in a jurisdiction. Crown courts hear only 4% of criminal cases, and trial is before a judge and jury.

you know, I suppose, potentially. She was only in there, because it seemed to be the thing to do to satisfy the family that was hurting. She didn't need education, she didn't need rehabilitation, and she did show remorse for the victim's family and everything else.

My analysis of this interview supported by independent research seems relatively clear, although admittedly, this is a very complex debate, and a "one-size-fits-all" approach to punishment and resettlement is definitely not suggested. Rehabilitation can and does work, but CM is clear that, rather than throwing opportunities at all prisoners (which might have been palatable in times of financial plenty), targeting receptive and genuinely motivated individuals early in their offending does seem sensible and rational. Perhaps, the swinging cuts to the government's budget will achieve this refocus of resources, although the money saved through less prison sentencing and prison building has certainly not been reallocated to support community sentencing yet, leaving the impression that this change of direction in the sentencing ethos in England and Wales is clearly not an ideological reform but simply a decision founded purely on checkbook imperatives.

Another conclusion from CM's experience is that, sometimes, prison does work and individuals who get adequate support, retraining, and help with housing and reemployment have the greatest expectations of prison being a one-time, "growing-up" experience. However, once a person is considered a career criminal or has multiple convictions, their chances of resuming a socially acceptable life reduce rapidly.

CM described himself as a "glass half full" type of person. My impressions are that this is a prerequisite for working with prisoners, as for each success story, there are multiple failures. I do interpret the trend to invite volunteer members of the community to befriend prisoners to be an unexpected but exciting initiative. It seems logical that, if we aim at releasing prisoners back into communities and expect them to live by the norms of societies, then reinforcing their links to society throughout their sentence and afterward is a logical starting point. As Kenneth Clarke noted, just "banging up" ever more people was "what you would expect of Victorian England" (*The Guardian*, June 30, 2010).

Conclusion

13

JENNIE K. SINGER
EILEEN M. AHLIN
DILIP K. DAS

This first volume in the new series *Trends in Corrections: Interviews with Corrections Leaders Around the World* presents interviews with 12 correctional leaders in nine countries. The interviews were conducted by accomplished scholars/researchers throughout the world and serve to present the personal views of those who lead agencies within the corrections systems of their respective countries. It is evident, by reading these in-depth stories about their careers and correctional philosophies, that there are striking similarities between the leaders, despite the vast differences in social and political environments in which they work.

The most prominent feature common to all 12 leaders is their ability to rise through the ranks, often arriving at their high-ranking post through happenstance and following paths discovered accidentally. For example, Dr. Antal Kökényesi (Hungary; Chapter 4) took advantage of a hiring burst in the police department as they sought new, young leaders with potential to improve the field. After spending almost 30 years with the police service, he followed his desire to learn more about prisons and the larger correctional system and is now the commander of the national prison service in Hungary. Sue Hall (United Kingdom; Chapter 10) entered the field of probation after completing her degree. She was enjoying her volunteer work and replied to an advertisement for the probation department because it sounded interesting. Hall did not have prior knowledge of the corrections field but enjoyed working with people. She has been working in probation ever since.

For other correctional leaders who also rose through the ranks in the criminal justice system, it is obvious that many took advantage of training programs and educational opportunities and simply persevered over time to gain knowledge and credentials essential to their work. For example, whereas John Rougier (Trinidad and Tobago; Chapter 5) was motivated by his brother who was working in the field of corrections, he sought out educational opportunities and waited for opportunities to present themselves within the prison system. He first worked as a prison officer, eventually becoming commissioner of prisons. John Pastorek (Vancouver, BC, Canada; Chapter 6) climbed his way through the federal system, working as a correctional officer and then a parole officer and become a deputy warden and, eventually, a warden. Luke Grant (New South Wales, Australia; Chapter 2) also held a variety of positions in the corrections system, including inmate classification and oversight of prison programs and industries. These experiences provided him with a vast knowledge and understanding of the challenges at all levels of the corrections system, which he draws on in his current role as assistant commissioner of Offender Services and Programs. Grant's original career trajectory focused on offender rehabilitation, but he saw a need for a better understanding of the prison system as a whole, and he sought to make prisons more effective and improve offender outcomes.

The correctional leaders interviewed in this volume did not always begin their careers in the field of corrections, and many arrived at their positions by working for many years in related areas such as psychology and education. Timothy Leo (Singapore; Chapter 9) is a psychologist by training, and CM (Northern England; Chapter 12), a reentry resettlement specialist, found a need for their expertise in the corrections field. Their knowledge and skills provide a valuable resource to their respective agencies and the corrections field as a whole. The rehabilitative and reentry programming spearheaded by these professionals takes a case management (or throughcare) perspective, focusing on the whole individual and his/her needs, to assist offenders as they transition from prison to the community. However, many of the leaders who were trained in the criminal justice field and spent their careers in corrections also support holistic approaches to working with offenders. For example, Robert Jennings (Western Australia; Chapter 8) believes in employing a multidisciplinary team of social workers, medical personnel, and teachers to support offender rehabilitation efforts.

All of the correctional leaders profiled in this volume often took advantage of educational opportunities that increased their capabilities and broadened their views about corrections. Prevalent features across the 12 leaders include self-motivation, hard work, and challenges that they sought to further their careers and improve the field of corrections. Luke Grant (New South Wales; Chapter 2) describes his interest and motivation to enter corrections as "voyeuristic." He capitalized on this interest in the field and has risen to the rank of assistant commissioner of Offender Services and Programs. As a police officer, Dr. Antal Kökényesi (Hungary; Chapter 4) saw how people became incarcerated. This piqued his interest, and his desire to learn more about what happened to them once they left police custody motivated him to become involved in corrections. Other correctional leaders took advantage of courses available to obtain qualifications needed to work in the field. Sue Hall (West Yorkshire, United Kingdom; Chapter 10) enrolled in the Home Office training program for probation officers. Robert Jennings (Western Australia; Chapter 8) took the accelerated prison administrator's course while working as a prison welfare officer. Robert Ambroselli (California, United States; Chapter 11) believes that corrections leaders need to be inquisitive and proactive seekers of knowledge to keep the field moving forward. He regularly attends conferences and works closely with law enforcement to incorporate a variety of ideas into daily practice.

These correctional leaders also have an interest in moving the field forward through staff and facility improvements. Dusko Sain (Republic of Srspka, Bosnia and Herzegovina; Chapter 3) provides training for his staff that allows them to keep abreast of practices and policies from the European Council and other international organizations. Dr. Antal Kökényesi (Hungary; Chapter 4) sought to modernize the prison system. He achieves this by seeking funding and grant money to improve the prison guards' working and living conditions and uniforms, as well as the vehicles used in the course of prison operations. John Rougier (Trinidad and Tobago; Chapter 5) sees a need to modernize the prison staff promotion system. He advocates one based on merit rather than longevity. He believes that this would motivate officers to develop their skills, which would benefit the inmates.

The passion these leaders evoke for their work and sense of vocation are inspiring. After completing his degree, Hazael Ruiz (Mexico City, Mexico; Chapter 1) found his calling while working with delinquents. While conducting personality tests with youth, he decided that he wanted to understand the etiology of criminal behavior. Another theme throughout this volume is that these leaders truly enjoy helping others. Dr. Antal Kökényesi (Hungary; Chapter 4) felt a need to help those less fortunate and speaks of this desire as omnipresent in his educational background and training. In a similar vein, Michael Boileau (Vancouver, British Columbia, Canada; Chapter 7) believes that inmates can be helped more if his correctional officers got to know them and understand their situation and needs. CM (Northern England; Chapter 12) speaks about how he enjoys working with ex-offenders who move forward with their lives through the reentry work program, which helps people pursue education and training opportunities and gain employment.

Through their experience and dedication to the field, they often developed an understanding that offenders' time spent in the corrections system is only one piece of the criminal justice puzzle. Many adopted philosophical views consistent with a holistic approach congruent with reentry efforts essential to the mission of corrections. These leaders view their role as consisting of not only keeping the public safe but, more so, of preparing offenders to become law-abiding citizens who will not return to the criminal justice system. Michael Boileau (Vancouver, British Columbia, Canada; Chapter 7) endorses programming for inmates and understands the need for reentry programming at the outset of the reentry process (while incarcerated) to prepare inmates for release. It was clear that the 12 correctional leaders appreciate the roles of other agencies that support correctional goals such as the police, rehabilitation efforts (e.g., mental health and substance use), and community programs that provide offenders with opportunities to improve their skills and gain employment. Dusko Sain (Republic of Srspka,

Bosnia and Herzegovina; Chapter 3) discusses the relationship between the Department of Corrections and Parole. Parole signifies a transition from incarceration and represents a continuation of the sentence that originated in prison and the two agencies work closely to ensure successful reentry. As a psychologist, Timothy Leo (Singapore; Chapter 9) supports rehabilitative initiatives and encourages the use of evidence-based practices to improve offender programming supportive of reentry efforts.

These correctional leaders are also concerned about the well-being and professional development of their staff. They encourage and support the education and training of the line staff who work on a more direct basis with offenders. For example, Sue Hall (West Yorkshire, United Kingdom; Chapter 10) takes an active interest in staff development and training, instilling a sense of vocation and ensuring her staff are experts at managing relationships with offenders. Similarly, Robert Ambroselli (California, USA; Chapter 11) provides his parole agents with a sense of ownership over their work and encourages them to track their effectiveness. The leaders involved in this volume believe that the staff are an essential component to a successful corrections agency and often seek to better their circumstances so that the staff members enjoy their work. This management approach benefits the entire agency. Leaders invest in their employees who obtain ownership of their role in the system, whereas inmates receive better treatment from an educated staff. A prime example of this management style is evidenced by Robert Jennings (Western Australia; Chapter 8) and his staff. He notes that they have a united team mentality. Everyone, from uniformed line staff to nonuniformed staff such as psychologists and educators, has input into the management of inmates and a vested interest in the welfare of the institution as a whole.

Over the course of their careers, these correctional leaders not only learned to appreciate evidence-based practices but also sought to find a balance between correctional experience and scientific support for the programs they implement in their facilities. The 12 leaders embrace the knowledge they gain through personal experience, but they also desire to bridge the gap between theory and practice and improve their programs and institutions by applying methods supported by research. Hazael Ruiz (Mexico City, Mexico; Chapter 1) encourages working relationships between scholars/researchers and practitioners as a way of improving programs and methods used in the corrections field. Similarly, John Pastorek (Vancouver, British Columbia, Canada; Chapter 6) understands the need for both evidence-based practices and tried-and-true line staff experience. The philosophical mindset of staff is based on tradition and is slowly becoming open to new methods such as evidence-based practices. However, many leaders acknowledge the need to incorporate both traditional and scientific programs to maintain staff and public satisfaction with the overarching goals of keeping inmates safe and returning them to society.

These leaders also consistently seek out opportunities to understand how other countries implement their corrections systems by attending conferences and trainings and visiting similar institutions to observe first-hand alternative methods for handling correctional populations. Dr. Antal Kökényesi (Hungary; Chapter 4) is proactive in the European community, where correctional leaders from many countries engage in trainings, tours, and discussions to learn about practices from similarly situated countries in the region. Likewise, John Rougier (Trinidad and Tobago; Chapter 5) has traveled to Canada and the United States to attend training programs and implemented practices that would also work in his country. These experiences provided these correctional leaders with alternative methods to expand their current programming and move their agencies forward. The lessons they learned may not be directly applicable to their institution because of social and political circumstances. However, the knowledge they gained by opening their minds to a different way of doing things served to boost creativity and encouraged leaders to make positive changes that would work in their own country.

The correctional leaders also face challenges and persevere by maintaining a positive attitude about their role in the corrections system. Many experienced budget cuts and were operating with outdated facilities and infrastructure. Limited resources and unmotivated staff can be obstacles to effective change. As Hazael Ruiz (Mexico City, Mexico; Chapter 1) reflects on the conditions of his prisons and how they negatively impact staff and inmates, he discusses the problem of overcrowding and the need for more community-based sentencing options. System changes can be difficult to implement and often require buy-in from other correctional agencies and government officials. However, as good leaders, they work with what they have available to them in efforts to modernize and bring positive changes to the system. Some leaders encourage staff input on organizational changes, whereas others proactively generated positive media about the corrections system to encourage public support for reform. Luke Grant (New South Wales, Australia; Chapter 2) engages the local media to espouse details about prisons (e.g., costs and reentry outcomes) to balance the negative information the public continually receives about corrections. These leaders not only understand that the field is dynamic and often political but also believed that modification and improvement is necessary. They recognize that the field of corrections is steeped in tradition and has an institutional culture that is not easy to change. However, they persevere, because they also greatly desire evolutions in the field they have embraced, because they know that the corrections system can be better for offenders and staff alike.

The 12 correctional leaders interviewed in this inaugural volume unequi-vocally seek to modernize their corrections systems and lead their institu-tions through the 21st century. They are forward-looking, forward-thinking individuals who care about improving the corrections system as a whole. An understanding that corrections is a field that needs to evolve away from tra-ditional practices is a common attribute among these leaders. This volume provides a detailed glimpse into the mindset of successful correctional lead-ers who are passionate about their work. They embody the key traits essen-tial for an effective correctional leader and serve as models for other leaders in the criminal justice system worldwide. Researchers, scholars, and practi-tioners stand to learn a great deal from correctional leaders in the field. Future volumes will continue this inquiry and broaden our understanding of cor-rections from insiders' perspectives on a transnational level.

International Police Executive Symposium (IPES) www.ipes.info

The International Police Executive Symposium (IPES) was founded in 1994. The aims and objectives of the IPES are to provide a forum to foster closer relationships among police researchers and practitioners globally, to facilitate cross-cultural, international, and interdisciplinary exchanges for the enrichment of the law enforcement profession, and to encourage discussion and published research on challenging and contemporary topics related to the profession.

One of the most important activities of the IPES is the organization of an annual meeting under the auspices of a police agency or an educational institution. Every year since 1994, annual meetings have been hosted by such agencies and institutions all over the world. Past hosts have included the Canton Police of Geneva, Switzerland; the International Institute of the Sociology of Law, Onati, Spain; Kanagawa University, Yokohama, Japan; the Federal Police, Vienna, Austria; the Dutch Police and Europol, The Hague, The Netherlands; Andhra Pradesh Police, Andhra Pradesh, India; the Center for Public Safety, Northwestern University, Evanston, IL, USA; the Polish Police Academy, Szczytno, Poland; the Police of Turkey (twice); the Kingdom of Bahrain Police; a group of institutions in Canada (consisting of the University of the Fraser Valley, Abbotsford Police Department, the Royal Canadian Mounted Police, the Vancouver Police Department, the Justice Institute of British Columbia, Canadian Police College and the International Centre for Criminal Law Reform and Criminal Justice Policy); the Czech Police Academy, Prague; the Dubai Police; the Ohio Association of Chiefs of Police and Cincinnati Police Department, Cincinnati, OH, USA; the Republic of Macedonia; and the Police of Malta.

The most recent annual meeting with the theme "Policing Violence, Crime, Disorder and Discontent: International Perspectives" was hosted in Buenos Aires, Argentina, on June 26–30, 2011. The 2012 annual meeting will be hosted by the United Nations in New York with the theme "Economic Development, Armed Violence and Public Safety" on August 5–10.

There have also been occasional special meetings of the IPES. A special meeting was cohosted by the Bavarian Police Academy of Continuing Education, Ainring, Germany, the University of Passau, Passau, Lower Bavaria, Germany, and the State University of New York, Plattsburgh, NY, USA, in 2000. The second special meeting was hosted by the police in the Indian state of Kerala. The third special meeting, with the theme "Contemporary Issues in Public Safety and Security," was hosted by the Commissioner of Police of the Blekinge Region of Sweden and the President of the University of Technology on August 10–14, 2011.

The majority of participants in the annual meetings are usually directly involved in the police profession. In addition, scholars and researchers in the field also participate. The meetings comprise both structured and informal sessions to maximize the dialogue and exchange of views and information. The executive summary of each meeting is distributed to participants and to a wide range of other interested police professionals and scholars. In addition, a book of selected papers from each annual meeting is published through CRC Press/Taylor & Francis Group, Prentice Hall, Lexington Books, and other reputed publishers. A special issue of *Police Practice and Research: An International Journal* is also published with the most thematically relevant papers after the usual blind review process.

IPES Institutional Supporters

African Policing Civilian Oversight Forum (APCOF; Sean Tait), 2nd floor, The Armoury, Buchanan Square, 160 Sir Lowry Road, Woodstock, Cape Town 8000, South Africa. E-mail: sean@apcof.org.za.

Australian Institute of Police Management, Collins Beach Road Manly NSW 2095, Australia (Connie Coniglio). E-mail: cconiglio@aipm .gov.au.

Cliff Roberson, managing editor, *Police Practice and Research: An International Journal*. E-mail: managingeditorppr@gmail.com.

College of Basic and Applied Sciences, Fayetteville State University (Dr. David E. Barlow, Professor and Dean), 130 Chick Building, 1200 Murchison Road, Fayetteville, North Carolina 28301. Tel: 910-672-1659; Fax: 910-672-1083. E-mail: dbarlow@uncfsu.edu.

College of Law, University of South Africa (UNISA; Professor Kris Pillay, School of Criminal Justice, Director), Preller Street, Muckleneuk, Pretoria. E-mail: cpillay@unisa.ac.za.

College of Natural and Social Sciences, University of Maine at Augusta (Mary Louis Davitt, Professor of Legal Technology), 46 University Drive, Augusta, ME 04330-9410. E-mail: mldavitt@maine.edu.

Cyber Defense and Research Initiatives (James Lewis), LLC, P.O. Box 86, Leslie, MI 49251. Tel: 517-242-6730. E-mail: lewisja@cyber defenseresearch.com.

Defendology Center for Security, Sociology and Criminology Research (Valibor Lalic), Srpska Street 63, 78000 Banja Luka, Bosnia and Herzegovina. Tel and Fax: 387-51-308-914. E-mail: lalicv@teol.net.

Department of Criminal Justice (Dr. Harvey L. McMurray, Chair), North Carolina Central University, 301 Whiting Criminal Justice Building, Durham, NC 27707. Tel: 919-530-5204/919-530-7909; Fax: 919-530-5195. E-mail: hmcmurray@nccu.edu.

Department of Criminology and Criminal Justice, University of the Fraser Valley (Dr. Darryl Plecas), 33844 King Road, Abbotsford, British Columbia, Canada V2 S7 M9. Tel: 604-853-7441; Fax: 604-853-9990. E-mail: Darryl.plecas@ufv.ca.

Department of Police Practice (Setlhomamaru Dintwe), University of South Africa (UNISA), Florida Campus, Cnr Christiaan De Wet and Pioneer Avenues, Private Bag X6, Florida, 1710 South Africa. Tel: 11-471-2116; Cell: 83-581-6102; Fax: 11-471-2255. E-mail: Dintwsi@unisa.ac.za.

Department of Psychology (Stephen Perrott), Mount Saint Vincent University, 166 Bedford Highway, Halifax, Nova Scotia, Canada. E-mail: Stephen.perrott@mvsu.ca.

Edmundo Oliveira, Prof., PhD, 1 Irving Place, University Tower, Apt. U7A, New York, NY 10003-9723. Tel: 407-342-2473. E-mail: edmundooliveira@cfl.rr.com.

International Council on Security and Development (ICOS) (Andre Souza, Senior Researcher), Visconde de Piraja 577/605, Ipanema, Rio de Janeiro 22410-003, Brazil. Tel: 55-21-3186-5444. E-mail: asouza@icosgroup.net.

Justice Studies Department, San José State University, 1 Washington Square, San José, CA 95192-0050 (Mark E. Correia, PhD, Chair and Associate Professor). Tel: 408-924-1350. E-mail: mcorreia@casa.sjsu.edu.

Kerala Police (Jacob Punnoose, Director General of Police), Police Headquarters, Trivandrum, Kerala, India. E-mail: JPunnoose@gmail.com.

Molloy College, The Department of Criminal Justice (Dr. John A. Eterno, NYPD Captain-Retired), 1000 Hempstead Avenue, P.O. Box 5002, Rockville Center, NY 11571-5002. Tel: 516-678-5000, Ext. 6135; Fax: 516-256-2289. E-mail: jeterno@molloy.edu.

National Institute of Criminology and Forensic Science (Kamalendra Prasad, Inspector General of Police), MHA, Outer Ring Road, Sector 3, Rohini, Delhi 110085, India. Tel: 91-11-2752-5095; Fax: 91-11-2751-0586. E-mail: director.nicfs@nic.in.

National Police Academy, Japan (Suzuki Kunio, Assistant Director), Police Policy Research Center, Zip 183-8558: 3-12-1 Asahi-cho Fuchu-city, Tokyo, Japan. Tel: 81-42-354-3550; Fax: 81-42-330-1308. E-mail: PPRC@npa.go.jp.

Royal Canadian Mounted Police (Helen Darbyshire, Executive Assistant), 657 West 37th Avenue, Vancouver, British Columbia, Canada V5Z 1K6. Tel: 604-264-2003; Fax: 604-264-3547. E-mail: helen.darbyshire@rcmp-grc.gc.ca.

School of Psychology and Social Science, Head, Social Justice Research Centre (Prof. S. Caroline Taylor, Foundation Chair in Social Justice), Edith Cowan University, 270 Joondalup Drive, Joondalup, WA 6027, Australia. E-mail: c.taylor@ecu.edu.au.

South Australia Police (Commissioner Mal Hyde), Office of the Commissioner, South Australia Police, 30 Flinders Street, Adelaide, SA 5000, Australia. E-mail: mal.hyde@police.sa.gov.au.

The Faculty of Criminal Justice and Security (Dr. Gorazd Mesko), University of Maribor, Kotnikova 8, 1000 Ljubljana, Slovenia. Tel: 386-1-300-8339; Fax: 386-1-2302-687. E-mail: gorazd.mesko@fvv .uni-mb.si.

University of New Haven (Dr. Richard Ward, School of Criminal Justice and Forensic Science), 300 Boston Post Road, West Haven, CT 06516. Tel: 203-932-7260. E-mail: rward@newhaven.edu.

Suggested Guidelines
for Interviewers

Contents

Brief Description of the Proposed Book

Information will be presented on a group of 20 countries using the personal views and experiences of a correctional leader in each country. In each country, a corrections scholar or researcher will be asked to conduct a comprehensive interview of the experiences and thoughts of a high-ranking corrections official in his or her country. The interviews will be edited to emphasize personal experiences, ideas, and detailed examples of issues (both positive and negative) in their country's correctional system. The relationship between theory, evidence, and practice will be highlighted.

Suggested Guidelines for Interviewers

Goals and Information

The general goal of the interviews is to present the views and interpretations of the developments, crises, and current issues in the correctional system *by experienced practitioners.* What do those directly involved in the corrections profession see happening in the correctional system in their countries and internationally? How do they evaluate or interpret developments (either positive or negative) in corrections? There are many books and articles that analyze and interpret the state of current correctional policy, programs, and prisons by scholars and policy makers from outside the correctional system. What we would like to have are views and interpretations from within correctional organizations. What do leaders in the field of corrections who work in the jails and prison systems see happening in corrections? What are the issues they consider important? What changes do they see as successes or failures? What aspects of the system are likely long-lasting versus those policies or programs they see as more transient?

The main goal of the interviews is to capture the views of correctional officials. Your role should not be to criticize or interpret what the officials meant to say but to write as accurately as possible what the officials told you. The chapter will be based on their views, experiences, and thought processes. We know what scholars think about corrections, but we know less about what the people who work in the corrections field think about and how they evaluate trends, developments, and issues in corrections.

The basic reason for doing the interviews is that we firmly believe that corrections officials possess a wide variety of information and that practitioners can make significant contributions to our insight into the issues and problems of current correctional practices. The knowledge these individuals possess is not easily captured, but our goal is to describe their personal information for this book. The practical reason that we are asking scholars to conduct the interviews is because leaders in the field of corrections do not have the time to write and reflect on their experiences, views, opinions, and perspectives. We think that in-depth interviews are one means to depict the knowledge of correctional practitioners, and it is why we are requesting researchers like you to record their views.

We want to emphasize one major point. *We do not want the official rhetoric (or the official success stories)* that high-level people sometimes fall back on during interviews; we want their *personal views and thinking.* If you have the sense that you are getting the formal language and official views on correctional policy and issues, see if you can get the officials to go beyond the official story and push them for their own views. The interviewer should seek to get the person being interviewed to move beyond simple answers and get them to analyze and reflect on their experiences, ideas, and knowledge. Our trust in your interviewing skills is why you were asked to do the interview.

Topic Areas to Be Covered

- In some situations, there may be areas of importance in your country or community that are different than the questions posed below.

In those cases, you should focus on these areas more completely and ask about these issues in addition to the questions listed. For example, questions for correctional leaders in transitional countries will likely deal more with changes in correctional philosophy and in organizations than questions for leaders in stable democracies. Even in stable democracies, however, a particular area or locale can be in a state of prison crisis, and we hope that these specific issues will be addressed as well. Being familiar with the correctional policies and situations (such as any lawsuits) in your country will enable you to tailor your questions toward the dominant local issues that have had to be dealt with by the countries' leaders. Be creative while sticking to the main issues at hand.

- We have listed a number of general and specific questions that should be covered in the interview. Please try to cover the topics mentioned below as the flow of the interview dictates. Please add, elaborate, and use follow-up questions as you see necessary to clarify points, expand on ideas, or pursue an insight offered.

- All the topics below should be asked, but the specific questions listed for each main area are suggestions. Interviews have their own dynamics. Follow them down their most productive paths. Since each of you will be interviewing officials within different organizations, the list and sequence of questions will have to be adjusted for each interview.

- How you word each question is up to your own preference. When asking follow-up questions, please try to get specific examples or details of any generalizations made by the official. (Specific examples of over-arching problems or situations in the leader's country are probably among the most useful and interesting pieces of information to readers.)

Career

Tell us a little bit about your career: length, organizations worked in, movements, specializations, trajectories in your career that might differ from those expected, etc.

- What motivated you to enter the field of corrections?
- Did the way your career developed surprise you?
- Did your work prove as interesting or rewarding as you thought it would?
- Do you have any regrets about an opportunity you pursued or chose not to pursue during the course of your career?

Changes Experienced

What do you see as the most important changes that have occurred in the field of corrections over the course of your career (philosophies, organizational arrangements, specializations, policies and programs, equipment or technologies, methods of rehabilitation, methods of community supervision, intermediate sanctions, personnel, diversity, etc.)?

- What changes in external conditions (support from communities, legal and legislative powers, relations with minority communities, resource provision, political influence, etc.) have had a significant impact on current correctional practices and policy?
- Overall, has the quality of prisons, jails, and community supervision in your country/community improved or declined over the past 10 years? (such as the number of personnel per inmate ratio, amount and type of training offered, programs offered to inmates, rehabilitation strategies and the amount of money available to implement these programs, what percentage of inmates are able to have access to programs, how recidivism of both technical violations and new criminal activity has been affected, interagency cooperation, the effectiveness of top management providing quality control and directing managing and line personnel, inmate and staff safety, and inmate suicide rates)?
- In general, is it more or less difficult to be a correctional officer (or supervisor, warden, regional management) now than in the past?

Personal Correctional Philosophy

What do you think should be the role of prison, jail, and community supervision officials in society?

- What should be their job, functions, and roles? What should be left to other people or organizations? What about line staff such as corrections officers? Prison/jail/community supervisors and wardens?
- What organizational arrangements work and which do not?
- What policies does your country have in regards to relations with the community, political groups, and other criminal justice organizations? Do these policies work well? What hampers cooperation with other agencies and groups?
- How should corrections institutions be run? What programs should be provided, and how would you prefer sentencing laws to be modified so as to have prisons and jails include the individuals most deserving of incarceration? What are the best correctional strategies to ensure the safety and security of the inmates, staff, and community? What services should prisons and jails provide that are currently not offered? What services are provided that you believe should be cut?

- How should supervision post-prison or post-jail (or in lieu of prison or jail) be dealt with? Is the procedure used in your country working, or do you see an increased recidivism rate due to issues those supervised in the community experience? How would you improve this problem or why is this process working in your country?
- Do you feel that your country uses appropriate intermediate sanctions when needed or is there a lack of such sanctions? Are intermediate sanctions such as treatment programs, intensive supervision, or electronic monitoring utilized, and do they reduce recidivism while keeping those in the community safe? If not, what do you feel is the problem?

Problems and Successes Experienced

In your experience, what policies or programs have worked well, and which have not? Can you speculate for what reasons?

- What would you consider to be the greatest problem facing the correctional system at this time?
- What problems in corrections do you find are the most difficult to deal with? What would be easy to change? Internal problems (culture of the organization, managerial deficiencies, allegations of corruption, or gender-related problems) or externally generated problems (resources, community support, parole or probation procedures, or lack thereof)?
- What is the most successful program you have worked with in corrections? What is the most successful policy in regards to the positive improvements that have been made to prisons, jails, or community supervision?

Theory and Practice

In your view, what should be the relationship between theory and practice? What can practitioners learn from studying and applying theories, and what can those who create theories of punishment gain from practitioners?

- What is the relationship between theory and practice right now? Does it exist? Does it work? What holds collaboration or interactions back?
- What kind of research, in what form, and on which questions would you find most useful for practice? If not very useful, what could or should creators of theory do to make their ideas more useful to you?

- Where do you find theory-based information? Where do you look: journals, professional magazines, books, publications, reports?
- Does the department of corrections you work for conduct research on its own? On what types of issues or questions?

Evidence-Based Corrections

In your experience, has your country's correctional system made use of various evidence-based programs? Do you feel that it is best to use evidence-based practices (or "what works") or that this focus is not important?

- What evidence-based practices are used now in prisons, jails, for intermediate sanctions, or in community supervision? Do you agree with the use of these practices? Do you feel that using more evidence-based practices would benefit the correctional system?
- Do you read information on evidence-based practices? Where do you get this information? If you do not have this information, would you be interested in having access to these practices? What programs have been proven to work best in your country?

Transnational Relations

How have you been affected by the following in your organization's work by developments outside the country: human rights demands, universal codes of ethics, practical interactions with corrections officials from other countries, personal experiences outside the country, programs developed by other countries, new sentencing laws, political strife or war in your or neighboring countries?

- Have those interactions been beneficial or harmful? What kind of external international influences are beneficial and which ones less so?
- How have international relationships with other countries or other political influences had an impact on correctional policy or practice in your country?

General Assessments

Are you basically satisfied or dissatisfied with developments in the field of corrections?

- What do you think of the relationship between sentencing laws and public opinion to the functioning of prisons, jails, and community supervision?

- How do you view the release procedures in your country and do they contribute to or inhibit recidivism?
- What rehabilitative programs could be offered either in or out of prison or jail that could decrease recidivism?
- How are intermediate sanctions (such as house arrest, ankle bracelets, rehabilitative programs in the community, or intensive supervision, among others) in your country used, and how are they working or failing to work?
- Which intermediate sanctions would you increase or create, and why?
- How could changing the balance between intermediate sanctions affect prison and jail environments? Would that be an improvement?
- What are the developments you see as most likely to happen in next few years, and which developments would you prefer to see happening?
- What is most needed now to improve prisons, jails, community supervision, and the overall punishment process in your country?

Preparation for the Interview and Instructions for Writing Your Chapter

Before the Interview

- Get a sense of how much time you are likely to have and what questions you will be able to ask during that time. No interview will enable you to ask all the questions you want, so it is best to choose your priorities based on who you are interviewing.
- You will have space for about 6000 to 8000 words (on the average) when writing your interview. It is important to pick the most interesting information that you have obtained (in your opinion). Our top priorities are the officials' reflections on the changes experienced during their careers, how they evaluate these changes, and the interrelationship between theory and practice. Thus, these areas are high priorities for the interviews.

After the Interview

1. Please write a short introduction to the actual interview. The introduction should
   - Briefly describe the basic structure of corrections in your country. You have to be the judge of how much an informed reader is likely to know about the country and how much should be explained.

- Briefly describe the interview itself. Where and when was the interview conducted, how long did it take, was there one or multiple sittings, and how honest and open do you feel the discussion was? What was the demeanor of the interviewee?

2. You should, if at all possible, record the interview by audiotape. For publication, edit the interview to bring out the most important discussion and answers. You will likely have much more information from your interview than we will have space for in the proposed book.

3. Write a short conclusion about your impression of the interview. What were the major themes? Briefly describe how accurate the leader's views were in accordance with known literature, without being overly critical about any lack of knowledge.

4. Write a glossary of terms or events mentioned in the interview a reader might not be familiar with. For example, if you interviewed a California correctional official and the *Plata v. Schwarzenegger* lawsuit was talked about, please define this lawsuit so that readers without knowledge of a country's specific terms and laws might be able to understand what is being referenced.

5. We have had two basic styles that are used to write up interviews. Both are acceptable, but we prefer the second style.
   - The first style is to simply transcribe the interviews—questions asked, answers given.
   - The second style, which requires more work, is to write short statements about the topic of a question and then insert long excerpts from the interviews. The main point is to have the voice and views of the leaders being interviewed, not your own.

6. Send the completed interviews to Dr. Jennie Singer (jksinger@saclink.csus.edu) and Professor Dilip Das (dilipkd@aol.com).

The total interview, including the introduction, body of the interview, conclusion, and glossary, should be approximately 6000 to 8000 words long.

Index

For Product Safety Concerns and Information please contact our EU
representative GPSR@taylorandfrancis.com
Taylor & Francis Verlag GmbH, Kaufingerstraße 24, 80331 München, Germany